STRADIVARIUS

STRADIVARIUS

Donald P. Ladew

Carroll & Graf Publishers, Inc.
New York

First Carroll & Graf edition 1995

Carroll & Graf Publishers, Inc.
260 Fifth Avenue
New York, NY 10001

Library of Congress Cataloging-in-Publication Data

Ladew, Donald P.
  Stradivarius / Donald P. Ladew.
     p.   cm.
  ISBN 0-7867-0136-6 : $21.95
  I. Title
PS3562.A262S77   1995
813'.54—dc20   94-22395
                                                    CIP

Manufactured in the United States of America

For my Mother, Harriett Glendine MacElwee Ladew Bernier
who but for the duress of life might have written a better
story than this.

Prelude

The Northern Italian Town of Cremona, Fall 1685

The maestro slid back from his bench and stretched. He pushed his cloak away from his face and ran callused fingers through thick coal-black hair. The afternoon sun washed the medieval town of Cremona with crimson. It poured through the two arched windows on the west side of an ancient tower built by invading armies from the north. In the distance the river Po turned gold. The autumn sun brought little warmth to the maestro's hands.

The tower wasn't really a tower, but in Cremona, where buildings were stacked so close one could have leapt from one to the other, it stood apart. In the vaulted room the slowly shifting beams of light changed from rose to honey: lucent, liquid, filled with fine particles of wood that swirled in the afternoon air.

This was a supreme moment. There had been other such moments, each magical.

The maestro picked up the violin and smiled. The wood, so intimately his, was true. He had endowed it with his art, his skill, his love. Now the result, many times magnified, flowed back to his callused hands.

He tucked it between shoulder and chin, took it away, repeated the movement, pleased with it.

Around the shop, master carvers, apprentices, stopped their efforts and held their breath. Antonius Stradivarius, the Maestro of Cremona, picked up a bow, touched the horsehair with amber-colored resin, put it back down.

1

The drama of the moment reached every corner of the room. With birth there is always anticipation, hope, and fear. No Italian with an ounce of passion could allow such a moment to pass unmarked.

He plucked each string in turn. The four perfect notes hung in the air, reverberating. They sang with power.

He picked up the bow again and held it over the strings. He paused, let his eyes scan the shop. His friends, his men of genius, transformed wood into instruments whose voices were alike unto the voices of saints.

He closed his eyes and brought the bow close to the strings. The maestro chose a simple country song: lush, romantic, melodic. As he played, he smiled, his worn face beautiful to behold.

The power of the instrument reached beyond anything he'd ever created. The violin's voice filled the space effortlessly. When the song ended, every man and boy let out a sigh, then stood as one and cheered.

The maestro bowed. A look of surprise covered his face. He could not believe he had created such a wondrous thing.

"My friends, I shall name this one . . . Hercules."

Chapter 1

South Korea, February 1951

A relentless gray-brown world. Aching cold, a cruel wind driving clouds of debris. War in winter: a hard-rock, vicious war; paranoid, xenophobic, wasteful, mean.

There was no relief from one broken horizon to the other. Not one leaf, not one full standing tree.

Amid a barrage of artillery and mortar fire, Master Sergeant Martin Luther Cole stumbled out of the trench that zigzagged down the south ridge of hill 406. It was one o'clock in the afternoon.

Luther had slept four hours in the last thirty-six. During the hours he was awake, waves of North Korean soldiers battered the narrow ridge. By one o'clock in the afternoon he commanded the remnants of two companies. Every officer and senior NCO had been killed or wounded.

Of the twenty-seven men he trained and brought to Korea, the last, Private Rodriguez, had been killed in hand-to-hand combat an hour before.

He searched the length of the trench for one, just one of his men that he could help. A dozen times he carried wounded men to safety, only to have them killed in the next assault.

That was what he was supposed to do. He had failed.

The explosion was so close, he couldn't hear it. It forced him to his hands and knees amid a hailstorm of earth and stones. He tried to think. He tried to remember his name and could not. He felt pain.

3

Not minor pain, not bruises or scratches, not even the bayonet wounds on his arms.

A hole went in the front of his shoulder and out through the large bone in the back. It burned with a terrible heat.

Luther trembled like an animal beaten beyond understanding. His eyes locked onto his right wrist. He tried to comprehend what he saw. A three-inch wound filled with congealing blood in the shape of a half circle on both sides of his wrist.

Teeth marks! He remembered. A Chinese soldier clung to him, clawing and biting until Luther strangled the man with a length of barbed wire.

He should do something; act, move, but he couldn't force his body to respond. Awareness had been compressed, pounded, beaten inward. The spirit that was Martin Luther Cole was blind, hidden behind a wall of reality as dense as the center of a star.

An enormous explosion preceded by a giant metal-tearing screech, ripped into the hilltop, and Luther, still kneeling, was thrown backward off the hill, down the steep, rear-facing slope.

He rolled and tumbled away, a helpless mote on the surface of a world gone mad. At the bottom of the hill he staggered to his feet.

The explosion and fall down the hillside added no more than bruises to a litany of harsher wounds. And as if his flight down the hill was but an incomplete journey to oblivion, he rose and stumbled away to the south.

His knees buckled and unlocked. Still he trudged onward, gaze fixed on the. ground. All that was left was movement and a dull awareness of his body. He was utterly alone.

The sun, dim in a flat pewter sky, shifted from above his head to the horizon. He stopped. Something opened a narrow vent into his world. His head came up. He looked around slowly.

He stood in a bowl between low hills. To one side were twenty acres of rice fields, deserted, dry, the dikes crumbled as a Persian ruin. Beyond the paddy a small farmhouse, its once-whitewashed walls blackened and shattered by a direct hit from artillery fire, blending into the dun-colored landscape. The front room still stood.

Luther sensed rain. He stumbled toward the farmhouse, a burned-out farmer-turned-soldier in a burned-out land.

He walked around the building, rifle ready. Somehow he'd held on to it through the madness of the past three days. In the rear he found a well filled with water, clear and sweet.

Inside the farmhouse were two rooms, every piece of furniture gone, all evidence of former life vanished. Although the front room was intact, the rear wall of the back room had a large hole from a few feet above the dirt floor to the roofline. The broken roof sagged and chunks of shrapnel jutted from the mud and plaster walls.

Luther salvaged wood from the fallen ceiling and built a fire in the middle of the front room. Over it he hung a square tin filled with water. As the water heated, he removed his clothing inch by agonizing inch down to bare skin. His large, spare body was surprisingly white against the purple-black streamers of dried blood.

From his knapsack he removed a worn brick of army soap and washed slowly, carefully. He barely noticed the scalding water as he cleansed his wounded wrist.

This was Luther's second war. He'd learned to survive in the first. Routine is good: Routine plus pain prevents thought, and Luther did not want to think. He washed his wounds, under his arms, his crotch, his feet, and between his toes. As patient and thorough as a cat.

From his pack he removed bandages, and where he could reach, sprinkled penicillin powder before taping the field dressings in place. At times the pain caused him to cry out. It didn't occur to him to use the morphine syrette in his pack. War is supposed to hurt. It wasn't a game, never was. The hole in his shoulder burned. It gnawed impatiently at his strength.

From his pack he took khaki shorts, socks, T-shirt, trousers, and dressed. He would wash his clothes the next day. Martin Luther Cole was an orderly man. He heated a can of K rations and ate, chewing each mouthful carefully, before swallowing.

Still, he did not think, attempt to understand. He was where he was. He was alive. He could move. It was enough.

In the distance, at every point of the compass, the war muttered and snarled, Old Testament cruel, but did not approach his sanctuary.

Darkness came. He didn't notice. He made coffee and sipped slowly. The fire died. Using strips of reed blasted from the walls, he built a shelter in the corner of the room.

He gathered his gear and dragged it within. He crawled inside, curled up in his poncho, and slept.

Two hours later a North Korean patrol moved past the farmhouse. One soldier, a sergeant like Luther, slipped into the ruined building and carefully shone a flashlight around the interior. He didn't smell the foreign odors, and seeing nothing but debris, hurriedly rejoined his squad.

An hour later a fierce firefight flared several miles to the south. Not long after, the North Korean sergeant stumbled by Luther's hide-out, headed north. He carried one man, terribly wounded. It was what he was supposed to do. Minutes behind the Chinese soldier and his wounded burden, a column of American soldiers roared by, headed for the ridge Luther had been forced to abandon. In his cave Luther did not move.

At dawn Luther's eyes, thick with an unhealthy residue, opened a fraction at a time. The accumulated injuries awoke him and he jerked upward in pain. He tried not to scream and groaned deep in his belly. It was an eerie sound, like a steer lowing.

Twenty minutes later he crawled from the shelter, and, rifle in hand, staggered outside. He scouted the area. He was alone. In the distance the glowering gods of war, muttered insanely.

He looked toward low, dun-colored hills and fragments of the past three days came unbidden to his thoughts. He had gathered the men into smaller and smaller defensive positions. More men are killed running away than facing the enemy.

Luther moved through a twilit maze of trenches and bunkers, from hole to hole, reassuring here, making a joke there. He came to Bobby Roy's hole at the end of the line. Bobby Roy stared straight ahead. He didn't hear Luther arrive. Every so often he shivered like a man with fever.

"Bobby Roy?" Luther spoke his name softly.

The boy twisted around violently, carbine coming up to shoot.

"Easy, boy, easy." Luther slipped into his fighting hole, deflected the rifle away from his chest.

Luther waited for the terror to leave Bobby Roy's eyes. Luther reached out and placed his hand on Bobby Roy's shoulder. The boy calmed down immediately. Luther knew what was wrong. He always knew.

"Bobby, ain't nothin' you do will make me ashamed of you. You ain't a coward, won't never be one. You been out here six months, and you never ran backward once."

Luther looked toward the torn slopes becoming blurred with darkness.

"Tonight yore agin the wall. One side duty, tother is something you fear worse than dyin'. Either way I won't never be ashamed of you."

Bobby's head dropped and his shoulders shook. All his fears washed away in tears. He held Luther's hand to his shoulder. When it was done he looked up at Luther, grateful and ashamed.

"You won't tell no one I cried, will you, Sarge?"

"Nothin' to tell, Bobby Roy. Y'all stay sharp, heah? They'll be coming 'round midnight."

"I will be here, Sergeant Cole." Bobby Roy Pettis spoke with finality.

"Never doubted it, Bobby."

Luther disappeared into the night. The North Koreans attacked at twelve-oh-four. It continued till dawn. At first light the battered, hollow-eyed remnants of Sergeant Cole's squad looked around at the devastation. They looked at themselves to confirm what could barely be believed. Some were still alive. There were many dead and wounded.

Luther made his way down the line, his left arm tied to his body with an undershirt. A battle-crazed North Korean had broken it with a rifle butt during the night. At the end of the line he came to Bobby Roy's hole. It was empty. He called out Bobby's name softly. There was no answer. Nothing stirred.

He crawled around the hole and found Bobby Roy, his hands sunk into the throat of a dead soldier. There were others, many others, spread around the hole.

Kneeling in the brown mud and debris, Luther looked over the carnage. He lay down and put his head on his folded arm. After a few moments he got back to his knees.

"I ain't ashamed of you, Bobby Roy, I ain't no ways ashamed," Luther whispered.

He fought off the memories with effort. Portions of Luther's mind still functioned; heat water, eat K rations, drink coffee. Sit, slow as an arthritic old man. Clean rifle, reload, survey wounds and re-bandage; check contents of pack—all in robotic silence.

When these things were done, he sat in front of the fire. Again memory relentlessly retrieved the past. Bitter tears washed down his bearded face.

Martin Luther Cole was twenty-four years old. He fought the Japanese for two years in the South Pacific. Now he fought North Koreans and Chinese in the Land of the Morning Calm.

He made no sound. He wept not for himself, but for his men. He was responsible. All his adult history was defined by a deep sense of obligation. He promised to care for the men in his small command; boys really, and they were dead, all of them.

A promise made is a promise kept. His daddy told him that when he was a little boy.

He tried desperately to shut them away in that place where men store the faces of war. Survival first. He was still alone in a terrible and hostile land.

He looked around. Something he'd seen when he arrived at the farmhouse wanted his attention, but he couldn't remember what it was.

Luther struggled to his feet and walked into the back room with its gaping hole in the rear wall. Something wasn't right. The wall! It was unusually thick: two, maybe three feet. He moved over to it, stumbling over broken beams and blasted hunks of hardened mud. Near the bottom edge where the explosion had burst open the wall was a shape too natural to have been caused by a bursting shell. A cache had been built into the wall, the size of a large suitcase. Without the explosion it might have remained hidden for centuries.

Luther looked inside cautiously. Two feet down, near ground level, he saw, faintly, a dark, oblong object. He thought, first, booby trap. He took out his bayonet and used the tip to delicately pry around the edges.

Reaching in with one hand, he lifted first one corner, then the other, never more than an inch. Nothing happened. There were no booby traps. He lifted the case out of the cache and carried it to the front of the farmhouse, his curiosity strangely muted. He put the case down near the fire, walked to the front door, and looked in every direction. He wondered if taking it meant he was a looter.

Luther went to the well and got more water, wincing with each pull of the rope.

He sat in front of his small fire and made another cup of coffee, glancing at the case from time to time. Finally he lifted it to his lap and examined it. A worn case but well made. He wet a rag and wiped away the dust. It looked like a case for a musical instrument, but why here, why in a farmhouse in the middle of Korea? He popped the three snaps, one at a time, and lifted the lid slowly.

A violin—he thought of it as a fiddle—lying in a bed of rose-colored velvet. A small square box had been built into the narrow end of the case. He lifted the cover. A hard block of golden material nestled in a tangle of discarded strings. He touched it with his fingertips, then smelled it. Nothing: It had a waxy feel. Fiddles in the mountains of West Virginia were as common as trees in a forest. He'd never seen a violin—a fiddle such as this. A beautiful golden brown, so well finished he could see his reflection in the surface.

He stared at it for a long time, his large, square hands resting lightly on the body and slack strings. He felt calm. This was right. This was good. This perfect thing had to survive, he would see that it did. Amid all the horror, one beautiful thing must live.

Chapter 2

The rain poured from a grim sky in sheets. Luther sat in front of the farmhouse wrapped in a poncho as the first elements of the column entered his small valley. The shelling became louder. The war returned.

A battered jeep pulled off the road and skidded to a stop in front of Luther. He struggled to his feet. Barely conscious, all that remained he controlled with instinct and duty.

Major Welter stepped out of the jeep and peered at Luther curiously, trying to fathom how he could exist. The few survivors of hill 406 said they had seen him blown off the rear slope.

Major Welter cleared his throat, coughed, a racking, sickly cough. His eyes were dark pits sunken into the recesses of his skull. He was gaunt, unshaven, and filthy. He rubbed his face hard.

"How ..." He coughed again. "How did you get here, Sergeant Cole?"

For a few minutes Luther didn't answer, trying to remember how to talk. "Ah don't rightly know, Major Welter, concussion maybe? Ah don't know. I'm shot up some."

Luther propped himself against the wall, but his knees wouldn't lock. He forced them straight with his hands.

"Major, you look poorly. There's water around back in the well. It's clean. Why don't y'all take ten? I'll heat water, you can have coffee, get cleaned up." Luther's voice faded with each word.

11

The major turned and hollered for a medic to come forward on the double. "I missed having you around, Sergeant. I haven't been looked after proper since I left Oregon." Sergeant Cole's head drooped heavily to his chest.

Major Welter hobbled over to Luther. He still suffered from the effects of frostbite. He put his arm around Luther's waist and helped him inside the farmhouse.

"I'll do like you say, Sergeant. Let's sit. I have been rained on hard and hung up wet."

Inside the small room, Luther stumbled to the nearest wall and leaned against it. "I lost track of things, Sergeant Cole. What about your men?" the major asked.

Luther's head came up. Major Welter saw his expression and wished he hadn't asked.

"Damn! Sorry, Sergeant, had to ask."

Luther's voice was a whisper. "Major, you don't look too good. I bet you ain't took care of your feet neither." His voice rose and fell with his fading strength. "Soldier lives on his feet: Man don't take care, he ain't gonna last."

The major nodded. "You're right, Sergeant. I promise, I'll do it."

The major's aide, a young first lieutenant, and the top sergeant stood in the doorway, waiting orders.

"Lieutenant Terry, see that everything keeps moving. I'm staying with Sergeant Cole for a while. Sergeant Keene, tell those corpsmen to step on it."

"Sir."

Luther waited for the major to sit. When he had, he half sat, half fell down. The major jumped to his side and eased him into a comfortable position.

"Easy man, take it easy. You've done your share."

Two corpsmen entered the room running. "You all right, Major?"

"I'm all right. This is Sergeant Cole, back from 406. He's been hit." He turned to Luther. "Where'd you get it, Luther?"

Luther's head was slumped forward on his chest. He didn't move. The corpsman knelt by his side and examined him.

"He's unconscious, sir."

Two men brought a stretcher and laid him on it. The corpsmen carefully removed his shirt. Lying on his back, unconscious, Luther moaned. Tears ran down his face.

A younger corpsman, just arrived at the front, looked disgusted. "Christ, he's crying."

The major, his sergeant, and the other corpsman turned on him at the same time. Their combined anger was like a fist in the boy's gut. The major had to make a physical effort not to hit him.

"Sergeant, someone should instruct the child regarding the facts of life before it becomes necessary to kick the child's ass through the top of his head."

The major turned to him. "You'll cry, boy, before you're done with this place, you'll cry if you're any kind of man."

The major knelt beside Sergeant Cole and gently wiped his face with his handkerchief. He spoke in a whisper.

"Any fool can see the sergeant is sweating. Probably fever."

The corpsman began to apologize. A look from Sergeant Keene stopped him. As Luther's uniform was removed, the young corpsman grimaced. It looked as if he had been beaten with a baseball bat. The bayonet wounds on his arms and shoulders were jagged, bloody, oozing pus. Around the bullet hole in his chest the skin puckered, waxy and yellowish-black.

The other corpsman spoke. "Looks septic, and these"—he pointed to the jagged cuts—"bayonet, ugly wounds." He lifted Luther's wrist.

"Jesus, I've seen this before. Teeth marks! It was hand-to-hand for two days on 406. If we keep him alive, it'll be a miracle."

The major turned to his sergeant. "You get the MASH unit on the hook." He had a hard time controlling his voice. "Tell them! Don't ask! They're to send a chopper. Now! If they screw around, you tell them I'll send a squad back and shoot every damn one of them."

The sergeant was surprised. The major didn't curse.

"Tell them we've got a survivor from the hill. Damn bastard war!" He turned away so the men couldn't see his face. "We had two hundred and eighty-six men up there and so far we've got six back, and they were shot up; seven counting Sergeant Cole. Sergeant Keene, get some water heated. I'm going to take a bath, and wash my feet. I don't intend for Sergeant Cole to come around and find I didn't do like he asked."

Chapter 3

Military Hospital, Japan, March 1951

Luther's eyes snapped open—a soldier's reaction driven by instinct. It took another ten minutes before the mind, pushing through drug delay, followed the body into wakefulness.

A hospital. Not a MASH unit. All white and chrome. The unmistakable odor of antiseptic. It had a smell, acrid and threatening. From the mind's eye he examined his body cautiously, an inch at a time. A dull ache in the shoulder, lesser aches and soreness down the length of his body.

I took one, he thought, *in the shoulder.* He felt hunger as something good, basic, but before he could explore being alive, a dark wave of fear filled his mind and nearly overwhelmed him. Panic, raw and violent. He couldn't locate the source. He felt hollow, nauseated.

First the violin case, then the violin began to form in the darkness of his mind, becoming clearer and clearer.

"Where?"

He tried to sit up and couldn't. He tried to speak out, to shout, but no sound came, just a hoarse gasp.

A nurse came into the private room, saw his face distorted with effort, and rushed to his side. His hand shot out and grabbed hers.

"Where is it?" It came out as a whisper.

She had been a nurse for five years, and knew the wounded the way a good sergeant knows his squad. She patiently asked him what he wanted.

15

"Where is my knapsack, my gear?"

When she understood, she gently disengaged his hand and went to the closet. She knew about him. A communiqué from SCAP head-quarters—Supreme Command Allied Pacific—preceded him. He was the lone survivor of a battle for another godforsaken hill, and no less than General Alton Taylor had recommended him for the Medal of Honor. Usually private rooms were reserved for majors and above.

She brought his knapsack and rifle from the closet. She stood the rifle against the wall near the bed. The knapsack she put in a chair next to the bed. She went back to the closet and dragged his duffel over to the bed.

He whispered hoarsely, "Please, ma'am, in the bottom of the duf-fel, there's a black case."

She'd handled a thousand strange requests from patients and knew they had to be taken seriously. It took more than cutting and stitching to heal a man.

She removed an odd assortment of gear, personal mementos, worn clothing, then the case. She placed it on the bed alongside his body, where he could feel it.

"Shall I raise the bed so you can sit up?"

"Please, ma'am." His voice was getting stronger.

She cranked the handle on the bed until he was upright. He pulled the case onto his lap and picked at the clasps. His hands were numb, weak. They didn't work right. He frowned, not understanding. She came to his side and reached down to the case.

"May I do that, Sergeant Cole? I'll be very careful."

He nodded. She popped the clasps and lifted the top.

It was there! Luther felt a visceral charge of relief. He stared at the violin, put his hands on the slack strings, reassured himself it was real.

"That's a beautiful instrument, Sergeant." She looked closer. "My brother plays the violin with the San Diego Symphony."

She peered down through the top, then stood up with a gasp. She quickly bent down for a closer look. Scarcely changed since the day it came from the hands of the Maestro of Cremona.

"ANTONIUS STRADIVARIUS CREMONA."

"Jesus and saints preserve, it's a Stradivari! No wonder you were worried."

What's she talking about, it's just a fiddle. It's made real fine, that's a fact. He had saved it. That mattered.

He closed the lid and the snaps himself.

"Does that closet lock, ma'am?" he whispered.

"Yes, it does. I'll put it away if you like."

"Please."

She put his things back in the closet and locked it. Then she came back to the bed.

"I'm going to check you over before the doctor comes." She proceeded to check his temperature and pulse.

"Uh, ma'am, that stuff in the closet is private."

She looked at him, nodded, and smiled.

"My name is Janice Pell, or just Nurse Pell if you like. You're going to be here awhile, so we might as well be friendly. Don't worry, I won't mention that." She pointed toward the closet.

"Thank you, Miz Pell." He fell asleep, one part of the terrible storehouse of his mind at peace.

Chapter 4

The dreams began in the hospital. They terrified him. During the day he hid the terror from everyone except Nurse Pell. He feared he might be mad. Luther answered the doctor's questions, even talked with a psychiatrist, though afterward he had no idea what the man asked, or what he answered.

He tried to be what he thought other people would think sane. He wasn't sure if he succeeded. The anxiety ate at him constantly.

How could anyone look at him and not know? he wondered.

He struggled not to dream. It was another war, and he wasn't strong enough for it. Luther confided in Nurse Pell his fear of the shrinks. He hated them more than he hated any battle-maddened North Korean soldier.

When he was a boy, his auntie Rebecca had been forcibly committed to the state facility for the insane. Her husband, a cruel, many-times-born-again Baptist, insisted she'd been possessed by the devil.

The poor woman talked to people she couldn't see. No one in the family minded. She never harmed anyone. Folks would just agree with her and treat her gently.

In the first year they gave her the electricity so many times she couldn't remember her own name. He went with his father to visit and she asked his daddy who is the nice little boy. He never forgot.

Whole days disappeared. He wondered if he was dying. Nurse Pell explained that he had done and seen more than he could deal with;

that there were automatic mechanisms in the mind trying to help him cope with the hurt done to his spirit. She suggested he find a quiet place when he got back to West Virginia and rest.

Luther believed her. Whenever the army shrinks wanted to interview him, she scheduled it for the early morning. He felt better in the morning.

Luther started life with a strong, resilient body. Once begun, the healing went rapidly. A week before he left Japan for the States, Major Welter arrived from Korea.

Luther started to snap to attention and the major waved him back to his chair. A worn Bible sat on a table next to the bed.

Welter looked around the room and raised his eyebrows. He smiled. "Nice billet, Sergeant Major Cole." He handed him the three-up and three-down cloth patch signifying his new rank.

Luther held the patch but felt no real pleasure in it.

"Ah thank you, Major. I ain't, I have not earned these stripes, but I'll take them, seein' as you're givin' 'em."

Major Welter nodded. "I know, I do know." He sat down in a chair across from Luther.

"It doesn't seem right, does it? You're alive and your men gone." The major looked out the window for a long time. Luther's hands writhed in his lap, knuckles white. "I'm still working on that one, Sergeant Major. Maybe someday we'll get the answer." He looked at the Bible on the table. "I read the book too." He nodded toward Luther's Bible. "I look forward to one day, just one, when my soul is at peace, when I'm at peace."

Major Welter leaned forward. "Luther, don't give up on yourself. You think you're not a good man. You think you didn't do it right, if you had, your men would be alive."

Luther watched Major Welter with complete attention.

Welter sat back in his chair. "I'm a professional soldier. It's my business to judge men. I judge them against the harshest environment there is. You and I were given commands far beyond what a soldier could normally be expected to accomplish. We might have died too, but we didn't. We have to live, to go on, if for no other reason than to live long enough to figure out why it turned out this way. You and I deserve peace as much as the next man.

"Another reason I'm here is to counsel you on what's going to happen when you go back to the States."

For an instant a terrified look passed over Luther's face. Major Welter didn't see it.

"General Taylor has announced your Medal of Honor. Before you give me any trouble"—objection was written across Luther's face—"you listen. I've seen a good many medals handed out. Many were deserved. I'm of the opinion you deserve yours as much as any man I've ever soldiered with. You don't want it for yourself. I understand that."

Major Welter saw Luther's despair.

"You and I can't give them back their lives. Christ knows, we want to. It's out of our hands. You will be a good soldier as you have been since you were seventeen years old, Sergeant Major Martin Luther Cole. You will obey your commanding officer, me, and stand in front of the President of the United States while he hangs that little bauble around you neck.

"And if I'm there, which I hope I will be, we will think of all the good men who should be there with us. We will not forget when the rest of the country has, as they always do."

"Sir, I 'preciate your comin' here, a lot."

"Good, good. I talked with Nurse Pell before I came up. Nice woman, pretty, thinks a lot of you. You might think about asking her to go back to West Virginia with you."

Luther flushed and stammered. "Now, Major, no call to talk like that. She is a fine woman, but she's educated. Me, I didn't get past the seventh grade."

"I know. I also know education hasn't got anything to do with how a woman feels when she 'being held by a man she cares for. You're twenty-four years old, Luther, plenty of time to learn what you need. It was just a thought, Sergeant, I don't mean to push."

Major Welter stood up to leave. Luther stood also and came to attention. Major Welter took his salute, then shook Luther's hand.

"In years to come, when I talk of soldiers, your name will always come up, Sergeant Major. Despite what you think, you're more than a good soldier, you're a good man, and I am proud to have soldiered with you.''

After the major left, Luther opened his Val-Pak and removed the violin case. He held it in his lap for a moment, then opened the case. He laid his hands on the wood and talked to God, who never seemed to be far from him.

A Villa North of Rome, 1715

Count Domenici Paisello was dying, alone except for a manservant and his cook. He had fallen prey to the adage that the worst punishment in life is to outlive one's children.

Plague, wars, and politics had tormented and finally killed them all. A man who devoted his entire life to music at the expense of his family, he felt shame. Yet he could not find regret for a part of life he'd never really experienced.

All his true memories were of music. He had heard them all. Bach, Boccherini, Haydn, Gluck, Scarlatti, Vivaldi. He drank with them, argued with them, and always played their music.

Count Paisello had been the greatest violinist of his age. They all came to him, asked his advice, wrote pieces especially for him, and he for them. Life enough for any man. He wanted no more. All the rest had been a surprise. In years long past he occasionally noticed his children waiting to see him. They were strangers. He wondered where they came from; surely they couldn't all be his?

Now they were gone. The last had died during an influenza epidemic twenty years before. Yet, Count Paisello wasn't ready to die. He had one more thing to do; one more thing he must do. He had been the king, and with kings there is always the matter of succession.

His servants were puzzled. He saw it in their eyes. They waited for him to die. A great joke. He laughed at them and they didn't understand.

23

Thirty years before he traveled north and received into his hand the great violin called Hercules. It was a mountain of a memory; the linchpin of his musical life. All things were measured as coming before or after that moment. It had been given into his hand, reluctantly, by the Maestro of Cremona himself.

Now he would do his duty, a most honorable duty. He had been twenty years making up his mind. Three weeks earlier he received a letter from the one selected saying he would come as soon as possible.

Count Paisello slept as the "Master of Nations," as Giuseppe Tartini was called, arrived.

All the long trip from Padua to Rome Tartini worried he would be too late. The count said he was dying, but that he would delay the event until he, Tartini, arrived. He went on to say that that which he would give Maestro Tartini must be placed into his care by his own hand.

Tartini, called by the count's manservant, that northerner with the nose, was led to the count's bedchamber, where he settled himself in a comfortable chair. The servant brought him a carafe of wine and left.

When the count woke, he saw his old friend, wrapped in his cloak, dozing, glass still clutched in his hand.

"Tartini . . ." His voice was too weak. Tartini did not stir. "Tartini . . ." Louder this time.

Tartini woke with a start, looked at the glass, and put it on a side table.

"Tartini . . ."

He got up quickly and went to the bed. He took the old count's hand in his own. "Count Paisello, my old friend." He smiled. "It appears that I am not too late."

The count smiled the smile of a child. What evil he had done in his life had been confessed or forgotten.

"You are not too late, old friend, though it has been a trial to stay alive when I have been so ready for death. When I was younger, it was 1685, thirty years ago, I commissioned the Maestro of Cremona to make for me a great violin."

He sighed, remembering the event.

"He excelled himself to such an extent, he did not want to give me what he had made. There, on the settee, bring it here."

Tartini got up and brought the violin case to the bed.

"Open it, Giuseppe."

Tartini opened the case. Count Domenici Paisello and Giuseppe Tartini looked at the golden perfection of a great violin.

"I have thought long about this moment. Who would be worthy? Not only in ability, but in character. I knew from the beginning its possessor must be more than a great musician.

"The maestro named it Hercules. It is strong. It has mythical power. I give this to you, Giuseppe, and I ask you to do the same someday. I ask you to give it to another when you can no longer be the one to make it sing...."

The count coughed weakly. *"It is good. I have done what I wanted to do. I think now it is time to die."*

"Hear me, my count," Tartini pledged, *"I will do all that you ask. I pray God help me be worthy of this gift."*

Count Domenici Paisello's eyes closed. His last breath joined the small breezes of the Roman dusk.

Chapter 5

Luthersville, West Virginia, June 1951

Mud, thick and black as molasses. Boy Patterson's blond hair was matted with it. The great wound in his chest blossomed like an evil flower pouring out the essence of his young life.

"I have to git you outa here! C'mon, Boy, try," Luther pleaded, "you gotta help me."

The bus driver shook Luther's shoulder and shouted in his ear. Luther's terrible struggle went on, all within the small space of his seat. His dreams held him in place like a straitjacket.

Across the aisle, a middle-aged woman with cruel eyes and a pinched face pulled her runny-nosed child closer.

"You'd think the army'd put people like that away. It's men like him who run wild killin' and rapin' decent women."

An older, colored man came down the aisle and gently moved the driver out of the way.

"Y'all give us a minute. I were a soldier, I know what to do."

He bent down and whispered in Luther's ear. "Sergeant Major, Sergeant Major, snap to, you're needed on the double."

Luther let go of Boy Patterson, nineteen years old, good-natured and full of laughter. He dragged himself into the present. It took all his strength. His unfocused eyes looked at the black man for a long count.

"What ... what is it? He coughed and pounded his knees with bony, clenched fists.

"You're home, Sar'n Major. It's time to git off the bus."

The black man reached out and touched the four rows of medals, especially the one with the blue background and white stars.

"No more war for you, young fella." He pulled Luther to his feet. "You gonna be all right, boy?"

Luther focused on the man's face. He saw concern and respect. "Was I bad?" Luther looked around nervously.

The older man's face creased with a smile. "Uh-huh, you was talkin' some. Don't you worry none. These folk don't unnerstan. Jus' 'cause the fightin's done don't mean the war's ovuh.

"Y'all go home now, find a place where folks won't mind if'n you talk strange for a while. Find you a big ole rock. Talk at it. It helps to know it'll be there the next day. This pain will ease, time an' family'll do it."

He pulled Luther's Val-Pak down from the overhead rack. "Go on now, I'll bring this. Time someone fetched for you, you done fetched for them." He nodded toward the passengers.

The bus stopped in front of a run-down gas station with a diner attached. Outside, the air was hot and humid. A faded Coca-Cola sign drooped across a slab of plywood. Someone had hand-painted RAY'S FINE FOOD on it.

Luther's father stood by a pickup truck parked next to a Texaco pump. A twentieth-century stoic: raised to work twelve hours a day, hide his feelings, and fear God.

Luther stood in the sun while the driver removed another bag from the storage compartment. The black man stood nearby. Luther turned to him and put out his hand.

"You musta been a good soldier."

They shook hands. Two solemn men closer than their neighbors or family would ever allow.

"I were, Sar'n Major. Y'all take it easy, heah?" He got back on the bus.

Luther's father walked over to the bus. They looked at each other, assessing the changes.

"It's real good to have you home, Luther." Luther's father did not embrace his son.

They shook hands. "I'm tired, Daddy, real tired."

Over the next few days Luther tried to explain himself to his father but couldn't find the words. A day came when he blacked out and fell off the tractor. He lay in a dark red furrow of dirt, groaning and dreaming.

His father sat in the field with him. He didn't know what to do, so he sat with his son and prayed. He prayed for what every father who watches his child suffer prays for.

"Let it be me, Lord. Let me have the pain." Fathers always imagine they are stronger than their sons when in fact they are only older.

Luther finally fell into a restless sleep. His father moved the tractor close to put the boy in the shade. It didn't occur to him to go for a doctor. There wasn't anything wrong with his son's body.

Luther woke up at dusk. Minutes passed before he realized where he was, what had happened. His father held his hand as he had when Luther was a little boy.

"I'm sorry to trouble you, Daddy, real sorry."

"Don't matter none. There's just you an' me. Y'all need time. Done too much, always did, even when you was a little boy."

"I don't know how long this is goin' to take." Luther looked across the fields to the purple mountains behind. "I'm glad Mama didn't see me this way."

"She'da been fine, boy. That woman had grit, and a gentle nature. Don't know that I evuh heard her say an unkind word to anyone." He smiled at Luther, then looked away into the distance.

"Musta been a thousand times I wondered what she seen in me. I weren't winnin' no beauty contests in those days. She was the accountant at Tolliver's Mercantile: finished high school too! Imagine that. You know up in the north they call us rednecks like it was a dirty word. As if we don't do nuthin' but drink moonshine likker and hang black folks."

He didn't let go of his son's hand. He worried Luther would go away if he did.

"Your mama didn't mind my red neck, which it sure 'nuff is," he chuckled.

Luther looked at his father with surprise and affection. They hadn't ever talked about Luther's mother that he could remember.

"I'da like to been better educated, but it weren't in me. Then the Depression and all, trying to keep food on the table. Got this here red neck workin' the farm, raisin' crops for other folks. Lord, I ain't

had a decent drink of 'shine in more than three years; and as far as
black folks go, I couldn't get so mad at a man, black or white, I
wouldn't go out and take care of business personal. Don't need no
dang fool bedsheets and burning crosses. It ain't Christian.''

   Luther looked at his father. He didn't remember his mother very
well. She had died when he was three. He never realized how much
his father missed her.

Chapter 6

Luthersville, West Virginia, Summer 1951

A month after Luther returned from Korea he knew it wasn't going to get better. He'd blacked out three times that he could remember. He couldn't concentrate long enough to do a decent day's work.

He went looking for his father and found him in the barn, putting up hay, his face sweaty, streaked with dirt and chaff. Nathan Cole stuck the pitchfork into the hay and motioned Luther outside. They sat on a wooden bench and looked across the fields.

Luther's father wiped his face with a checkered cloth and slowly rolled a cigarette. The leaf was rough-cut and pungent. He grew and cured his own tobacco like his father had before him.

"Not goin' too good, is it, Luther."

"No, Daddy. I feel worse 'cause it troubles you. I know you don't mind, but it bothers me somethin' terrible." His father waited patiently. Luther went on.

"What kinda shape is Granddaddy's place up on the mountain?" Luther looked toward the hills turning orange in the sunset.

"Why, boy, I don't rightly know. Been four, maybe five years since I been up there. Went huntin' with Cousin Joe Barkwood up that way." He took a drag on his homemade, and watched the blue smoke catch on the wind.

"He built it good, mostly stone, red oak, and pine. Door still worked: Roof weren't broke. 'Course that slate probably last three hundred years. Went down to the spring. Big jack pine fallen down

31

and messed it up some, but the water's still sweet. Man could make good whiskey with that water." He paused to stamp his cigarette out in the dirt. "You fixin' to go up there, are yuh?"

"Uh-huh."

"Bothers me some to think you might come on one of yer spells out in the forest with no one to look after yuh."

"Figured it would, Daddy, but I got to do it. I just cain't stay here no more. I'll be all right, stay close to the cabin 'n all. Gonna go to Elkins, get me a new pickup, some tools, and such. I've got me the money from the medal and my mustering-out pay. Don't need much. I've got to live simple, not be no trouble to no one."

Luther raised his hand as his father started to speak. He reached out and took his father's worn hand.

"I know you don't figure I'm trouble, but I do, and it makes it harder, a lot harder."

Luther's father looked down at his son's hand, so much like his own. "All right, boy, you do what you want, you've the right."

Padua, Italy, 1719

The night was hot, close. The "civilized" world was still tortured by the idea that windows must be kept closed to prevent the night air, source of evil humors and of a multitude of diseases, away from the body.

Against the advice of his wife, Tartini had eaten two game pies. Now he paid the price. He went to bed early. It took a long time getting to sleep.

The dream came slowly, without form, and then there he was, making a pact with the devil. It went well. He felt no remorse, no faustian indecision.

The devil asked if he might play his violin, the Hercules. Tartini gave it to him out of curiosity. Then he was amazed to hear the devil play a sonata so miraculous that it exceeded all imagination.

It enchanted Tartini. His breath stopped and he awoke. He reached for his violin, the Hercules, to reproduce some of the sounds he heard in his dream.

As he told the French violinist, Lalande, sometime later: "The music I composed at that moment is no doubt the best I ever wrote—and I call it the 'Devil's Sonata'—but it is a far cry from what I heard in my dreams."

Chapter 7

Luthersville, West Virginia, Spring 1952

The maple log in the fireplace settled on the grate with a small exhalation of sparks. The flickering light exposed a large, stone-walled room as spartan as a monk's cell.

Luther turned up the gas on the Coleman lantern and sat at the red oak table in the middle of the room. On the table, a disassembled twelve-gauge shotgun, gun oil, brushes, and rags had been pushed aside. Beyond the gun a stack of worn books.

The woman at the library told him there were ten or fifteen books that famous men read: men like Napoleon and General Grant. Privately, Luther didn't think being a Union general or a French general much recommendation, but he wasn't of a mind to argue, so he took what she gave him.

Adam Smith's *Wealth of Nations* lay open on the top of the stack. Reading was hard, but with a dictionary and patience he began to get the hang of it. Her choice had been good. He liked Montaigne's *Essays,* and read some of them three and four times.

But this night he wouldn't read. A stack of writing paper and three or four yellow pencils lay in front of him, waiting. He wrote three words on the first piece of paper.

Dear Miss Pell. He stared at the paper. The pencil, dwarfed by his large hand, was forgotten. He'd written the letter a hundred times in his mind. Alone on his mountain in West Virginia, he blushed with shame.

He didn't write longhand. He printed, and the letters were large and awkward. He started again.

I thought of you often since I got back and wanted to thank you again for being so nice to me. It has been hard. I stayed with my pa for a while but after a month couldn't do that no more. He was real good to me and didn't mind that I fell off the tractor and lay in the field all day having terrible dreams. So I have come to live on Cole's Mountain which was my granddaddy's. I have a nice house and work in the lumber mill in Elkins now and again. I take the fiddle out most evenings and try to imagine how it got to that farmhouse in Korea. It feels good to look at it and touch it. I feel sure God meant for me to find it and take care of it. I have been practicing reading most every evening. It is getting easier but I am sorry I write so poorly. I remember you didn't make fun of me or the way I talk which is why I decided to write. I am not proud of this writing but I am going to get better. I would be real pleased to get a letter from you if you had the time. If you don't I will understand. I admired the way you got yourself educated. Wouldn't many men have done as good. I still have them spells from time to time but I think it is getting better. Sometimes it is funny like the time I woke up with a squirrel on my chest making an awful racket. He was madder than all get out cause I fell across his storehouse of nuts. We were both nuts! Ha-ha. Well, I sure hope your feeling good and not having no trouble of any kind.

> Your friend,
> Martin Luther Cole

The next day Luther took the letter down the mountain and mailed it from the post office in Luthersville. The little children looked at him and whispered.

He smiled at them. *They think I'm crazy.*

He didn't mind, kids were like that.

Luther was amazed to receive a letter ten days later. Mrs. Ames, the postmistress and owner of the five and dime, smiled at him and asked if he had a girlfriend all the way across the country in San Francisco. Luther blushed, too embarrassed to answer.

He took the letter back to the mountain and didn't read it until the end of the day. She said she was happy to hear from him. She talked of her work at the hospital and life in the city, and said she missed the small town where she was born.

Their letters criss-crossed the country for a year before she sent him a picture of her in uniform. He'd never seen anyone so pretty. He didn't think about love. That wasn't permitted. In his own mind he was still crazy.

Then came the letter that she said she was coming to West Virginia. He secretly yearned for just such a visit, but faced with the fact of it, was terrified.

As the day of her arrival drew close, he imagined all kinds of things going wrong. He'd have one of his spells while driving his truck and kill them both. Maybe she would be embarrassed to be seen with a hillbilly like himself.

The day before she arrived, he went to Luthersville and got a haircut. He bought a couple pairs of decent pants and shirts. Back on the mountain he spent the afternoon cleaning the truck.

The next day, as he waited for the Trailways bus, he thought of his own arrival back from the war and his father waiting for him. He decided to take her out to the farm. She said she wanted to stay a few days. It'd keep tongues from waggin' more than usual.

When the bus came to a stop in front of the Texaco station, Luther was sweating and praying he wouldn't have one of his spells. He didn't remember her being so small, but then, most of the time he'd seen her he was flat on his back. She wasn't in her uniform. She wore a neat print dress with a perky hat and shoes with heels. He'd forgotten how blue her eyes were.

She came right to him and took his hand like it was the most natural thing in the world.

"Hello, Luther." She smiled and it almost burst his heart on the spot. "I don't remember you being so tall."

He smiled and smiled but said nothing. Luther watched curiously as the driver brought out three large Samsonite bags from the storage bin. But not knowing anything about how women traveled, guessed it must be okay.

He put them in the back of his truck, helped her in, and drove toward his father's farm. He tried to think of something to say.

"You look so pretty, I can't think to look at the road." It just burst out, and he blushed. She gave back a blush and looked at him steady.

"Now I know I wasn't foolish to come. I worried you would think I was too much trouble, or that you didn't have any feeling for me, you know that way." She looked down at her hands, which were clasped in her lap. "Luther, will you pull over for a minute?"

"Sure." He pulled in underneath a stand of pine.

"Luther, I guess I better tell you right off. I came with the intention to stay. I have most everything I need in those suitcases. If you think I'm being too forward, I'll understand. I don't have anything in San Francisco I want, and seeing you, I know what I want is right here."

Her hand lay on the seat between them, waiting to be held. He took her hand.

"Miss Pell, I would surely like to hold you."

She came into his arms and they held each other, and kissed each other there in his pickup beneath the pines. They talked and romanced until the moon came up, then drove along to his father's farm.

A month later Martin Luther Cole married Miss Janice Marie Pell at the Faith and Redemption Baptist Church in Luthersville. Luther took her to his mountain, and they stayed. Occasionally he took out the violin. He held it and remembered, and it hurt, but he could bear the pain.

Luther Cole and Janice Pell Cole had five good years on the mountain before fate in the guise of something called the Asian flu came and took beauty from his life. Not satisfied with taking his wife, his father also died that year.

Folks below the mountain who had been getting to know Luther and Mrs. Cole didn't see him for two years. Some thought he'd died of heartbreak. In the mountains they knew a man or woman could be taken that way.

He came finally, to buy supplies, and people whispered. His hair hung below his shoulders and it was gray. Luther was still in his early thirties. He spoke to no one, even those who spoke to him.

It wasn't a stretch of the imagination for folks to think him crazy. Being poor in the mountains of West Virginia often led to madness, great and small.

Chapter 8

Luthersville, West Virginia, Summer 1978

Ailey Barkwood played in the dust alongside an ancient sway-backed barn. As he played, he sang "Rock of Ages" at the top of his voice. Sammy Sue, the old black woman who looked after Ailey and his grandfather, sat on the porch and shelled peas. She gazed across the fields to the forest, occasionally glancing toward the barn where Ailey sat in the dust and sang.

Against the mountains behind the forest, massive thunderheads marched away forever. Sammy Sue smiled. Her hands, separate from her thoughts, popped fresh peas from their green sheaths. The day before, Ailey asked her how far up the biggest cloud went: Did it reach the moon?

She told him it went forever.

He nodded, his serious eyes looking toward the sky. He believed her.

Sammy Sue hummed along with the boy. "You're a caution, Ailey Barkwood. I do believe you're tuned sweeter'n the piano at the church."

It was true. He slid over every third word and changed those he wasn't sure of, but each note, each tone, was faithfully rendered. He could have tuned the piano by ear. Ailey Barkwood wasn't quite five years old.

Ailey's grandfather, Joe Barkwood, pushed open the screen door and walked onto the porch. The wooden door slammed noisily behind

41

him. Joe Barkwood once stood six feet four in his stocking feet; now he was bent by age and rheumatism. Despite the wear of sixty years in the sun and a thick shock of hair gone pure white, he and the boy were quite similar: long, narrow faces, square chins, and deep-set dark eyes.

Grandpa Joe sat on a bench near Sammy Sue and rubbed his legs with large, square-knuckled hands. After a while he pulled a watch and chain from a pocket in the front of his overalls and snapped it open.

"About two minutes, Sammy Sue."

"Uh-huh, Mistuh Joe."

They both looked toward the boy playing in the dust. Two minutes later Ailey got up and banged his hands against his shirt and jeans. A cloud of dust rose in the still air and settled back like fleas to a hound. He ran toward the porch on legs too long for the rest of his body. He went immediately to his grandfather and stood by his knee.

"Can I git it, Grandpa?"

"You ain't gittin' nothin', Ailey Barkwood, till you washes yo face and hans," Sammy Sue said.

His grandfather nodded. "You do like Sammy says, boy."

Ailey frowned at such foolishness and muttered, "What do my hands and face have to do with 'it.' "

When Ailey came out of the house two minutes later he looked like a raccoon. The front half of his face was reasonably clean, but farther back was a brown ring of dirt. He stood in front of Sammy Sue impatiently.

She laughed, warm as sunshine, and put the bowl of peas on the porch by her chair.

"What's the matter with you, boy?" He shifted from one foot to the other. "Couldn't you find the rest of your face?" Ailey didn't answer.

"Did you bring the cloth?" she asked.

He held it behind his back, and the instant she said cloth, handed it to her. She washed his face, all of it, then his arms and hands.

"There, I knew there was a little boy 'neath there somewhere."

"Grandpa?"

"Okay, Ailey, bring 'er here."

He dashed into the house and came out a moment later with an old Philco Transoceanic portable radio. An extension cord dragged behind. It was so big, Ailey could barely carry it. He bit his lip with concentration and lifted it to a low table along the front of the porch.

"Go ahead, boy, find yer music."

Saturday afternoon, and every Saturday afternoon at two o'clock, for two whole hours, WNEW New York played the classics, featuring the New York Philharmonic Orchestra.

Neither Grandpa Joe nor Sammy Sue liked it much, but from the first moment Ailey heard it, he screamed and shouted when they tried to change the station. They were too old to fight such total anger.

Ailey handled the radio like a religious artifact, carefully turning the dial until he heard the familiar voice of the announcer. When he was satisfied, he turned the volume up as far as it would go. By some oddity of atmospheric conditions and location, the station came in perfectly.

Ailey sat down and leaned against the wall of the house, an acolyte in the presence of the master. He had been doing this every Saturday for more than a year.

He learned the names of the instruments from a children's concert conducted by Leonard Bernstein. Ailey's intensity unnerved Grandpa Joe and Sammy Sue. Old Joe Barkwood figured a boy ought to get worked up about a good Barlow knife or a baseball glove.

For Ailey, the rest of the world disappeared. The universe revolved around the porch of his grandpa's house at the foot of Cole's Mountain, West Virginia.

The opening piece was "The Moldau" by Smetana, the most perfect evocation of a river from source to fullness ever set to music. He had listened to it three times. He knew every note.

As the lilting sounds of the flutes marked tiny rills in the forests of Bohemia, he formed the word *flutes* silently. And when the massed violins burst forth with the theme, his small body leaned forward, trembling like a hunter on the point.

He whispered, "Violins" as others would call the names of saints.

Two hours later, his head tilted back against the clapboard covered walls of the farmhouse, Ailey was still lost in the music. He would replay every note in his mind, over and over.

He got up, turned the radio off, and took it back in the house.

Another Saturday had come and gone, the standard against which he measured the ebb and flow of life.

On his fourth birthday his grandfather bought him a worn-out fiddle for five dollars from a tinker, a wandering gypsy who sold pots and pans, cloth and needles out of the back of a battered pickup.

The man was old like his grandfather, but short with curly black hair and dark, laughing eyes. He showed Ailey how to tune it and hold the bow. Ailey began to practice immediately and found himself in the barn with five milk cows, two draft horses, and twenty Rhode Island Red chickens.

Sammy Sue said the scratching made her teeth ache. His grandfather's two Bluetick hounds sat in the doorway of the barn and howled mournfully. Ailey allowed as how they weren't a righteous accompaniment and chased them into the woods with a dozen well-thrown rocks to make sure they understood. After that, when the hounds saw Ailey with the violin they headed for the woods without being asked.

The scratching lasted about a week, and then to his grandfather's and Sammy Sue's surprise they heard a melody: not pure but recognizable. The old violin was all one might expect for five dollars, but somehow Ailey coaxed music from it.

Life now had other markers to define and measure the passage of time. He broke strings. These were the catastrophes that ruined the harmony of his child's existence. Then he had to wait for his grandfather to go to Elkins, the nearest town with a music store.

There were other children on the farms nearby, but he'd become so used to living with Grandpa Joe and Sammy Sue he didn't walk the mile or two to meet and play with them. If he'd had a mother and father living at home, they might have seen that he had a more normal childhood. But it wasn't to be.

His father, Little Joe Barkwood, had been killed in a sawmill accident when Ailey was one, and his mother ran off to California with a soldier when he was two. He didn't remember his father or his mother.

He had Sammy Sue and Grandpa Joe, and he had his violin. That was enough.

Padua, Italy, January 1770

"You weren't my first choice, Monsieur La Houssaye, though I admire your playing as much as any violinist I've heard in many years. I fear the French love themselves first and their music second." Tartini paused. *"You were a good student, I'll give you that."*

Giuseppe Tartini looked down at his gnarled hands, twisted with arthritis.

La Houssaye, elegant and vain, waited for Tartini to go on. He resented the Italian perception of Frenchmen, and that a great violinist like Tartini shared this perception hurt doubly.

"Please do not be offended by what I say. This is, as they say, a moment of truth. Whether I am wrong or right, it will soon not matter. As you can see, time has given me the greatest punishment. I hear perfectly, yet I cannot play."

They sat across from each other in Tartini's drawing room. Between them on a small round table of walnut a violin case lay open. In it, the Hercules reflected the golden glow of candles spread around the room.

"Not so long ago Count Domenici Paisello gave me this instrument. He charged me to select the next man to have it with great care. He further instructed me to find not just the greatest virtuoso of my time, but a man of equal character; one who would preserve it and pass it on to another equally worthy when the time came.

"That time will come, monsieur. It comes to us all as these

45

wretched claws have come to me." He looked at his hands with profound loathing.

"I will not try to extract a promise to uphold the count's wishes. I will hope for that, but I will not ask for the promise. It is yours and I freely give it. Let as many hear it as possible, for it truly has a majestic voice."

La Houssaye bowed solemnly to the older man.

"I am French, Tartini, that is true. I am also consumed by my music. To that I plead guilty. I do know the value you place on this beautiful thing and I shall carry out your wishes."

"Good, that is enough."

Tartini reached out and touched the strings gently. A look of deep sadness crossed his face. "I wish that I might hear it again, for I think God has touched this thing, and I would hear his voice before I meet him in person."

"My dear Tartini—" La Houssaye's voice broke. "I am not God, but I would be delighted to play whatever you would like to hear."

"You would do that? Ah, that is good. Play me something of yours, I have heard too much of my own."

La Houssaye smiled. He stood, took the Hercules from the case, and rapidly adjusted each string.

"Let me hear an adagio. I am too old for the pyrotechnical. Something sweet, the long bow, the cantilena ..."

La Houssaye put bow to strings and Tartini closed his eyes.

Tartini's last thought before La Houssaye gave himself to the music was a comfort. "There can be no doubt of it, he is the best I have heard, and they say he is an honorable man. ..."

Chapter 9

Luthersville, West Virginia, August 1979

Miss Iris Bentley taught elementary school in Luthersville. Every summer around the first of August she went over the county lists and wrote down the names of children ready for the first grade. She made it a point to go to the home of every family on the list and make certain the parents sent their children at the appointed time.

Sitting as erect as a soldier, her hands squarely at the three-quarter points on the steering wheel of a 1963 Ford station wagon, she drove through the ripening fields of corn, tobacco, and beans to the Barkwood farm.

When she arrived, Ailey was in the barn practicing. Grandpa Joe Barkwood had gone to Elkins to buy feed, which left only Sammy Sue.

Miss Bentley sat on the porch with Sammy Sue and drank lemonade. Sammy Sue wore her Sunday dress. In the hills the older people still had great respect for a teacher.

"Who's that playin the fiddle?" Miss Iris asked.

Sammy Sue smiled. "Oh, that be little Ailey, ma'am. Ain't he somethin'? Ole Joe, that's Ailey's grandpa, give him that fiddle on his fourth birthday, him wantin' one so bad 'n all."

"Who's his teacher?" Miss Iris asked.

Sammy Sue laughed. "Sakes alive, Miz Iris, he don't have no teacher. We's poor folks, ma'am. He done taught himself. Ever Satur-

47

day he listen to that WNEW from New York, then he go to the barn and try to play everything he hear.''

"That's amazing. Do you suppose you could ask him to come over here, I'd like to meet him.''

"Uh, Miz Iris, I can't do that. He won't come. When he like that, he won't come till he done, and that could be three, four hours.'' Sammy Sue was apologetic.

"I see. Well, you see that he is ready for school come September, Sammy Sue.'' She gave the old black woman a list of what Ailey was to bring with him. "Maybe someday he'll be a great violinist, but he can't do that unless he learns to read and write.''

On the first of September, Ailey stood by the road to Luthersville with his grandpa and waited for the bus. His clothes were worn but clean. He carried a cigar box with two pieces of chicken, an apple, and a wedge of sweet potato pie. He had one new yellow pencil and lined notebook. He was frightened and he didn't want anything to do with school.

On the bus the little girls giggled at his clothes and the boys teased him. He didn't say a word. Sammy Sue said into each life a little rain must fall, which he understood very well. School, however, was a thunderstorm.

Ailey was a poor student. He understood what school was. Torture. He learned right and wrong from Sammy Sue and Grandpa Joe. Sammy Sue was a shoutin' Baptist with a real colorful idea of heaven and hell. Grandpa Joe had a more quiet view of things, but even so he had a pretty severe picture of the punishment awaiting man or woman after life.

Ailey went over everything bad he'd ever done, even the things he'd thought of doing. Throwing rocks at the chickens and cows, spearing frogs in the brook, stealing molasses cookies from Sammy Sue. But that was a game. She hid them and he was suppose to find them. The list grew and grew, and he was sure he was a very bad boy. Why else would God punish him?

Miss Bentley tried to understand, but he wasn't talking. She told the class how he played a fine fiddle, and asked him if he wouldn't bring his fiddle in and play for the class. He was too embarrassed to even consider that, so the children chased him around the school yard shouting at the top of their voices.

"Liar, liar, pants on fire."

He didn't understand, only that it hurt. In his second year he fell far behind the other students and Miss Bentley wondered if she would have to hold him back. He was smarter than anyone in the school, but he hated being there so bad, he didn't try.

Ailey didn't go out to play with the other children. At lunchtime he wandered off by himself or stayed in the schoolroom and looked at pictures in the encyclopedia. The other teachers got so used to seeing Ailey wandering around, they stopped paying attention to him.

He found a closet in the basement, full of used books, sporting equipment, and broken musical instruments, among them a violin. There wasn't anything wrong with it, there just hadn't been anyone to teach it for years. His own violin had been without strings for a month and Grandpa Joe didn't have money for new ones.

Ailey wanted that violin more than anything. He thought about taking it but couldn't face the idea. That was a sin for which he might never be forgiven. He thought about it for days and finally admitted he would have to ask Miss Bentley.

What if she says no? he thought.

He wandered through the halls to Miss Bentley's classroom, where he and fourteen other first-graders were punished. He stood on his tiptoes and looked through a pane of glass in the door into the room. She sat at the desk, grading papers. She looked alien, a stranger, someone who wouldn't want to talk to a little boy.

He wished he were as old as his grandfather. Everybody liked to talk to Grandpa Joe Barkwood. He didn't say much, but he was nice and people just wanted to talk to him. Old people didn't want to talk to children, not about things that mattered. Ailey wondered why.

His ankles got tired and he stood flatfooted outside the door, frustrated, desperate. Old Moses, the handyman, said he intended to clean out that closet and throw all the junk away. Ailey didn't realize Moses had been saying that for ten years.

Recess would be over soon and he would have to go back to making perfect circles and lines that slanted at perfect angles.

"Who cares, dumb circles, dumb straight lines," Ailey muttered.

The bell rang. Torture again. "Class, this afternoon we will learn about the directions. We must know them or we'd never get home, would we?" Some of the students giggled obediently.

Mercifully, an hour and a half later the schoolday was over. Ailey hung around, fussing with his copybook, until the other students left. He had twenty minutes before the bus came. He had to choose the exact correct moment. He would do it! He would ask her now. He watched her out of the corner of his eye, trying to guess if it was time.

Just when he thought the moment was right, the principal came into the room. They started talking about the school garden, the principal's favorite project.

Ailey scowled with frustration. *Why don't you go away,* he thought. *You look like a goat with that white hair on your chin.* Ailey drummed on the desk with his yellow pencil. Finally the principal left.

Ailey started to get up. Miss Bentley glanced up and gave him the "look." It startled him and he headed for the door, forgetting what he wanted.

"Ailey?" He looked back at her fearfully.

"Have a seat, I'll be back in a moment."

Ailey sat, wishing he'd left with the other kids. She came back in a minute.

"Now, Ailey, we can talk."

"I'll miss the bus." Last chance.

"No, I told the driver to tell Sammy Sue I'd drive you home, that you and I were doing some extra work." She sat quietly and said nothing, waiting for Ailey to speak.

"Ailey, this isn't punishment. You wanted to tell me something, didn't you?" she asked.

How did she know? "Yes'm." His voice descended to a whisper. She waited for him to go on. He took a deep breath.

"Miss Bentley, you know the closet where the old music things are?" She nodded. "There's a violin there. It's been there a long, long, forever long time. No one uses it. No one cares about it."

"There is? Well, I'll be, I didn't know that." She smiled, and to Ailey it was a real nice smile.

"Is that it? You want to use the violin. Of course you do. Is something wrong with yours?"

"Yes, ma'am. It's busted, the strings all broke except the big one."

"You should say, 'The strings are broken,' Ailey," she reminded him. "All right, let's go look at your violin." She got up and walked out of the room. Ailey followed like a shadow.

At the closet she told Ailey to get it. He brought out the case and held it protectively against his chest. "Wait a minute." She went in the closet and rummaged through a stack of paper. Finally she found what she wanted.

"Bring it along, Ailey."

Back in the classroom Miss Bentley sat at her desk. Ailey stood in front, still holding the case. It was very large next to his small body.

"Do you know what is in these books, Ailey?"

"No, Miss Bentley." He held the violin tighter, afraid she'd change her mind.

"Come here and I'll show you."

When he stood by her side she opened one of the books. He leaned forward. Suddenly he was very interested. There was a picture of a man holding a violin. He forgot that this was Miss Bentley, master of punishment.

She turned to the next page. It showed a large picture of a hand holding the bow in different positions. Ailey's eyes were wide and his attention total.

"Oh, I don't do it right." Without thinking, he put the case down carefully and moved in close to Miss Bentley's side.

She opened another book of songs. He looked at the lines and notes, trying to imagine what they meant.

"What is it?" Ailey asked, not realizing he'd actually talked to Miss Bentley.

"This is music," she said.

"Shoot, you're funnin' me." He looked at her with disbelief.

"Here, I'll read it for you." She put her finger under the words at the top of the page. "The name of this song is 'Black, Black, Black, Is the Color of My True Love's Hair.'" She sang the words in a high, sweet voice, following along with her finger under each note.

When she finished the first verse he understood. On his face was a look of utter delight and astonishment as one would expect from the most profound religious experience.

"Would you like to be able to read this so you can play all these songs?" She touched the stack of sheet music with her finger.

"Yes." Total commitment.

"Good. I can teach you how to read music, but if I do, you must do something for me," Miss Bentley said.

Ailey looked away. Is she going to take back the violin if I don't do something, he worried.

"What do I have to do?"

"Learn to read and write better than anyone else in the class. I know you can, Ailey. I know how smart you are. Up till now you haven't been trying because you don't want to be here."

Ailey looked at the stack of books and sheet music longingly. He looked at and saw a friendly woman, much younger than Sammy Sue, but like her in many ways. He knew if he said yes, it would be a promise.

"Do I have to promise?"

"No, Ailey, you do not. I want you to learn to read and write, but I cannot make you do it if you don't really want to. But I believe in being fair, do you?"

"Yes, ma'am."

"Good, I thought you did."

"I will learn to read and write and all the other stuff." There it was, he'd promised to do it.

She put out her hand. "Let's shake on it. This is our bargain."

Her hand felt warm and dry. She smelled faintly of lilac. It was nice. She handed him the stack of sheet music.

"All right, you will stay every Thursday afternoon for an extra hour. I'll drive you home afterward. I'll tell you something else, Ailey. In this book"—she pointed to the book with the picture of the man playing the violin—"in this book the words you learn to read tell you how to play the violin better."

Ailey felt suddenly shy, like when his grandfather gave him his first violin.

"Thank you, Miss Bentley."

"You are very welcome, Ailey Barkwood."

Chapter 10

Luthersville, West Virginia, 1980

If Miss Bentley thought Ailey would do better, she wasn't prepared for how much better. She never before had a student who learned faster than she could teach. He was raw, impatient, and she, a southern lady of quality: patient, perfectly mannered, and intelligent. She had taught little anarchists for twenty years. She met his demands with her own and in the process he learned manners more fitted to the nineteenth century.

It never went smoothly. If he was rude, she ignored him until he apologized. He would scowl, sulk, and cry bitter complaints. Stubborn, volatile, and finally penitent when he realized she couldn't be swayed by drama. He had to know and she had the knowledge.

In a year Ailey learned every song in the music books, played every scale. The quality of his tone improved beyond recognition. Miss Bentley taught him the basics of music, how to read notes, the values of tempo. He grasped musical concepts so fast, her well-prepared methods of explanation weren't necessary.

Miss Iris spun in a whirlwind, helpless to do more than hang on and see where it all went.

The summer when Ailey was almost seven, Grandpa Joe Barkwood went to sleep on the porch and never woke up. There being no other relatives, Ailey stayed with Sammy Sue. She was going on eighty and had all she could do to keep him fed and clothed. No one grasped the reality of the old man's death.

Sammy Sue said he had kin around somewhere, but she didn't know how to get in touch. She knew the story about Nathan Cole's strange son who went to live on the mountain behind the farm, but she wasn't having her Ailey looked after by no crazy man.

At the beginning of the school year, Miss Bentley made her usual visit to the Barkwood farm, not because Ailey might not show up that fall—he was far and away the best student in the class. She knew Uncle Joe Barkwood had died, and she knew what would happen when the busybodies in town found out.

Sammy Sue put on her Sunday dress and made lemonade. Ailey joined them on the porch.

"Well, Sammy, I heard in town that Mr. Joe died. I am sorry for you both. I didn't know him very well, but people spoke well of him, very well."

"Yes, ma'am, he wuz a fine man. Ailey and I miss him."

"Sammy, I don't mean to pry, but how have you been getting along, what do you do for money."

"Mistuh Joe, he knowed he was goin' to the Lord. He sold some land a few years back, and he left the farm to the boy. I been gettin' my government check regular. My daughter comes by once a week and does the shoppin', and her husband, George, the fixin' that needs doin'. I been leasing him a hundred acres down by the grove. That give me some income to look after Ailey. We don't have a lot, Miss Bentley, but we gets along."

Sammy Sue shifted in her rocking chair nervously, as though she could see what was coming.

"Sammy Sue, I'm not saying you've done anything wrong. I think most people would have done less. You've done fine with Ailey, but don't you think he'd be better off living in town?"

"Who he goin' to live with? He don' have no kin over there."

"He could stay with me, if you don't mind. I have plenty of room. Sammy, you have to admit you aren't a young girl anymore. What if something were to happen to Ailey?"

Sammy Sue didn't say anything. Two big tears formed in the corners of her eyes.

"Now, Sammy, please don't be upset. I'm saying these things because I am truly concerned about Ailey."

"I don't want to live in town." Ailey moved closer to Sammy Sue.

"Oh, Ailey, of course you don't." Miss Bentley looked across the fields. "It's very nice here. But there are problems you don't understand. Sammy Sue knows what I mean." The two women looked at each other.

"Miss Bentley, I knows you mean to do right by Ailey, but I'm more kin to the boy than you or any of the white folk in Luthersville. Babies are babies, white or black. They needs their own. Strangers don't smell raht, don't sound raht."

There it was, on the table. Ailey looked puzzled. This wasn't something he understood. He'd heard the kids making jokes about niggers, but he ignored them. He didn't know what they were talking about. Sammy Sue was Sammy Sue, as close to a mother as he'd ever have.

"Sammy, supposing he was to stay with me through the week and I brought him here on the weekends? What I want to do is stop trouble before it has a chance to start."

Sammy Sue barely whispered. "All right, Miss Bentley." Ailey started to protest.

"Ailey, you do like Miss Bentley says. She's right, I cain't do as good for you as I should no more." She chuckled, not one to stay sad. "Boy, I get tired jus' watchin' you. Don't you worry none, Miss Bentley be quality folk, she'll look after you proper. You come home Saturday and Sunday, I make you greens and chicken, maybe even a big batch of 'lasses cookies. We can sit on de porch and listen to WNEW New York. I swear, ah'm gittin' so I like that music."

So Ailey went to live with Miss Iris Bentley during the week, and each weekend she drove him to his grandfather's farm.

Ailey needed the forest and fields. They were as much a part of his existence as his music. When he wasn't practicing or eating all the things he missed during the week, he walked in the forest on the mountain. There was a pond halfway up the south side full of catfish and bream.

Perfect Indian summer; air crisp and leaves just beginning to change. Ailey went to the farm for his weekend.

He walked through a stand of cattails and the squishy black mud was cool on his feet. He carried a cane pole and an old tomato can full of worms. Near the edge of the pond he waded to a flat rock close to the cattails. Line in the water, worm working hard down near the bottom, bobber making small circles on the mirrorlike surface, Ailey sang in a loud voice.

This was life as sweet and right as it ever got. A half mile up the mountain in a stand of ash and maple, Luther moved quietly, as comfortable in the forest as the deer. A buck had been hanging around the area and there wasn't much meat left in the cave behind his cabin. Luther was partial to venison.

Squirrels chattered, and the click of their claws on tree bark fit well with the other sounds of the forest. Faintly in the distance Luther heard singing. At first he thought some fool had brought a transistor radio into the forest. People did that from time to time, though for the life of him he couldn't understand why.

He moved in that direction, then realized it came from the pond. He didn't hurry, he didn't need to. He sensed the source wasn't going anywhere.

Luther came out at the edge of the pond a hundred yards from Ailey, who leaned back, resting on his elbows, and sang at the top of his voice. Loud as it was, it seemed natural in the amphitheater formed by the pond and the surrounding trees.

Luther stayed back out of sight in the trees. He sat down and took an apple from his pocket and cut chunks from it with a bone-handled Buck knife. He watched Ailey lazily in the afternoon sun.

Ailey was oblivious. He didn't even notice the twitch in his line. Luther smiled and whispered.

"You are about to get a surprise, boy, an' you don't even know it."

Something tugged the line again, hard, then headed for the other shore with no intention of stopping. Ailey was so surprised, he dropped the pole and the fish dragged it into the water.

Ailey reached for it and fell into the pond, sputtering and thrashing. He grabbed the pole and tried to stop the fish.

"Whoa, you damn fool fish. Where you goin'?"

In the trees Luther laughed out loud. Ailey clutched the pole awkwardly and wasn't about to let go. The water was up to his waist. Ailey pulled the line in as fast as he could.

Luther realized he must have a real granddaddy of a catfish on the line, might go ten pounds or more. All of a sudden Luther stopped laughing, dropped the apple, and ran through the trees toward the edge of the pond. He'd been in there a year ago stalking a bear. By that same rock he'd stepped in and sunk into the mud over the top of his boots. Like to never got out. Boots were still there as far as he knew.

Through the trees he saw the boy sink in deeper; couldn't go forward or back, but he wouldn't let go of the pole.

From the edge of the rock Luther leaned forward, hands held out to Ailey.

"C'mon, boy, gimme your hands or your gonna sink right on down to China."

Ailey reached out with one hand; he wouldn't let go of the pole. Luther pulled slowly. He could feel Ailey coming free, still holding the fishing pole. Once Luther got him up on the rock he sat him down.

"Now, pull that fish on outa there before he pulls you in agin," he laughed.

Ailey pulled with all his might, muttering dark threats all the while. He got up and stepped backward off the rock to the shore. Once there, he dragged a fat catfish, close to ten pounds, after him. Still towing the fish, he walked back through the cattails onto solid ground. He thumped the fish six or eight times on the head with a rock until it quit wriggling.

"Boy, oh, boy,"—his eyes were big—"that's the biggest one I ever caught. Must weigh"—he had to think about it for a minute—"twenty or thirty ton." Ailey hadn't been paying that much attention when the class learned about the weight of things.

Luther didn't correct him. "You got a knife so's you can clean him?"

Ailey frowned. "No, sir, I don't. I'll take him on down't the house."

Luther took out his Buck knife and opened it with what Ailey thought was a very satisfying snap. He handed it to Ailey haft first.

"It's real sharp, so have a care."

Ailey admired it for a moment. He took the fish to the edge of the pond and cleaned it and the knife carefully. He figured out how to close the knife, then brought it and the fish back to where Luther sat.

"You must be little Joe Barkwood's boy. I knowed your daddy

many years ago. Hear your granddaddy passed a year back. I am
sorry to hear it, I liked that man, though he could be some stubborn.
Reckon you got some of that from him.''

"Are you the cr—the man that lives up top the mountain?''
Ailey asked.

"I am. You think I'm crazy, boy?''

Ailey wound the fishing line around a piece of cardboard. He
looked directly at Luther, considering.

"Nope.'' He went on rolling up the fishing line. "Is your name
Cole?''

"Uh-huh. I'm Martin Luther Cole. What's your name?''

"Ailey, Ailey Parkman Barkwood.''

"Well, Ailey, you 'n me are cousins. 'Cept for some distant folks
over by Elkins, you're my only kin.''

Ailey thought about it for a minute, then smiled.

"Aren't you too old to be a cousin?''

"Nope, but you can call me Uncle Luther if it'd be more
comfortable.''

Ailey guessed Luther meant to have fun with him, but he didn't
mind. He'd already decided without reservation, the way children do,
that he liked Uncle Luther. He hadn't offered to pull in his fish. That
showed a nicety of understanding about what's important that few
adults would have known.

"Okay.''

"Who you live with now your grandpa's gone?'' Luther asked.

"On weekends I stay with Sammy Sue on the farm down yonder.''
He pointed off to the south. "Weekdays I stay with Miss Bentley in
Luthersville. She's the schoolteacher.''

"Is she agreeable?''

"Uh-huh, she's nice. She let me have a violin someone left in a
closet over at the school, and all kinds of music. Been teachin' me
to read that music too.''

Luther looked at Ailey for a moment, like someone he'd been
expecting but didn't know what he'd look like.

Luther stood, stretched, and looked around slowly.

"You got strong legs, Ailey?''

"Sure.''

"You hungry?'' Luther asked.

"Yes."

"Well, I'm goin' along home, get that deer tomorrow, I guess. You come with me, I'll cook that catfish in cornmeal, make a few dozen biscuits. Got twenty pounds of new honey from the broken oak over by forty-mile crick."

"Okay, Uncle Luther."

Luther set an easy pace so Ailey could keep up. Unlike most boys his age, Ailey didn't feel the need to chatter. He felt at home with the natural sounds of the forest. And since no one else, including the dogs, seemed to like his loud singing, he figured Uncle Luther might not like it that much either.

When they had walked two miles or so, Luther heard Ailey puffing like a truck with a busted gasket. Luther stopped and looked at the ground, pretending he'd seen some tracks.

"Deer come through here this time of year," Luther said. They were in a grove of oak, and acorn husks littered the leathery carpet of leaves.

"They eat the acorns, least those the squirrels don't git."

Luther took his time looking around, watching Ailey out of the corner of his eye. When he thought Ailey was rested, he pointed up through the trees.

"Not much farther, maybe five hundred yards." He moved slowly in that direction.

It was in Luther's nature to lead. He knew the condition, the state of mind of those he led, and adjusted his intentions to ease and preserve.

Ailey stopped at the edge of the clearing. The cabin was tucked in next to a pile of granite boulders. A faint trail of smoke came from a chimney at one end. There was an abundance of flowers Mrs. Cole had planted soon after she arrived. Luther tended them faithfully year in and year out. Wild rosebushes climbed the wall near the door.

Ailey thought the cabin would be a lot smaller, like some of those places south of town. It was big, five or six rooms, and made of stone.

Later, filled with catfish, green beans, and four biscuits with wild honey washed down with cold goat's milk, Ailey could barely hold himself up. His head drooped with the sheer weight of Luther's cooking.

Luther had built a bench all along the front of the cabin. Ailey sat beside Luther and watched him roll a cigarette. He did it much as his father had before him. Ailey's eyes closed and he lay down on the bench as limp as a fed cat. He slept within minutes.

Luther got up after a moment, went in the cabin, brought out a blanket, and spread it over Ailey. He sat at the other end of the bench and watched the boy. He thought of his wife buried by the garden in back of the house.

They wanted a baby, but it hadn't happened. Luther looked out across the spread of green turning gold.

"Lord . . . I'd sure like to know what you're up to. I knowed you are testin' me, like you done Job. This little boy plays the fiddle. Ain't no way that's an accident. You want I should give him the one you put in my care? Is that it?"

Luther listened for the voice of God, as he often did.

"All right . . . I will wait. You know I can do that, but you're makin' it awful hard." Luther looked down at Ailey and spoke aloud.

"You've got grit, boy. I like that. That big ole catfish like to pulled you all the way across the pond." Luther smiled. "And you sing louder'n anyone I ever heard."

Ailey smiled in his sleep, probably catching the catfish all over again.

An hour later, at two minutes till two, Ailey woke with a start. He looked around, saw his uncle Luther sitting at the end of the bench, dozing.

"Excuse me." Luther didn't stir. "Excuse me," he said in a louder voice. Luther woke up.

"Darn, I guess that catfish got to me too," Luther said.

"Do you have a watch, Uncle Luther?" Ailey asked.

"Uh-huh." He went in the cabin and came out a few minutes later. "It's almost two o'clock."

Ailey jumped up. "Uh, Uncle Luther, I'm sorry, but I got to be goin'. It's time for my music. Sammy Sue will be a-waitin' for me."

"Well, if you got to hurry, I can drive you down in the truck. Shouldn't take more'n ten, fifteen minutes."

In Luther's pickup, Ailey explained all about WNEW and the

New York Philharmonic. Luther listened. Mrs. Cole liked that kind of music.

"Well, you know where I live, boy. We're kinfolks. You're welcome up on my mountain anytime. Might be, sometime you could bring your fiddle, play me a tune."

Paris, France, 1818

The lawyer Morency read the spidery scrawl of Pierre La Houssaye with difficulty: Last Will and Testament, August 10, 1818.

I, Pierre La Houssaye, being of sound mind and failing body, do separately bequeath the violin, Hercules, given into my hand in the year 1770 by Giuseppe Tartini, to Niccolò Paganini.

I have heard all that is bad of him and all that is good. As in my own case, I think the good outweighs the bad. I do not know when Monsieur Paganini will come to Paris, but I am assured that he will. They all do.

For some years now I have been going deaf. But for the fear of God, I would have taken my own life when I knew.

I am, as l'Avocat Morency knows, a pauper. My greatest fear is that he will use the Hercules to settle my bill for authentication of this document. It is difficult to place something this important at the mercy of God. I fear the whimsical nature of a supreme being who would permit my legacy to fall into the hands of Satan's servants.

I have seen his manifestations and I am not comforted. God allowed the government of France to be formed. I have seen their greatest creation, the guillotine. And Napoleon! How can a Christian accept such evil. Were I a saint, which I hasten to add I am not, I would cry out, Enough!

63

Now I must place that which I value above all things in the hands of fate. The Hercules is the greatest instrument I have ever heard or played. It must not be possessed by one unworthy, by one unable to match the beauty of its creation.

In despair I pray that my dying wishes be carried out.

Pierre La Houssaye

Morency rattled the paper angrily. "Arrogant swine. Rest assured, Monsieur La Houssaye, I will do the right thing."

Morency called to his assistant. "Bertran, who is the leading dealer in musical instruments in Paris?"

Chapter 11

Luthersville, West Virginia, Fall 1981

After his Saturday music, Ailey practiced extra long. He felt guilty for having missed part of it. Since he'd gone beyond what Miss Bentley could teach him, hours of daily practice was as close as he got to having a lesson. He thought about going back to the mountain. He liked his uncle Luther. He listened better than anyone he knew. But playing the fiddle for him, he wasn't sure about that. He'd never played for anyone, not even Miss Iris, though she'd been after him for a long time. He'd finally gotten around to calling her Miss Iris at her suggestion. He practiced in his room on the third floor of her house, but he didn't actually play listening music for her.

She wanted him to perform at the school for all the students and parents. He'd told her a hundred times he wasn't good enough. Seems like she'd understand that. He thought he'd play for Uncle Luther. He's family. He didn't say anything about it to Miss Iris.

During the week Luther went down to the Barkwood farm and talked with Sammy Sue. After that she allowed as how there really wasn't anything wrong with Luther at all, he just liked living off by himself on his mountain.

Before he left he made an arrangement with Sammy Sue. He'd give her some money for the boy, for clothes and other necessities. He went to Rawling and bought Ailey a bike and brought it back to the farm for Ailey when he came for the weekend.

Ailey began to go up the mountain whenever he had a chance. He liked the feeling. It was the same as when his granddaddy was alive.

Six months passed before he brought his violin. Luther, like Sammy Sue, asserted nothing, demanded nothing. Ailey figured he'd listen, and that would be that.

After supper Ailey got out the violin and tuned it. Luther sat at the old oak table, cleaning his shotgun.

Ailey was shy.

"If you want, I'll play something."

"That'd be fine, boy. You go ahead."

Luther wasn't ready for what followed. He figured it'd be some childish songs he'd learned at school.

Ailey, with the violin tucked into his shoulder, stopped being an eight-year-old boy who liked to fish at Blair's Pond, chase squirrels, and sing at the top of his voice.

Awkwardness disappeared. He changed before Luther's eyes. As he played, he leaned forward and the tension transmitted by his small, wiry body filled the room.

Not having any idea what Luther would like, he played a series of practice pieces by Vieuxtemps. He made mistakes, held the bow incorrectly, and some of his fingering was creative to say the least, but the music was powerful and compelling.

It was a mediocre instrument, but he drew from it every ounce of sound. Luther had no experience to measure the extent of Ailey's genius. But he sensed the thing that made Ailey different. His focus was total, and he loved the making of every note.

When Ailey finished, it took Luther a moment to respond.

"That was mighty fine, Ailey. You've done real good to teach yourself."

Ailey smiled shyly. "I ain't"—he hesitated—"I'm not nowhere near good enough. I have a tough time figuring out from the books how some of the songs should be played. They's all kind of Italian words on the music, and I don't know what they mean."

Luther chuckled. "I wish I could tell you, but I don't even know English that good. I don't guess there's anyone who could teach you, is there?" Luther asked.

"No, Miss Iris give up teaching me a year ago. I done"—he corrected himself—"I learned everything she knew."

"Lord, I imagine so. I doubt there's anyone in West Virginia who would teach you very much."

After Ailey had gone down the mountain, Luther sat in front of the cabin, having his sunset. This was a situation that required some thought.

"What's to become of him," Luther wondered. "It's like keeping a butterfly in a room full of moths. If he's left, he'll become like them."

Luther went to his bookshelf, now lined with books from floor to ceiling. He selected a book of essays by the Englishman Bulwer-Lytton. He thumbed through the pages, searching for a remembered quotation. His finger came to rest on the piece he was looking for. He read out loud.

Talk not of genius baffled. Genius is the master of man.
Genius does what it must, talent does what it can.

"I think I ought to go down and have a talk with that teacher, Miss Bentley. No reason genius shouldn't have a little help now and agin."

Chapter 12

Luthersville, West Virginia, Winter 1982

Ailey ate four strips of bacon, three eggs, a heap of grits smothered in butter and honey, then drank two glasses of milk without noticing any of it. A stack of sheet music sat beside his plate. He read it with the same thoroughness and interest that a banker reads his *Wall Street Journal*.

He hummed a phrase now and again, looking disgusted when something didn't satisfy and pleased when it did. Miss Iris moved around the kitchen, put food back in the refrigerator, washed dishes, and occasionally glanced at Ailey, who was oblivious.

Ailey wasn't aware of his good fortune to live with Miss Iris, to be looked after by a woman of her character. Parents, like husbands and wives, usually won't stand to be ignored.

Not long after Ailey came to live in the old Bentley place on Ferris Avenue, Miss Bentley knew she'd done the right thing. Ailey practiced every day, sometimes through supper, and no amount of coaxing could drag him away. If she tried, he would shout at her.

"No! No! No!" His comments if he was bothered again were colorful. The latest had her chuckling for three days.

"I'm going to South America, by jingo. I'll live in Macchu Pichu with heathens, idolatrous Indians. I'll bet they won't bother me!"

She didn't take offense. Music lessons, usually piano lessons, were known as a form of adult torture against children, forced on them by mothers and fathers who couldn't or wouldn't learn themselves.

She recalled her own experience. I was six years old, Miss Bentley remembered. Such a tomboy. It was summer, I think. I went to the piano teacher, Miss Piper's house at the end of Maple Street. She laughed at the memory.

That horrible Victorian monstrosity, it was more suited to a Boris Karloff movie. According to another boy, Timmy, who had already suffered for three years, Miss Piper's lips were so dry, she had to pry them apart with a screwdriver when she talked.

Timmy said if I looked on top of the piano, I'd see the screwdriver. He was right. It was the first thing she looked for and saw. She was very disappointed when Miss Piper used it to tune the piano instead of pry apart her lips, which were indeed very dry.

She remembered those days clearly. The window of the music room had been left open and she heard her friends in the meadow below playing kick the can, or on their way to the river for a swim. They called out to her, adding to the torment.

Ailey was the exception. He had an unseen, unforgiving muse. It demanded and got total dedication. If he skimped, he would slink around guiltily until the time had been made up.

Miss Iris understood, and being a generous soul, without vanity, gave Ailey the room he needed. Besides, she'd never seen anyone practice for six hours at a stretch.

Almost four years. Ailey would be ten in seven months. All hands, wrists, and feet. He would be tall like his father and grandfather, but that was years away. Hair now thick and black as a raven's wing. When most boys wore their hair short, he didn't. It was long and pretty as a girl's.

He had a couple of fistfights over it, but not many. Those who gave him a try found out he was all boy. A windmill of sharp elbows and fists when angry. And he had the strongest hands in the school.

The little girls his age thought he was romantic and took considerable interest. It was not returned. When he noticed them at all, it was with the puzzled distrust of human meets alien.

He asked Miss Iris what was wrong with *them,* and she tried unsuccessfully not to laugh.

"Girls are different, Ailey."

"Well, shoot, I know all that," he said with the superior knowledge of nine years. "But they won't leave you alone. Seems the more you ignore them, the more they come around, chattering, acting ignorant as hounds. I never heard so many dumb questions in my whole life. You're a girl! You don't ask dumb questions.''

Miss Iris had to turn away to take a breath.

''Ailey, girls, and boys, even men and women, often want those who don't want them. It's like the cookies you couldn't have for breakfast, which you sneaked in and took while I was out watering the lawn this morning.''

Ailey's eyes got big.

''I'll bet they tasted better than the same cookies I give you for lunch,'' Miss Iris said.

Ailey didn't say anything for a minute, then he laughed. ''They sure were, best cookies I ever ate.''

''Have ever eaten,'' she reminded him. ''You think about that, Ailey Barkwood, and note there's no cookies in your lunchbox today. You go along now, or you'll be late.''

Ailey didn't argue. He had a keen sense of fairness, and Miss Iris never punished without saying why.

She drove her old Ford to school, which gave her ten minutes after Ailey left to sit and drink a cup of tea. She took the letter from Professor Morton out and read it again. Miss Iris had a plan.

A month earlier Luther Cole had paid her a visit. She knew his story, as did everyone in town. Yet in all the years he lived on the mountain she never met him. There was a good deal more fiction about Luther than fact.

On Saturday morning Luther's old pickup appeared in her front yard. He tried a knock on the front door, and when no one answered walked around the side of the house.

Miss Iris knelt in the rose garden. She wore a heavy jacket, and an apron to kneel on. Atop her head a straw hat, worn and frayed at the edges, was held in place with a scarf tied over the top and under her chin.

Luther thought she looked pretty, natural, a proper part of the setting.

She was dismayed to have anyone see her in such a state, especially a man. Even so, her poise never failed. She'd always been uneasy around men, and had decided that was why none had come courting. There was a time she wouldn't have minded a visit even if she knew it was because she was modestly wealthy.

Although Luther was in his fifties, Miss Iris thought he was a handsome man. *Why, he looks just like Gary Cooper,* she thought.

She wiped her hands on her apron nervously. Luther had his fedora in his hands. It had to be a serious visit, Luther was wearing dark slacks, a white shirt and jacket. People in the hills didn't usually put such clothes on unless someone had died or was getting married.

"Miss Bentley, I am sorry I come without letting you know ahead of time, but it has been on my mind and I didn't want to put it off."

Miss Iris invited him in as if he'd been expected for weeks. Hers was a grace developed over generations. Once in her parlor, she excused herself and said she'd be back in a moment. She came back in ten minutes. She'd fixed her hair and changed into a more suitable dress.

"It's about Ailey, Miss Bentley," Luther said once tea had been served.

Miss Iris went back to bring out a plate of cookies.

"You may already know it, but Ailey is blood kin to me."

She knew, Ailey had told her all about meeting his uncle Luther.

"He's got talent, which I guess you already know. I like that boy, and I mean to see him do well. Now, in case you get the wrong idea, I'm real pleased you're lookin' after him. It appears to me you've done a right fine job. I don't see no reason to change things none.

"A few weeks ago Ailey brought his violin up the mountain. I knew he played, but I thought it just a childish fancy." Luther took a drink of tea. Miss Iris's best Meissen china cup disappeared in his hands.

"He played for me, Miss Bentley."

She let it hang there for a moment. Miss Iris was surprised, then hurt. She tried not to be, but there it was, she was hurt.

"Miss Bentley, I don't know nothin' about that kind of music, but I know if something's fine when I hear it."

Miss Iris nodded. She knew, she had known all along. Luther simply confirmed it.

"He has genius. He gets more music from a simple song than

anyone I've ever heard. When he played it filled the room till there wasn't space for anything else. I reckon you know what I mean."

It burst out before she could stop it. "He's never played for me! Oh, he practices all the time up in his room, but he never played for me!"

Luther understood immediately. The pain was obvious in her voice.

"He will, Miss Bentley. You were his first teacher. He's almighty hard on himself. He don't think he's good enough."

Miss Iris began to protest, and Luther held up his hand to stop her. "Don't matter what we think, ma'am, it's what he thinks. We don't set the measure on that part of his life. Aren't many folks in the whole world could do that. I'm his family. He can make a mistake, not do it the way he wants, and I'll make no notice. Family, leastwise his family, won't be critical.

"Y'all are his family too. So you ask yourself, how come he don't play for you? Miss Bentley, teachers are held in a high place, for man or boy. He holds you qualified to judge. Me, he don't. You got to be patient."

Miss Iris took a deep breath, then sighed.

"You are a wise man, Mr. Cole. I don't have children of my own, and I guess I do look on him as almost mine." She smiled sadly. "You've been a help to me, Mr. Cole. We're both interested in his future, so I think you better call me Iris."

Luther gave her a small bow. "Miss Iris. Y'all can call me Luther."

They sat quietly for a while, drinking tea.

"Me and Janice didn't have any children either. Now she's gone, it ain't likely I ever will. But we, you and me, even Sammy Sue, are his family. Thing is, we got different parts of his life where we can each do some good. From Sammy he gets hugs, a clean face, his ears boxed when he's bad, his scratches mended, and some good Christian teaching. Wouldn't surprise me none if he got some music from her too. She's a fine singer. I haven't known him long, but there are things I can give. I'll give him history. And a boy needs a man to teach him about a man's world. I'll look after that.

"You have the toughest job of all, Miss Iris. You have got to feed his love of music. You already done put a polish on him he'd never get from me.

"If he stays here in West Virginia, the light which makes him shine will burn out. These hills are hard on a man, or woman. You and I have got to do something about that."

"I know, I know. You're right, he has to be heard," Miss Iris said.

They sat together, taking tea, each thinking about Ailey. Luther broke the silence.

"I have an idea, but getting Ailey to cooperate may be difficult," she said.

They went on talking for an hour, then Luther drove back to Cole's Mountain. Miss Iris sat down and wrote a letter to Professor John Morton, dean of the School of Music at the state university in Wheeling. She told him all about Ailey. It was a long letter. She explained that she wanted to arrange a recital and she wanted him to attend. She knew exactly what she wanted to do and it was essential that he be there.

Miss Iris had known for some time that Ailey had to have a teacher, not just any teacher, but a person who could teach him at his level. She hoped there would be someone at the university. Perhaps arrangements could be made for a gifted musician like Ailey.

Chapter 13

Luthersville, West Virginia, Summer 1983

When Luther got back to the cabin on the mountain, Ailey met him with fishing rods in hand.

Luther smiled. "I see you're ready even if I'm not. Well, c'mon then, let's catch a fish for supper."

They weren't a hundred yards down the trail when Ailey announced he was going to Europe, get him a violin teacher. It took Luther a moment to figure out what he was talking about, then he burst out laughing.

"You are a caution, boy. I ain't laughing at you, just how when a thing's time has come, the rest of the world had better get in step 'cause they ain't gonna have much choice in the matter."

"I don't get it," Ailey said.

"I went down to Luthersville to talk with Miss Iris this morning. We talked about you."

Ailey hurried alongside Luther so he could look at him. He was almighty curious why anyone would be talking about him.

"Ailey, how come you never played for Miss Iris?"

Ailey looked at Luther, wondering where that question came from. "I ain't ready. I work real hard, but I know I can't ... I'm not getting it right."

"How come you played for me?"

"You're family!" He sounded impatient. Luther should know.

"Okay, I figured, just wanted to be sure. I mentioned you'd

75

played for me and her feelings were hurt. She thinks on you as family.''

Ailey said nothing and looked at the ground. He knew it was true.

"You know she wants you to do a recital?''

Ailey nodded.

"Well, I reckon you should do it. Listen to me, boy, if you're lucky, you'll never get it perfect. If you did, what would be left? Don't you worry none, you'll get close, so close only you and God know it can get better. You need a teacher, and you ain't goin' to find one around here. We understand that. Hell, boy, you don't need to go to Europe.

"Miss Iris has a friend, head of the music department over at the state university. She'll get him to come. Miss Iris is sure she can help you get a teacher. That woman likes you and wants to help. You be smart to let her do it.''

They walked on down through the trees toward the pond. Ailey didn't say anything for another ten minutes.

"All right, I'll do it.''

Luther was amused. "To listen to you, a man'd think you was goin' to be beat with a stick. Can't be that bad.''

Once Miss Bentley had Ailey's agreement, she moved ahead with quiet determination. She knew exactly what she wanted and set out to get it. The Elks lodge had a fine meeting hall on the road to Elkins. She got her students to make flyers and tell their parents to be sure and come. She was clever, appealing to local pride.

Ailey achieved overnight notoriety and hated it. Now it wasn't just little girls asking him silly questions. He was tempted a dozen times to go to Uncle Luther's and not come back till all the fuss was forgotten, but he couldn't, he'd promised.

Miss Iris sat with Ailey over breakfast and planned the selection of music. She asked Ailey if he knew any bluegrass songs, folksongs like the locals had heard since they were children. When he answered, she began to realize how far Ailey had evolved as a violinist and musician.

He rattled off a dozen songs she had never heard him play, all old favorites in the hills.

She decided there had to be a couple of short romantic pieces the ladies would like, and finally a technically difficult piece that showed what he could do. She wasn't sure about that, so she called Professor Morton in Wheeling and he recommended a few typical recital pieces.

Privately he thought the trip a waste of time, but Iris Bentley had been a memorable student and her plea was genuine. Besides, it wouldn't be that bad, might be nice to get away from the same old rounds for a while.

They agreed on several pieces Ailey had the music for, and with that done, Miss Iris made up a program and took it to the printers in Elkins.

They had their first big argument over the program. It wasn't that it was inaccurate, it had everything they'd agreed on, but Ailey began to get the idea how much money was being spent and he couldn't see how he'd ever pay it back. Then Miss Iris took Ailey to Elkins to get a new suit. And of course there had to be a shirt and tie, and fancy shoes.

Everything he'd been taught by his grandfather, Sammy Sue, even Luther, said a man didn't take charity. A man didn't take on debt he couldn't pay. Finally, when he couldn't stand it any longer, he rode his bicycle to the farm.

Sammy Sue didn't ask him why he'd come. She cooked him breakfast and waited for him to speak what was on his mind. It all came out in a rush and tears.

She folded him into her arms and he was safe. Here were the familiar smells of childhood. He could be a little boy again. After he calmed down she gave him another glass of milk and a sack of biscuits.

"Y'all got a problem, Ailey. I think you should go on up the mountain and see your uncle Luther. He be strange, a-livin' up on that mountain, but he do have good sense, and he's kin. You tell him ever thing, an' y'all listen to what he tell you, then you makes up your own mind."

It was nearly ten in the morning before he reached Luther's place, and he was tired, partly from the walk and part from worry. He could hear the sound of Luther's ax before he got there.

Luther chopped wood and stacked it against the cabin for winter. Ailey walked out of the forest across the clearing.

"How do, boy. Sit, get your breath, I'll be done in a bit."

Luther went on splitting big sections of pine. Ailey naturally took the pieces and began stacking them without thinking.

When Luther was done, they went over to the pump and got a drink. Luther walked around to the front of the house and sat on the bench. Ailey followed.

"You in some kind of trouble, boy?"

"I ran away from Miss Iris, and I'm supposed to be in school."

"Well, you must have a good reason. You want to tell me about it?" Luther asked.

"Yes, sir."

Ailey described everything Miss Iris had been doing. When he came to the suit, shirt, tie, and shoes, which he described in great detail, his distress was obvious.

"Do you like that suit and them shoes?" Luther asked.

"Well, sure I do."

"How would you have felt if you hadn't liked that suit and them shoes," Luther asked with a grin.

Ailey burst out laughing. "Shoot! I probably wouldn't have felt so bad. Anyhow, I tried to tell her she was putting a debt on me I couldn't pay back. You know. That suit cost ninety-eight dollars! The shirt, tie and shoes are another forty dollars. Then she spent money on the printing and the Elks hall over to Elkins. I'll have to work a thousand years to pay her back."

"A thousand. Uh-huh, could be. You do any work for her now?"

"Sure I do. I clean up around the house, wash dishes, mow the lawn, rake leaves, ever thing I can. But, Uncle Luther, that's for my keep. I'd do the same if I lived with you."

"I reckon you would. A man can't always give back in the same coin he gets. The question is, are you doin' your best?"

"Uh, yes, sure. I reckon I could do more, but I ain't ... I'm no lazybones."

"Didn't figure you were, boy. It's the cash money, ain't it?"

"Yes, sir. I went over to Pope's sawmill and asked Wiley Pope himself if I could have a job. He was nice about it. Said sure, he'd hire me in a few years, but the state wouldn't let him hire a ten-year-old boy, that was the law."

"I know about that. Can't do nothin' about it. Well, I'll tell you how it is. Until you're a few years older, you're goin' to be short of cash money, no way around it. So you got to do what you can. You've got to trust me, Ailey. The time will surely come when you have plenty of money and you can do for folks the way you want.

"You also got to understand it isn't always money, it's what the other person needs, or wants in exchange for what they give. That's why agreements are important. Wouldn't need lawyers if people could get their agreements straight, and then stick to 'em.

"If I was to tell you I'd feed you for a week if you'd cut timber for me, you'd cut timber for me. But supposin' I had it in mind you was to cut four cord of hard wood for me, and you cut two cord of pine, figurin' that was fair. I'd be upset and you wouldn't know why.

"If you was to do well at that recital and impress the professor from the university, Miss Iris would be the proudest woman in West Virginia. She'd feel right because she knowed all along you was good and worth the effort. She'd feel she got something a lot more valuable than cash money. Money don't always fix an agreement between two people.

"Time will come, boy, if you keep getting better, people will pay good money to hear you play. Might even make recordings. I've heard people pay as much as five dollars for them recordings."

Ailey couldn't comprehend anything that far in the future, but he did know that Miss Iris would be pleased if he did well at the recital.

"I sure wish I'd talked to you before I lit out."

"I reckon. Well, it's done."

Luther got up and Ailey followed him. "It's a fine day. Let's take a couple pails over to the blackberry patch. I'm thinkin' I might make a pie. Bet you didn't know I could do that? I'll take you on back to Luthersville this afternoon."

In Luthersville, Miss Iris discovered Ailey was gone. After her initial worry, her thoughts went to the argument. She hadn't understood, which made her wonder if she was doing the right thing, if she should be taking care of a boy like Ailey at all.

She was still worrying it back and forth when Luther arrived with Ailey late in the afternoon. Luther lifted Ailey's bicycle out of the truck and Ailey wheeled it over to the garage. Miss Iris walked over to the truck.

Luther's comfortable smile went a long way to easing her concern.

"Don't you be worried none, Miss Iris. Ailey's just being a boy tryin' to live accordin' to a man's rules. We've talked some. I think he understands things a little better.''

Miss Iris reached out and took Luther's hand. ''Mr. Cole, Luther, I want you to know it's a comfort to me knowing you're up there on your mountain, and that Ailey can go to you when he needs to. I just don't know what to do sometimes. I used to think I knew everything there is to know about little boys. Lord knows, I ought to know. I've taught two generations.''

Luther blushed. ''I surely don't know everything, ma'am, but I know men, I always did.'' The light faded from his eyes and he drifted into the memories that still haunted him.

It was a long time before he came back to the present, and Miss Iris saw pain in his eyes. In that instant she knew some of what had driven him to live on a mountain away from the world.

''Ailey needs to do for you. Man or boy, Miss Iris, no man does what's needed 'cause someone told him. He does it because he can't in his heart do nothing else.

''He ain't one to take charity. He needs to carry his share. You keep that in mind and things will go along just fine. I've got to be goin' back.''

''Thank you, Luther.''

When his truck disappeared up the road, Miss Iris could hear the violin from the house. She went inside satisfied that her plan was back on track.

Paris, France, Summer 1820

Paolo Gracchi and Dolpho Batino drank the local wine in a small tavern on the outskirts of Paris. They introduced themselves to the curious as lumber salesmen from Milano. Paolo and Dolpho were convincing.

In Verona they had passed themselves off as papal agents looking for works of art for Pope Pius VII's extensive collection. Before they left Verona they had indeed collected several fine paintings and a sculpture attributed to Bellini himself. However, they removed these works of art in the dead of night and neglected to make payment in the normal manner.

Even as they drank wine on the outskirts of Paris, the authorities in Verona were searching for two clerics dressed in the brown robes and white sashes of the Dominican Friars.

Paolo and Dolpho began life in a traveling circus from Naples. In their travels they acquired abilities that later suited them to their current profession. Both skilled actors and mimics, the addition of forgery and certain mechanical knowledge had put them among the elite of their profession.

They no longer sought out the objects of their particular brand of commerce. Now, through the offices of certain intermediaries, they took work only on commission.

One such agent had written them a seemingly innocent letter regarding a piece of property in Paris, and would they care to come to the city and discuss its disposition.

81

Their agent had been approached by a Polish gentleman known to be in the employ of a certain royal personage from Budapest whose love of music was legendary.

His instructions were that for a sum of money—quite extraordinary for the times—they were to acquire a violin now residing in the shop of one M. Berthaumé et Fils on the Rue du Faubourg.

The problem was that there might be as many as a hundred violins in this shop, but only one would do. They solved this problem by hiring an itinerant musician who loved strong drink more than music. They sent him to the shop with the request that he be allowed to examine the violin Hercules. He would tell M. Berthaumé he'd been asked to act as agent for a famous French violinist who did not wish to come in person.

He did as he was asked and performed with such accuracy, Paolo and Dolpho were able to enter the shop a week later and remove the Hercules. They left a copy in its place and the theft wasn't discovered for three months.

Following their instructions, they traveled to Berlin, where they passed on the Hercules to the Polish gentleman and received their pay. Later in a Gasthaus, *full of sausage and rhennish, they mused over the peculiarities of a man who would place such value on a simple violin.*

For the first time in its travels the Hercules found its way into the hands of an amateur. The royal personage placed it in the hand of his court violinist and asked him to play.

The king later admitted he was so overwhelmed by the voice of this great instrument, he had a severe attack of conscience. He contacted the same Polish gentleman and had the instrument returned to its owners in Paris.

There is some doubt as to the veracity of this tale. Others say the instrument was recognized by a visiting virtuoso. The king protested his innocence and straightaway threatened to behead the agent who purchased it for him.

The only fact that is certain is that it was stolen from Berthaumé et Fils and that six months later returned under mysterious circumstances.

Chapter 14

Luthersville, West Virginia, October 1983

Ailey walked home from school in the heat of the afternoon. The breeze wouldn't come until evening and now the stillness was oppressive.

Indian summer. Sweat-hot during the day and cool at night. Dogs lay panting beneath cars parked along the street, too tired to chase a small boy in dungarees, sneakers, and a faded New York Yankees T-shirt.

Leaves were heaped on every lawn and along the curb. When the trees gave up the last clothes of summer, men would come out in the evening after work. They would bring rakes, followed by laughing, shouting children. It was understood that children could dive into the piles of leaves and act silly.

The last rites of summer, chased along by nature's littlest pagans and their fathers, always present to ensure that the rituals were obeyed. When full dark came, the piles of leaves were set fire and the tangy, bittersweet smoke filled the air. Children and fathers stood around the bonfires, caught in the ancient fascination, taking heat against the coming winter.

Ailey barely noticed the leaves, which was unusual because he tended the ritual fires for Miss Iris. He was the man.

Tomorrow night he would have to stand in front of three or four hundred people. He would be alone. Miss Iris took him to the hall earlier in the week. He went up on the stage with his violin. She walked him through each step of the program, taught him how to bow and insisted he say thank-you.

No end in sight. God did not punish in half measures.

Isn't it enough I have to play for all those people? Why do I have to talk to them too?

He liked how the violin sounded in the high-ceilinged hall. So different from his room. Miss Iris tried to be agreeable. Ailey knew it, but she was strong-minded with a great certainty how each thing should be done.

She insisted he announce each song.

"Remember," she said, "the audience doesn't know the music you're going to play."

He could say whatever he wanted, but he must say something. She didn't want him parroting a speech written by her. And he agreed. What else could he do? She was family, and he didn't want to make her unhappy.

He wasn't good enough. He knew it. Didn't matter what Miss Iris said, didn't matter what might or might not happen in the future. He'd heard all the great violinists on the radio and Miss Iris's record player. He wasn't good enough.

When he thought of God, he thought of the picture of Johann Sebastian Bach on the front of one of his exercise books. And when he thought of Bach, he thought of Itzhak Perlman, the greatest violinist he'd ever heard.

In his world the connection was entirely logical. When he played Bach that good, he'd be ready.

An artist takes his measure from his teachers, his peers, and finally from himself. He loves his family and friends and he wants them to approve, to admire. But they do not measure his ability. Only the mediocre would accept the evaluation of a parent or a friend.

In the garage, Ailey stacked the music for the recital. He didn't need it. He knew every note of every song. He had put new strings on the violin the week before. He'd done everything he could.

Miss Iris came home an hour later and found Ailey curled upon the divan, reading a book on the lives of the great composers. She expected to hear him in his room, practicing. He answered her greeting distractedly.

"Aren't you going to practice, Ailey?"

"No, ma'am. I know the music as well as I can. I can't make it no better."

"Any."

"Yes, ma'am, any."

She smiled and nodded.

"You're right."

The day and a half went awfully slow. Finally the hour arrived. Ailey wondered if it would always be like this, waiting in a small room alone, not knowing what to expect.

The room backstage was hot and his suit was too new to be comfortable. The shoes, which he had polished to a high gloss, were tight. The smell of fresh leather was good, but they hurt. The man at the store said they were a perfect fit. He was tempted to take them off and play in his stocking feet.

That made him laugh. Miss Iris would be scandalized and Uncle Luther wouldn't approve either. He'd understand, but he wouldn't approve.

Ailey left the room, which had a faded star on the door. He didn't know what it meant. A heavy curtain closed on the stage, and Miss Iris in her Daughters-of-the-American-Revolution-once-a-year-ball gown checked every detail.

She ordered the man in charge of lighting about with the assurance of a general. It didn't occur to Ailey that Miss Iris had been a teacher to every man in a hundred-mile radius between six and thirty-five years of age. This gave her a powerful authority.

What boy or man who had been made to sit in the corner facing the wall for dunking a girl's braids in an inkwell would go against her. She discovered every culprit who'd put the frogs and toads in her desk drawer. Now these men and women were grown, but they would not forget. She demanded obedience and she got obedience.

She made the lighting man repeat exactly what he was to do for each song. She had even made provisions for mistakes. She gave him a stack of three by five cards with her instructions carefully printed on both sides.

He looked to heaven and sighed.

Ailey peeked around the edge of the curtain. Miss Iris had commandeered some of her students to act as ushers and they were busy taking people to their seats.

Uncle Luther sat right down near the front. He looked as uncomfortable in his blue serge suit as Ailey felt in his. He wished Uncle Luther could come backstage and wait with him. Luther smiled and looked around comfortably.

Everyone was there, even the mayor of Elkins.

For a while Ailey had thought no one would come, then they began to fill the hall in a rush. Miss Iris turned to where Ailey stood and shook her head no.

"You go along to the waiting room, I'll be there in a bit. It won't be long now. I must go out and meet Professor Morton."

Ailey couldn't suppress a scowl, the natural resentment a person feels when his future, his life, falls into the hands of another.

Ailey headed for the room, but as soon as Miss Iris left, he darted back to the curtain. In a few moments he saw Miss Iris with a tall gray-haired man in a nice suit, carrying an overcoat. He looked comfortable in his suit, one of the few in the crowd who did. Most of the people were hill folk and wouldn't be found in a suit except at church.

He stopped Miss Iris halfway down the center aisle and pointed to a single seat. Ailey could see his lips clearly.

He said, "I'll be able to hear better from here."

She nodded, and when he sat down, excused herself and headed for the stage.

Back behind the curtain, she put a folding chair in the wings and had Ailey sit there. A murmur rose from beyond the curtain. Miss Iris waved her hand at the man working the lights. He flipped a switch up and down three times after looking at one of the three by five cards.

Miss Iris visibly counted to ten. When she reached ten, the house-lights dimmed and the curtain opened.

There was power to the ritual. It had a strange effect on Ailey, opposite from what one would have expected. The grinding fear that pinched his gut and made his chest feel too small eased, replaced by excitement and anticipation.

A microphone had been placed in the center of the stage, already adjusted to Miss Iris's height. She left nothing to chance. She walked to center stage as grand as a queen.

Ailey was vastly impressed. This was a Miss Iris he had never seen. She waited a moment for the voices to subside.

"Good evening, ladies and gentlemen . . . former students." She smiled, and there was a ripple of laughter that spread quickly from the front to the back of the hall.

As she looked out at the crowd, her eyes rested on one individual after another, and two hundred middle-aged men and women felt a twinge of guilt, then awkward self-knowledge as those keen blue eyes, which in times past had found so many of them out, touched first one then another.

"Thank you for being here, thank you very much. We don't often get a chance to celebrate one of our own. I'm sure you won't be disappointed. Ailey Barkwood is most surely one of our own, raised and nurtured by our own fields, forests, and mountains.

"He is proof that excellence cannot be held back by circumstances. Ailey is eleven years old and he plays the fiddle. He's never had a lesson. I taught him to read notes, but my teaching didn't last long. In six months he'd learned everything I could give. Before and after that he has been his own teacher."

She turned and beckoned to Ailey. Carrying his violin by the neck in one hand and his bow in the other, he walked out onto the stage. He didn't look at the audience until he stood where Miss Iris told him to stand.

A quiet patter of polite clapping rippled around the room. Miss Iris took the microphone and carried it to one side. She left the stage into the darkness of the wings, where she stood, nervous fingers entwined in knots.

Ailey stood for a moment, then started to speak. He had to clear his throat first. He forgot the "ladies and gentlemen."

"I'm going to play some West Virginia music first. The first one is the Virginia reel."

Ailey lifted the fiddle to his shoulder. The awkwardness of the jacket made it impossible for him to get comfortable. It was something the formidable Miss Iris hadn't thought of.

"Dang coat," he muttered.

Though he spoke quietly, his voice reached all the way to the back of the hall. He didn't realize that it was the best thing he could have done for this crowd. The laughter rolled around the hall.

One old farmer called out. "Go ahead, boy, take it off. A man can't make music nor drink whiskey in no straitjacket."

Someone else hooted.

Ailey laughed with them, took off his jacket, ran to the wings, and held it out imperiously until a hand reached out of the darkness and took it from him.

Back in the center of the stage he looked, if anything, smaller. He immediately began tapping his foot, held the fiddle to his shoulder with the bow poised, ready. In that position so characteristic, he leaned forward and struck the first note, all doubt gone.

The lively, upbeat melody, telling of parties, dancing, and white lightning drunk beneath the moon, pulled the audience irresistibly. First fingers drumming on knees, then feet tapping, hands clapping, finally laughter.

This was mostly what they had come for, and to hear it coming from an eleven-year-old boy who was surely their own made it doubly fun.

Ailey couldn't keep still, all the pent-up energy of waiting and worry erupted with the music. He practically hopped up and down the stage, leaning forward and back, black eyes flashing, face wreathed in a huge grin.

The man on the lights was hard pressed to follow him. In the crowd, Professor Morton frowned. He wasn't interested in all this capering around. He came to hear the violin, not attend a hootennanny. But he wanted to be fair, so he waited. As he watched he realized it wasn't country showmanship. This little boy was happy, so the professor closed his eyes and listened to the music.

Revelation! It was country music, traditional fiddle playing, but much more. Thrown in among all the wild sawing of the bow were things not at all traditional. Arpeggios in triple time, harmonic variations whose roots were a continent away from the hills of West Virginia. Ailey even played a melody backward on the spot just for the fun of it, scales so fast they were hard to follow. Masterful violin playing no matter how it got done. And if he had taught himself, and that he was only eleven, it would be well worth the trip.

When Ailey finished the first set of songs and bowed as he was taught, the hall was alive with cheers and whistles. He had a fine sheen of sweat on his brow and looked pleased. This wasn't as bad as he thought.

He wasn't aware of his own gift, the ability to communicate his song, his emotion through music.

"Thank you very much."

Ailey plucked the strings, retuning the violin. Obedient to Miss Iris's wishes, he told them what he was doing.

"What I'm doing right now is tuning this fool thing. If I don't mind it close, it wanders around worse 'n a hound looking for a rabbit. There, that's got it.

"I'm going to slow down a bit 'n play some pretty songs. Some made for the violin and some made to be sung, but they work pretty good for the violin too. If nobody minds, I'm going to play these specially for my teacher, Miss Iris Bentley." He turned and smiled toward the wings.

"The first one is called 'Liebeslied,' then 'Marguerite,' then 'Songs My Mother Taught Me,' all arranged by Mr. Fritz Kreisler."

He waited until things had gotten very quiet, looked out toward the audience. He started, soft as a summer breeze, on a single string playing the melody in a strong, lush style. The women brought out the handkerchiefs and the men remembered their youth, and in the wings Miss Iris Bentley, gentle tyrant and a very romantic woman, shed secret tears, thankful that no one could see her.

After playing for nearly an hour, he stopped for the intermission. Chased by thunderous applause, Ailey went back to his small room. Within minutes after the curtain closed, Miss Iris came in.

"Ailey, that was wonderful. I don't think I'll ever hear anything as lovely. I knew you would be great, I knew it, but that was beyond my expectations."

Ailey blushed, embarrassed, and mumbled something unintelligible. There was a glass of cold water on the dressing table, two towels, one damp and one dry.

"You wash your face and neaten up. That was fine for all your friends around here, but Professor Morton is someone else. Try to wear your coat if you can, maybe if you unbuttoned it."

Ailey nodded and took a long drink of water. When she left he muttered.

"Miss Iris, you never give up."

There was a refreshment area outside the hall. Two long tables had been set up with punch, small sandwiches, cookies, cakes, and pies. It was a congenial crowd. Most of the men had said they knew he'd be good all along; after all, he was a hometown boy.

This wasn't near the truth. The men had been dragooned by their wives into going, and most figured they'd have to spend a miserable night listening to some half-baked kid making painful squeals on the fiddle.

Miss Iris made her way to the professor as soon as she could get away from all those wanting to congratulate her on her student. The women wanted to know when they could get him to play for their clubs and functions.

It was a relief to be pulled away from the chattering.

"Well, Professor Morton, I hope you weren't disappointed."

He shook his head ruefully.

"I'll tell you the truth, Iris. I thought it would be a dull night at best. You're sure he's never had any lessons? No, of course not. One look at his bow position, and the fingering—god-awful. But"— he laughed at her expression—"now, don't go and explode on me, Iris. I'm not one of your students, you can't cow me."

"Why, Professor, don't be silly, I never cowed anyone in my entire life." He decided not to comment on that bending of the truth.

"All right, Iris, I'll tell you. So far I am very impressed. That's got to be one of the worst instruments ever made, yet he gets an amazing sound out of it. It would be something to hear him play a really fine instrument. And yes, he has talent. Even if I didn't hear the rest of the program, I would do something to get this boy a decent teacher. Lord knows he needs one."

"Now, that, Professor, is music to my ears." Miss Iris sighed with satisfaction.

Fifteen minutes later they all filed back into the hall. Most of them had never heard of the music selected for the second half of the program. The houselights went down and the curtains opened slowly. Ailey put his coat on as a concession to Miss Iris, but left it unbuttoned. Almost everyone in the hall stood and spontaneously clapped.

Ailey bowed low and waited for the applause to stop. It was new for him to have admiration. This was a heady brew he had never tasted.

When the people were seated, he told them what he intended to play.

"These will be a little different. These are some pieces by an Italian named Paganini. I think he might have been a pretty fair player 'cause his music's real hard to play. They're real purty too. He wrote twenty-four of these songs. They're called caprices. He sets out a simple tune, then fools around with it in all sorts of different ways. Don't worry, I ain't gonna play all twenty-four."

The professor rolled his eyes in disbelief at Ailey's bland description of one of the finest violinists and composers who ever lived.

Ailey attacked with great skill. Where he'd been unable to figure out how to play certain parts, he reconstructed them to fit what he could do. Some of his innovations left the professor with his mouth agape. When he finished he was wringing wet. Most of the crowd were too stunned to react, then one man got up and started clapping. Soon they were all standing. The noise after the silence with only the violin was painful. He bowed over and over. Finally, mercifully, Miss Iris got the man to close the curtain and Ailey walked off the stage.

"Ailey, I know you don't want to do this, but I really think you should. You must go to the reception area and speak to people before they leave. Don't worry about what you say, just be gracious. It'll be over soon. Professor Morton is staying. We'll talk as soon as the people have left."

"All right, Miss Iris," he agreed tiredly.

He didn't want to do it, but he was learning the lesson of the limelight. Once in it, a part of his freedom was lost.

When the last few people straggled out of the building, Ailey made his way back into the hall. Luther had stayed and sat with Miss Iris and Professor Morton.

Miss Iris introduced musician and teacher. Professor Morton saw that the boy was so weary, he could hardly stand.

"You better sit down, young man." Ailey did, gratefully.

"I don't know why I'm so tired, I never get this way when I practice."

The professor nodded. "It's the emotion and the excitement, Mr. Barkwood. You don't withhold anything. An audience is like a huge unfilled bucket that just naturally wants to be filled. You haven't learned to pace yourself, but you will.

"Mr. Barkwood, you have a real gift for your instrument. Miss Bentley is hoping I'll bring you over to the university on a music scholarship. I could do that, but I won't.''

Seeing the disappointment on Miss Bentley's face, he laughed.

"Be patient, Iris. I swear, you can't wait any better than your students.''

Ailey's mouth dropped open and he sat up with a jerk. He'd never heard anyone talk to Miss Iris that way.

"I'll tell you what I think. Miss Bentley wants you to have a good musical education, which you could get at the university, if you were going to be a music teacher. Frankly, boy, I don't give a damn if you never learn to enjoy Chekov's plays or understand the politics of medieval Europe.

"I don't think you should come to Wheeling. What you must not do is wait until you finish high school to continue studying your instrument. By then you will be too set in your ways to change, and, Mr. Barkwood, if you want to get better, you have got to change.''

Professor Burton wasn't joking anymore. "Do you understand that?''

Ailey looked at him for a moment and nodded tiredly.

"Ailey, what you need is a teacher, someone special, someone tough and very skilled. What I have in mind is that you will go live with this person and study violin.''

Miss Bentley broke in.

"What about his other studies. A man can't handle his own affairs if he can't do any of those things you treat so lightly. There are other things in the world besides playing the violin.''

"Not for this young man there aren't. Mark my words, Miss Iris Bentley, there aren't! He'll be enrolled in a regular high school, well, not regular, a special school for the gifted, but where they understand the requirements of the artist. And of course he can go on to college when he's ready.

"I have someone in mind. I'll call him and see what he says. I haven't sent him anyone in nearly ten years. What will happen is this. He will go to New York and audition. If Maestro Everade thinks Ailey can be taught, that he is good enough, he'll take him as a student. I imagine he has ten or twelve other students living with him, so Ailey will have company."

Miss Bentley had a few hundred questions bursting to be asked, and Ailey had more.

"I know you all have questions, and I'll try to answer them." He turned to Ailey. "The real question is how badly do you want to become a violinist? Believe me, young man, it won't be easy. I wouldn't send my own son up there unless he had the hide of a rhino and the patience of a saint. You have acquired very bad habits. Some physical, some mental. When the teaching begins, and you're told to do something you think doesn't make sense, you're going to imagine your way is best. Why? Well, because you made it work when there was no one around to help or tell you different. You've had the satisfaction of tackling a difficult task, and instead of giving up, which almost anyone else would have, you took it to a successful conclusion. When someone tells you you're wrong, you're just naturally going to get angry and tell your teacher your way works. I hope you understand what I'm saying, young man."

It was hard for Ailey. "I think I do. I will sure enough try. I won't quit."

"I know you won't." The professor smiled nicely. "You wouldn't be here and I wouldn't be either if you did. Let me tell you something, Ailey Barkwood. If he takes you, and there's no guarantee that he will, and if you survive the first year, then perhaps another three years, there will come a time when you can play what you want the way you want. But first you must obey, you must do your apprenticeship. I'll tell you something else. If this man takes you, you won't thank me, but if you're strong enough to last, you have the potential to become a great violinist, and if nothing else, you will have been taught by a master.

"I'll be in touch, Miss Bentley, soon. Ailey, if no one tells you, let me be the first. You have talent, the real thing, and you have passion. When things get difficult, remember that and don't waste it."

Chapter 15

Luthersville, West Virginia, Spring 1984

Ailey could not endure waiting. He was an eleven-year-old boy about to make the biggest change of his life. He was going to live in Bronxville, New York. He looked it up in the atlas at school. It was too close to distinguish from New York City, and he knew all about that place from television and magazines.

He saw it as a filthy place of uncollected garbage, dead junkies lying in the doorways of battered tenements, and, of course, no trees or grass. He wondered if he'd have to get a pistol and a switchblade knife, join a gang.

Miss Iris and Uncle Luther held similar views, tainted by the prejudices a southerner holds for the North, especially a big city.

On weekends Luther put Ailey to work getting the cabin ready for winter. Luther would tell him what to do, then leave him to do it.

In the alien city of Bronxville, New York, Ailey was to play for the violinist and teacher, Antoine Joachim Everade. He ran the most famous school for musical prodigies in the United States. Many of his students went on to the great orchestras and concert halls of the world.

Professor Morton made it plain there were no guarantees. He would audition. If he did well and Everade thought he could be taught, he would stay, otherwise, back to West Virginia.

Ailey had the entire summer to worry, and in his imaginings he tried to adjust to what his life would be, success or failure.

Luther talked more than he had in all the time Ailey had known him. It was as if he needed to transfer all the things he'd learned to Ailey. Ailey didn't mind. He had hundreds of questions.

Questions about drugs, crime, northerners, gangs, sex, God's will, food, clothes, snow! The prospect of travel had set his imagination afire.

Luther said nothing about the Stradivarius. He pondered about Ailey going away to New York. From his view it wasn't much different from going to a foreign country. He wondered if now was the time to pass along the legacy.

It wasn't in his nature to force the idea. Luther was guided by a deep instinct, a sense of timing that couldn't be described in words. Years before, during blackouts, there'd been a terrible day. He woke at dusk, his feet in the spring, freezing. The day had vanished in a fog of dreams. He didn't remember how he got there.

He stumbled and crawled to the cabin. There, he finally made a fire. When the feeling came back to his feet, he shouted with the pain. He knew what happened, he'd had frostbite in Korea.

Later he sat in front of the fire and held the Stradivarius. A strange thing had happened. He felt himself float free of his body, above the cabin on Cole's Mountain, finally above the whole world. It spun beneath him like a child's ball. The surface was covered with a hundred colored strands of light. The strands marked the paths of his past and future. More than that, he sensed some of the strands represented possibilities. One line was brighter than all the others.

On that strand he recognized the place where the violin went out of his life. The time was not then or now. When it came, he'd know what to do.

Luther saw the violin on other strands and they were not his. It had been the same when he first opened the case. He was not meant to possess it. He was the caretaker and he took his stewardship very seriously.

After Ailey went back down the mountain, Luther went to the cabinet in his bedroom and removed the case. As had happened so many times in the past, he felt a sense of peace, a sense of purpose, as soon as his hand touched the case. He didn't do it often. Luther had an ascetic's knowledge and fear of indulgence. What he got from that which rested in the case was a commodity whose benefit had limits, and because of this he enforced rigid discipline even when the need was great.

It had been especially difficult when Janice died. If he hadn't felt responsible for the Stradivarius, he knew he would have joined her, for when she died the joy went out of his life and all that was left was resolve and waiting, for what, he wasn't sure.

Ailey's desire for a better violin didn't go beyond one he'd seen at the music store in Rawling. It cost five hundred and forty-six dollars and seventy-eight cents. He had thirty-five dollars and fifty cents he'd made selling wild strawberries to tourists along Route Six. The gap between desire and fulfillment was vast.

He tried not to have trouble with Miss Iris, but just because Uncle Luther wouldn't like it. He knew she cared about him, but there were some things she didn't seem to understand.

Ailey counted every penny spent on his venture north as a personal debt. A debt that somehow had to be settled. He couldn't get around the idea that what he received wasn't charity.

Miss Iris decided he could not go to New York by himself. She had no intention of letting him wander about that wasteland alone. For Miss Iris New York was a dumping ground for all the world's perverts, its sidewalks a refuse heap of dead mafiosi and other assorted criminals.

Privately, Luther told Miss Iris that if she hadn't decided to take Ailey, he'd have gone himself.

Paris, France, 1829

"Monsieur Berthaumé, you have a violin called Hercules. Is that not so?"

"Yes, it is true." Berthaumé *looked at the portly, well-dressed gentleman, trying to recall if he knew him. He had sold instruments to all the great musicians of Europe. No, he did not know this man.*

"You have the advantage of me, monsieur. I do not know who you are, but you know me."

"Only by reputation, Monsieur Berthaumé. I am Jean-Marie Diderot. As a boy I had the honor to meet the great violinist Tartini while visiting Italy with my father. He told me the story of the violin, Hercules.

"That evening he played, oh, how he played. Never have I felt closer to the gods ... until yesterday evening. I heard a young boy play. His name was Henri Vieuxtemps. Though he is but nine years old, he is worthy to possess the Hercules. I have it in mind to buy this instrument for him, as I am sure he could not afford it himself."

"Vieuxtemps, ah, yes, I believe I read something about him by the critic Fetis. You are aware we do not sell these things to just anyone," Berthaumé *said.*

"Of course, monsieur. I would be surprised, no, disappointed if you did. Only the very deserving should be brought to the marriage with such beauty. No, monsieur, I, like you, have heard all the great violinists of the age. This nine-year-old boy is deserving."

99

"I will consider selling it to you, Monsieur Diderot, with certain conditions. No, only one really. I understand he is Maestro Beriot's protégé. I will invite them both here, where you will present the instrument to the boy along with the certification of ownership."

"Monsieur, your attention to these details astounds me. It gives me comfort to know you care for more than the possible monetary gain."

Diderot was effusive in his admiration. Berthaumé bowed in acknowledgement.

"Before we go any further, I should tell you, Monsieur Diderot, it will be very expensive. Allow me . . ."

Berthaumé wrote a figure on a small slip of paper and handed it to Diderot. Diderot read it. His eyebrows rose with surprise. He grunted as though someone had struck him sharply in the solar plexus.

"Perhaps Monsieur would like to consider this purchase for a few days?"

"No . . . no . . . I will tell you, I would have gone through with it if the price were double. I am a rich man. But what can I buy that I do not already have? A better meal? A finer home? A more beautiful mistress?"

"Monsieur is wise. This gift and its affect will outlive you, and that is more important than any material thing. You restore my faith in the goodness of man and God."

The next day, in the afternoon, the violin Hercules was presented to the nine-year-old prodigy, Henri Vieuxtemps, in the shop of Berthaumé et Fils in Paris.

Chapter 16

Bronxville, New York, September 1984

Ailey had never been on a train or plane. Miss Iris feared flying, and on buses one had no choice as to one's fellow passengers. She was much too polite to suggest that traveling that way was for the lower classes, but she could no more help thinking it than she could bare being rude. It did not occur to her that first-class accommodations did not guarantee first-class traveling companions.

They were fortunate in not having to test the truism. There were only six other passengers in the first-class section of the train. Given the chance, Ailey would have felt more at home in third class, where the accents were more familiar.

The handsome countryside paraded the ripening of spring. It was fine to watch the world whip by at forty-five miles an hour. Miss Iris chattered on about things Ailey had no interest in.

"When you wear your suit coat, always carry a handkerchief." She showed him how to fold it. "Remember, we are not dogs, we do not chew with our mouth open." He muttered an acknowledgement, hoping she would stop.

"Avoid girls who chew gum. It is a disgusting, bovine habit. Ladies of good breeding simply do not do that. Remember, when you are introduced, don't look at the floor and shuffle your feet. We may not be wealthy, but we have good family and we have history. Your uncle Luther is a holder of the Medal of Honor, this nation's highest award for valor. Look at the person you're greeting, shake their hand once or twice, firmly. And don't offer your hand to a lady unless she offers hers first.''

Ailey was trying to memorize a Beethoven violin concerto and Miss Iris didn't make it easy to concentrate.

Grand Central Station in Manhattan was filthy like most of the big rotten apple. Exactly what Ailey expected. Miss Iris moved them from the arriving platform to the Westchester train as fast as she could, as if the very air of New York City were evil beyond redemption.

The steady rocking of the passenger car, the clatter of the rails, overcame Ailey's curiosity and he fell asleep dreaming about the Beethoven second movement. His head drooped onto her shoulder, and though it was uncomfortable, Miss Iris stayed still and never gave it a thought. She stroked his hair, long and black, and tried not to cry.

It wasn't dignified, she told herself, and after all, he's not my son, giving her heart the lie.

It had been difficult beyond what she imagined. One voice punished and one praised: one for sending a eleven-year-old away from his family to live with strangers, one for getting him out of an environment where he would not develop.

Long before Ailey became her charge, she had resigned herself to being the object of men's jokes and women's pity, of being a spinster. The only children she would ever have would be the sons and daughters of other men and women.

Ailey had lived with her for the better part of four years, and while she was by nature an orderly woman, neat and precise, a person who did not like noise and runny noses, he had, even with every bad habit known to eleven-year-old boys, edged slowly and certainly into her heart. Now, as she looked down on his sleeping face, she understood a mother's heartbreak.

Ailey slept on unaware until the train reached the Bronxville station. She sent him to the men's room to change into good slacks, a white shirt, and tie.

The tie! The devil's device, probably engineered to remind small boys of what would happen if they went wrong in life. At least he didn't have to wear the sweater. She had bought him a sweater with buttons down the front like a girl's! The shame of it! He'd have told her it was warm if ice formed on his eyebrows.

Ailey took out his grandfather's watch; six in the evening and already dark as they got off the train. Miss Iris had had several conversations with Mrs. Rose Everade, the maestro's wife. These conversations were the subject of much amusement between Mrs. Everade and her husband.

Ailey would stay at the school—also the maestro's home—for three days, during which time he would listen to Ailey and decide if he would take him for a student.

Mrs. Everade tried her best to get Miss Iris to stay, but without success. Miss Iris insisted this was Ailey's moment, that he would not want her underfoot. In this her instincts were sure. Mrs. Everade arranged a room at a local hotel, the best one.

Ailey and Miss Iris looked around the station awaiting the appearance of all the horrible things they were secretly sure were a part of living in New York City. The station was neat and the people surprisingly ordinary: businessmen returning from offices and meetings, professional men and women. Most were well dressed.

There were no derelicts drinking cheap wine in doorways. The nearby buildings looked solid and conservative, mostly stone. No gangs bent on theft and rape running amok in the streets. And through the darkness she could see trees.

The woman advancing on them was tall with a formidable bosom. She wore her graying hair in a loose pile that rolled down the back of her neck to her shoulders. She had a broad, handsome face and a mouth to match. Her dress was long, down to the ankles, tied with a brightly colored sash at the waist. She went right to Miss Iris.

"You must be Mrs. Bentley. I am so pleased to meet you."

"How do you do?" Miss Bentley smiled, giving nothing away.

"And you must be Ailey Barkwood." She did not offer her hand. "My husband and I are very glad you could come."

She turned back to Miss Iris. "I've sent someone to get your luggage and bring it around to the car park. Won't you follow me, please?"

Ailey tagged along behind, knowing everything was in the hands of the women and the best he could do was try to keep up and hopefully out of sight. He looked around at everything. Heck, it didn't look that much different from Elkins. They put Ailey's things in the back of a new station wagon and summoned a taxi driver to take care of Miss Iris's bags.

"Ailey, why don't you hop in the front seat. I'm going to talk with Miss Bentley for a moment," Mrs. Everade said.

They stood at the back of the car and talked. He couldn't hear what they were saying and guessed he didn't really want to. *Probably Miss Iris is telling Mrs. Everade to make sure I brush my teeth and say my prayers,* he thought.

"How does he feel about all this, Miss Bentley?"

"I'm not sure. He doesn't say much. He seemed miles away on the train. I asked him what he was thinking about and he said he was trying to memorize the second movement of a Beethoven violin concerto."

Mrs. Everade laughed. "They aren't like us at all, Miss Bentley, are they?"

Miss Iris joined in her laughter. "No, they aren't."

"I know you have a lot of important questions for me," Mrs. Everade accented the *me*. "When they are playing, they're like children. We need to make sure they eat and have a nice place to make music. I love them all, but they're really quite helpless. If you like, I'll come by the hotel before noon and we can have lunch. Maybe you'd like to go shopping. We can talk then. I have two women, family, who look after things. They'll see that Ailey knows what to do and finds his way around."

"That would be fine, Mrs. Everade."

Miss Iris went to her taxi and Mrs. Everade drove Ailey to the school. Ailey realized that Bronxville wasn't a very big town, and nothing like he'd imagined. It was a disappointment.

He'd made up his mind to deal with the criminals and drug dealers bravely. Instead, they were on a tree-lined road and the houses all looked like mansions. Many had fine stone fences with fancy cars in the yard.

They hadn't gone far when she turned in at a gate through a fieldstone fence. A small sign said EVERADE. The house was huge. Mrs. Everade hadn't said much except to smile at Ailey from time to time.

The property inside the stone fence stretched back behind the house for a long way. Ailey followed her into the house carrying his one piece of luggage. She carried another case that contained his violin and his music.

They headed for a central staircase, but Ailey stopped before he got there. He heard music from all over the house. Violin, viola, cello, even double bass. Fantastic! If he had asked for a greeting, this would have been it. This was real, not records or the radio. Live people made those sounds. All the questions he wanted to ask poured into his mind, and he knew he could get them answered.

"It's a wonderful sound, isn't it," Mrs Everade said.

He couldn't contain his enthusiasm.

"Yes, ma'am!"

His was a room on the third floor under the eaves with a dormer window that looked out over the yard. He saw several small cabinlike structures to the side and behind the house. The lights were on in one of them and he heard a violin. It was very good. He forgot about Mrs. Everade, who stood watching in the doorway.

"Are you hungry, Ailey?"

"No, ma'am. Thank you. Miss Iris and I had supper on the train."

"All right. The bathroom is at the end of the hall. You come down in the morning and someone will tell you where we eat. Will you be all right?"

"Yes, ma'am."

"Good night, then, Ailey. See you in the morning."

"Good night, ma'am."

She smiled as she closed the door. Even as she left, she saw him moving to the window.

They can't stay away from it, she thought. They truly are different.

Ailey sat on the shelf with his violin, trying to duplicate the finger positions that would create the scales he heard from below. He heard voices, and the scales started over again.

After the second time through he figured out what the teacher wanted. The higher notes well up the soundboard weren't as tightly bound as the lower. He could hear it. He'd figured out how to do that two years before.

He looked around. A shelf was filled with books and he found a stack of sheet music in the closet. The excitement made it impossible to sleep. He picked up a basic method for cello. He started reading, got interested, and didn't put it away until midnight.

Mrs. Berenson, the housekeeper, came around at one o'clock as she did every night and found him asleep on top of his bed. She went through his suitcase, found his pajamas, and got him into them. He hardly noticed.

Chapter 17

When Ailey woke in the morning he didn't remember anyone coming to his room. Obedient to Miss Iris's instructions, he put on his robe. He took his toothbrush, a towel, and soap and went looking for the bathroom.

A small towheaded boy of about eight ran by him with his toothbrush still in his mouth. He took it out long enough to shout.

"You better hurry or all the good stuff will be gone."

He dressed carefully. He'd been thinking about meeting Maestro Everade since he got up. No one gave him a schedule, so he had no idea what he was supposed to do or when he was supposed to play.

Downstairs he found the dining room. There were still three or four people eating. In one room there was a large ornate clock on a mantel over a fireplace. Nine-thirty. He thought he'd messed up, and worse, there wouldn't be any food left. Mrs. Berenson, who also doubled as cook, told him where to sit and quickly began piling food on his plate.

There were potato pancakes, some funny-looking sausage, cereal, fruit. He guessed he wasn't the only one who got up late. A tall, skinny girl with eyes like a Chinese sat next to him. She was really putting away the food. She smiled at him and asked his name.

She introduced herself as Myung Lee Pak and said, "You may call me My My."

It was all very informal. Food moving around, people asking for this and that, chattering about everything. But over it all music, always music.

What did he think of this piece? Had he ever played any of these sonatas, or so and so's studies?

They talked about other musicians and composers the way the kids at the Luthersville elementary school talked about baseball players. They criticized and praised with the complete nonchalance of long familiarity. He was happy. He couldn't help smiling.

"What do you play?" the girl asked.

"Don't tell us," another boy broke in. He was maybe a year or two older than Ailey. He got up and came around the table. Before Ailey could object, he grabbed Ailey's left hand and looked at his fingertips.

"Oh, God, another screecher," the boy giggled, and thought it very funny.

"Don't be such a pest, Tommy," the Chinese girl said. "He means you play the violin. He calls violinists screechers, violists moaners, cellists groaners, and double-bass players something rude. He plays the cello and I play the viola. Are you here to study or audition?"

"Audition."

"Are you scared? You must be. I came all the way from Seoul, and if I hadn't been accepted, it would have been terrible. Don't worry. Mr. Everade's very nice. He shouts sometimes, but it doesn't mean anything. He's the best teacher in the world."

Ailey took it all in without saying a word. He was beginning to wonder if anyone ever asked a question and actually expected an answer. He finished eating after the others. Without thinking he piled his dishes and carried them to the kitchen.

The women were astounded as they watched him rinse and put them in the sink. Mrs. Everade came in and watched, speechless. She tried to remember if she had ever seen a student carry anything but music.

"Ma'am, could you tell me what I'm supposed to do?" Ailey asked.

"Why don't you have a look around, the maestro has a lesson this morning. He'll be another hour or two. Someone will find you when he's ready. He doesn't keep a very tight schedule, so you'll have to wait until he's ready," Mrs. Everade said.

"Thank you, ma'am." He made a little bow to the other women and left.

Mrs. Berenson looked at the others and shook her head in disbelief. "Where does an eleven-year-old boy learn manners like that? The first thing we have to do is send all the other students to West Virginia for a year or two."

Ailey wandered out of the house. It was a fine spring day, and everywhere he looked there were trees, mostly huge old elms. Along the inside of the stone fence were shrubs and flowers. His fears about living in New York were obviously off the mark.

As it had been the night before, the air was filled with music. He could hear two people practicing the cello, and someone on the second floor played the double bass.

As he walked around the side of the house he heard a violin in the distance. As iron is drawn to a magnet, he headed in that direction.

He saw a patio around the back of the house with several tables. Two men and a woman worked on a stack of sheet music. They smiled at him and continued. He wondered what they were doing.

In the back of the house it was like a park. There were tall, thick pine trees everywhere, much larger than the ones in West Virginia.

Among the trees he saw two cabins, and as he walked toward them he saw a third farther back. The violin music came from there. The music stopped and started again, a difficult exercise that covered the full range of the instrument.

As he got closer he heard voices, first a young girl's then a man's. At first he thought the girl was speaking in a foreign language, then he realized she had an accent he'd never heard. The man was patient but firm. She played one part over and over.

Ailey sat down beneath the cabin window on a carpet of pine needles, like home. It smelled like his own forests. He didn't see the man come to the window and look down.

"Come along, Lucienne, tempi, tempi, the blue jays are listening." The man spoke impatiently.

Without thinking, Ailey's fingers moved, trying to duplicate the positions of the unseen student's fingers. Ailey thought her violin must be the best in the whole world. It had a voice like nothing he'd ever heard. He realized how poor his own instrument was.

He held his head in his hands. *How am I supposed to impress Mr. Everade?* he thought.

The girl's voice was soft and musical, her accent strange. He tried to imagine where she came from. He listened with complete attention.

Mr. Everade came to the window again and looked down at Ailey. "Well, Lucienne, your audience hasn't left yet, perhaps he hears something good that I've missed?"

Ailey jumped to his feet, embarrassed, and started to leave. Everade called out to him.

"You there, come in here."

Ailey looked around, hoping the request was meant for someone else. It wasn't.

"Yes, yes, you. Come in here!"

Ailey went around to the door reluctantly. The interior of the cabin was simple. A few chairs, a long folding picnic table, a couch, music stands, sheet music everywhere, and a small grand piano.

The girl was much like Ailey, slender as a reed, and awkward. Her eyes appeared too large for her perfectly oval face. They tilted up slightly at the corners and were sea green flecked with brown; gold to the more observing Ailey.

Her hair was long, wavy, a true, deep auburn. Skin dusky, tinged with rose. In one shy glance Ailey decided she was as beautiful as a wildflower.

Everything about the man was big. A large square head and face dominated by powerful nose that jutted out, then straight down, with large, flared nostrils. Ailey would learn that the nostrils were the key to his emotions; their movement told all. He had a fine, full beard carefully tended.

Ailey knew little of vanity. He had no mother or sisters or aunts telling him what a handsome boy he was, and Miss Iris, who certainly thought he was handsome, would never say so.

The man rumbled, his voice a deep baritone. "And who might you be, Mr. Blue Jay, who sits beneath my window?"

"Ailey Barkwood, sir."

Ailey wasn't afraid, though wary and certainly interested. This was the man he must play for.

"I thought perhaps." He stepped forward and introduced himself. "Joachim Everade. You will call me Maestro."

He looked Ailey over thoroughly as they shook hands once in the European manner. The look missed nothing. The maestro ignored the girl.

Ailey, his southern manners intact, turned to her with a small formal bow.

"I am very sorry to interrupt your lesson, miss. My name is Ailey Parkman Barkwood."

She was poised for an eleven-year-old. She took violin and bow in one hand and offered him the other.

"Lucienne Rosamond Ysaÿe, Monsieur Barkwood." He held her hand gently, as one would hold a great national treasure.

Joachim suppressed a smile. "Are you teaching me my manners, Mr. Barkwood?"

The idea startled Ailey, and it showed. He didn't know how to answer.

"No, I see you are not doing that. An ten-year-old virtuoso without guile."

"Excuse me, sir. I am eleven, and I'm not a virtuoso." He had trouble pronouncing the word.

"Hmmm, we shall see, we shall see. Tell me, Mr. Barkwood, what do you think of Miss Lucienne Ysaÿe's playing?"

Ailey did not hesitate. "Wonderful tone, excellent bow. She will be great." His statement was delivered with complete assurance.

The maestro's bushy eyebrows swept upward, and his eyes were full of laughter. "Will be? Explain, please."

Ailey looked at her, his serious eyes asked forgiveness. He hadn't learned how to dissimulate.

"Miss Ysaÿe is still your student. It's hard to be perfect when there is still so much to learn."

Lucienne smiled at Ailey. He was as totally captivated as a boy can be who has met his first great love.

"Well, it happens that I agree with you, Mr. Barkwood: that is, if she ever learns to join two notes together as if they were one. Do you know this exercise, Mr. Barkwood."

"No, Maestro."

"Come here, look at the music."

Ailey had to stand next to her. She smelled wonderful. Then he looked at the music. The maestro started to say something, then stopped. Ailey became instantly absorbed in the music. He quickly flipped the sheets back to the beginning of the exercise, then read through it again. His fingers, at his side, moved automatically against his pants leg as they tried to form the positions on their own.

He looked up at the maestro. "Will you show me the best fingering for these? Some of them are right purty."

The maestro wasn't put off by the boy's country accent.

"What do you mean, the best fingering?"

Ailey answered without looking away from the music. "There's always different ways to git there. Some's better'n others."

Miss Iris would have been upset with him for reverting to the accents of the hills; the maestro was not. He'd taught many students whose native language wasn't English, and many of them had been nowhere nearly as fluent, even in their own language.

"That is correct, Mr. Barkwood. Should it come to that, I will indeed show you what I think is the best fingering. Sometime in the future you may discover a better way. Leave room for the possibility.

"Miss Ysaÿe, would you mind if we took a bit of your time. I want to get to know a little more about Mr. Barkman."

"That's Barkwood, sir."

The maestro went on as though he hadn't heard. ". . . Maybe you would too. You share the same instrument. Perhaps you'll play a duet together someday."

The maestro liked to tease, and she blushed. Ailey did not. She looked at Ailey and agreed.

"Mr. Barkword, did you bring your violin?"

"No, Maestro, it is in my room."

"No matter." Joachim lifted a case from the top of the piano and handed it to Ailey.

Ailey held it like a ticking time bomb.

"I'd rather not, if you don't mind. If I were to mess it up, it'd be a hundred years before I could pay you back."

"I'll worry about that. It's not my best instrument."

Ailey opened the case carefully, took a handkerchief from his pocket, and wiped his hands. He folded the handkerchief to make a pad for his shoulder, then removed the violin from the case gently, his eyes devouring every inch of it. He knew it was very old and very fine. His hands trembled noticeably. It wasn't nervousness. It was a hunger to have, to possess such an instrument as his very own.

His longing was so obvious, both the maestro and Lucienne felt it. The maestro said nothing and watched. At this point, everything Ailey did interested him. The desire to be a violinist was more than ability, it was an attitude, and he was seeing that attitude sooner than he thought.

"Is it in tune?" Everade asked.

Ailey plucked each string once. "No, Maestro. The G and E strings are off."

"Would you like me to give you a G on the piano?" Everade asked.

"No, I can fix it."

Ailey plucked the strings and adjusted the appropriate pegs. Then he tested his adjustment, checking all the octaves. When he thought he had it right, he reached for the bow. It was a Tourte. He read about them but never held one. The balance was wonderful.

Perfect pitch, Everade thought. The maestro frowned at Ailey's hand position but suppressed the urge to correct. *Plenty of time to fix that if I decide to take him,* he thought.

Ailey looked at the maestro as if asking permission to put the bow to the strings.

"Go ahead, Mr. Barkwood, attack, attack, let's hear the big sound."

Ailey hesitated, then his face became oddly still. He struck the open G string, the lowest note on the violin, and held it, making full use of the bow. He took it out to the full power of the instrument and it filled the small cabin to overflowing, almost unbearably powerful.

He continued with the one tone, changing the volume and voice from harsh and angry to full and rich, filled with harmonics. The voice of the one note slowly changed its emotional quality. Ailey finally let the note die in a sigh as soft as the breezes beyond the window of the small studio.

When he lifted the bow from the string his face glowed. It was an expression of purest ecstasy, revelation, and awe.

After some moments Everade spoke.

"Do you like that instrument, Mr. Barkwood?"

Ailey was speechless. His mouth moved, but no sound came. "It is like . . . Jesus in wood."

The maestro, Joachim Everade, burst out with happy laughter. "Yes! Yes, young Barkwood. That is appropriate for a Guarnerius del Gesu."

Ailey held it away from his body, then made as though to put it back in its case.

"No, no, go along and play something for us. Would you like to hear something, Miss Ysayë?" he asked.

"Yes, very much, Maestro."

"Good. You and I will make tea. Do you drink tea, Mr. Barkwood?"

"Yes, Maestro."

"Good, good. Come along, Miss Ysayë, give me a hand."

There was a small sink at the back of the studio and a two-burner hot plate. Everade turned back to Ailey.

"Come, come, don't stand about. You have Jesus in your hand. Let us hear his music."

"If I may, sir. I will play something simple, just a song. I don't know this wonderful thing very well."

"That's fine, play what you like."

Ailey picked a song he'd heard the famous French chanteuse Mireille Mathieu sing on the radio. He instinctively turned toward Miss Lucienne Ysayë and played the first slow, utterly romantic notes of "Je Me Souviens."

The melody was simple and filled with longing. Both Lucienne and the maestro stopped what they were doing to listen, transfixed by the passion. The effect on Maestro Everade and Lucienne was quite different.

Everade was astounded by the amount of music the skinny boy pulled from the simple melody. Lucienne heard his voice alone. She instinctively knew this testimony was for her, though she was too young to know how to respond.

With the last note of the song Ailey took a deep shuddering breath, then looked at the instrument as if unable to believe he was holding such a thing of beauty in his own hand.

"Well, well." Everade cleared his throat. "Very nice. The French know all there is to know about romance, and you seem to have made the most of it. What is the name of that?''

Ailey blushed. ''I'm sorry, sir, I heard it only once on the radio. I don't think I can pronounce it right.''

Everade waited and said nothing.

''I'll give it a try. 'Je Me Souviens,' the singer was Mireille Mathieu.'' Very bad pronunciation, but neither one laughed.

''Miss Ysaÿe?' Everade asked.

She pronounced the name of the song and the singer properly.

''Fortunately, Miss Ysaÿe is from Paris, Mr. Barkwood. She can prevent us from ruining her wonderful language. Miss Mathieu is a fine singer. Look in that stack there, you'll find an exercise book that says *Kreisler* on the front. Play one or two of those for us, if you will.''

Lucienne turned back to the sink to make the tea. She didn't want Ailey to see her face.

''I have played one or two of these, sir, pardon me, Maestro.'' As Ailey started to study the others, the maestro stopped him.

''No, sight-read please. Take the first one. Andante cantabile.''

Ailey got a worried expression on his face.

''I'm sorry, Maestro, all of them Italian words weren't in my dictionary.''

Lucienne looked surprised. Everade laughed.

''You don't know, of course, do you, Miss Ysaÿe. Mr. Barkwood has never had a music lesson from a violinist. He taught himself to play.''

Lucienne was more that startled, she was shocked.

''Not to worry, Mr. Barkwood. That means moderately slow, as though being sung.''

Ailey nodded, smiled, one of the few. He held the bow over the strings and vanished inward as though sucked out of the room into a world completely his own. They could barely hear the first note. There had been silence, then it was there, as pure and sweet as a raindrop. He made the occasional error, ignored them, going on until he completed the piece.

Everade sat on the couch and drank his tea. Lucienne stood and watched him with an expression only another performer might interpret. They would have seen admiration and not a little envy.

When he finished, the maestro nodded approvingly.

"Good, quite good. Your bow position is atrocious, your fingering indescribable, yet you manage to extract excellent interpretive content from the music. Good intonation, quite fine."

Seeing Ailey's expression, he went on quickly. "Not to worry, my boy, not to worry. That can be fixed. You won't like it, but we will fix."

"It's your turn, Lucienne. What do you think of Mr. Barkwood's playing?" Everade asked.

She was silent for a moment, then, as if saying something very difficult, she answered, "I think Mr. Barkwood may become the greatest violinist that ever lived."

Ailey frowned, disbelieving.

"Yes, perhaps. Or maybe he's unteachable. Off you go, Mr. Barkwood. We will see you at dinner. Tie and jacket, young man."

Brussels, Belgium, 1873

The massive bedroom seemed to be filled with people gliding about as silently as disembodied spirits. Vieuxtemps wanted to shout at them to go away. If he were able, he would, but one whole side of his body was frozen, senseless, immobile.

The doctor said it was a stroke, that he was lucky to be alive. "Why do they say that," *he wondered.* "Isn't that my choice? Shouldn't I be the one to decide if I am lucky to be alive?"

Beside his bed on a small deal table, the Hercules lay in the open case, surrounded by its own couch of rose velvet. Next to the violin, a stack of sheet music, his own A-minor concerto on top.

He intended to rewrite the opening, when this latest malady struck. Things had been going so well. The Brussels Conservatory, where he taught, was prospering. He had several fine young students. His goal of making it the finest source of musical excellence in Europe was well on its way to being realized. Now he lay in bed, surrounded by people in white, who murmured like Shakespearean extras.

I must consider that which I cannot bear to think of . . . I must pass along the Hercules.

He wished the new maid would bring some hot broth. She would have to help him. She was young and as plump as a partridge, and she smelled delicious.

117

"Ahhh ... Henri, you fool. All you can do is dream of the two things you enjoyed most. Robust young women, and music. Forget all that. . . . If only I could." *He wasn't even able to sigh.*

"Who shall get the Hercules? Who deserves my treasure?"

Chapter 18

Ailey left the studio in the pines in a daze. Nothing was as he thought it would be. The maestro should be a male version of Miss Iris; imperious, tyrannical, stubborn. He thought the other students would be older, more assured, sophisticated, already famous.

"Lucienne." He tried her name several times. The shape of her name was magic itself. "Rosamond." He'd never known anyone named "Ros-a-mond." From Paris, he thought. Finally he said her last name aloud. "Ysaÿe."

He began to sing, realized where he was, and blushed with embarrassment. He looked around.

"Damn." He liked to sing loud when he was happy.

Ailey wondered when he would audition. How could he audition with his violin, a complete piece of junk, especially after playing the Guarnerius. It wasn't fair.

As he walked toward the back of the house, Mrs. Everade, who had joined the group on the patio, beckoned him over.

"Good morning, Ailey. Did you sleep well?"

"Yes, ma'am."

"I noticed your light on very late."

"I'm sorry, ma'am."

"Oh, no need to be. We don't keep strict hours here. I thought perhaps you couldn't sleep. I have trouble sleeping in a new bed, never seem to adjust to the shape."

"I read a book on the cello method and forgot what time it was, ma'am."

"I see."

She introduced him to the others. A younger man first. "This is Eric Herter, he's a theatrical agent." Ailey didn't know what that was.

A large, middle-aged woman with thick glasses, very unkempt, a cigarette dangling from thin lips, smiled at him and held out her hand. He noticed her fingers were tobacco-stained.

"This is Analise Clay. She's writing a book on twentieth-century classical music."

The third person was a diminutive man with white hair, beautifully dressed with a flower in his buttonhole.

"And this is Solomon Hirsch. He arranges concerts for Carnegie Hall." Ailey knew about Carnegie Hall. What musician who dreams doesn't?

Ailey shook hands with the men and bowed to the lady.

"This is Ailey Barkwood. He came all the way from West Virginia to audition for Joachim."

"You're violin, aren't you?" Miss Clay asked.

"Yes, ma'am."

"What do you think of modern music, Mr. Barkwood?" Mr. Hirsch asked. "We've been discussing it with Miss Clay, who is an exponent."

Ailey was having a difficult time adjusting to the idea that someone would ask him his opinion as if it really mattered.

"What is an exponent?"

"Someone who really likes a certain thing," Hirsch said.

"I don't care for most of it. It don't start nowhere, and it don't end up nowhere. I like some of the French composers, Ravel, Debussy, Fauré, and some of Erik Satie's music. Stravinsky is fun, but I don't guess that's really modern music. I am sorry, ma'am, I ain't ... haven't listened to very much."

"Why do you like the French composers?" the theatrical agent asked.

No one had ever asked him why. He was saved from having to answer.

"Don't badger the boy, Lise. Sit with us, Ailey. Would you like some coffee or tea?" Mrs. Everade asked.

"Tea would be real fine, thank you."

She went to a side table and poured for all of them. She piled a plate with small biscuits, then turned back to Ailey.

"I heard someone playing a beautiful song. I can never remember the name. Was that you?"

"Yes, ma'am."

"Then you've met the maestro. Good. And you've met your counterpart on the distaff side." She raised her eyebrows and glanced at the others.

Ailey had no idea what she was talking about.

"Ma'am?"

"Miss Lucienne Ysaÿe, the shy Ysaÿe." She laughed, as did the others. Ailey did not laugh.

"Yes."

His answer contained such finality, no further comment about Miss Lucienne Ysaÿe was possible.

"The Kreisler, lovely. Was that also you?"

"Yes, ma'am."

"You must play for us one evening soon."

Ailey looked alarmed, ready to tell her he couldn't, when she continued. "Each of the students plays a few selections after dinner nearly every evening."

"Yes, ma'am. If I am still here, I will play."

She assumed he'd already auditioned and realized Ailey could think of nothing else.

Ailey wandered away. The people on the patio went back to their discussion, frequently heated and always loud. One wing of the house contained a large old-fashioned library with shelves of books twelve feet high. A rolling ladder was attached to rails along the top of the shelves.

He found a whole section on the violin. He started counting the books and estimated there were more than a hundred books in that section alone.

He remembered what the maestro called the violin he played and found a book devoted entirely to the Guarnerius. He was still reading it with the help of the dictionary when the maestro entered the library.

Ailey, completely absorbed, didn't see him.

Earlier Mrs. Everade went to look for her husband after she met Ailey. There were household things to discuss, but what she really wanted was to ask about Ailey. She found him in his office at the back of the house.

"Did you give the boy an audition, Joachim?" she asked.

"Barkwood? Not exactly. I found him listening in on my lesson with Lucienne and invited him in. I had him play a few things on the Guarnerius. I don't know what he's been playing, but just holding it overwhelmed him. After he played one note he said it was like Jesus in wood. What do you think of that?"

"I think he's a remarkable young man. The question is, how good is he? He's still waiting for you to give him an audition. He doesn't know if he's been accepted or not."

"Oh! Damn, I didn't say anything about that." He thought about it for a moment.

"I must see him right away. He's not like the others. Oh, they love their music all right, but their futures have always been assured. Even if they don't become soloists, they are certain of good positions with a symphony.

"To answer your question, his bowing is awkward, his fingering"—he blew out a huge breath—"the best I can say is that it is creative, and his technique is terrible. That's the negative, and you will note, all of those things can be taught, can be corrected. On the plus side he has something only the very great ones have, an internal vision of music filled with passion, a singularity of voice. He has perfect pitch, what amounts to a total recall for music, and sight-reads like a dream. I asked young Ysaÿe what she thought, and she said he could become the greatest violinist that ever lived."

Mrs. Everade raised her eyebrows at that.

"Yes, indeed. She may be shy, even withdrawn, but she has a powerful ego regarding her own ability. I think they were both very taken with each other. And you know what? She may be right about his ability.

"In my own mind the audition was over as soon as he played that first big open G. He extracted more music from that one note than half the so-called great violinists now on tour."

"You must be very careful and very good, Joachim. You must not teach him technique at the expense of that passion."

He gave her an impulsive hug. "Just right, my dear. I think I will not tell him just yet." He pulled at one large ear reflexively.

"I'll have him play for all of us after supper. I'll accept him, of course, and take the opportunity to say some nice things."

"Are you sure? He has played in public once, and that wasn't a very discerning audience." She looked doubtful.

"I'm sure. I think that boy is strong, and I want to test his mettle."

In the library he watched Ailey for a moment longer, then left silently.

Ailey asked another student the time and went to his room to change. Shirt and tie every evening for dinner. He didn't like that much. He had only three white shirts and one suit jacket. Maybe if he was real careful and went upstairs right after dinner and changed, he could keep it clean for a week or two.

He was confused. In one part of his mind he was already a student, accepted and ready to go to work. How could one travel this far and not be? The other part said he hadn't been asked to stay, so he might get sent back to West Virginia. Isn't that what Professor Morton had said?

He had a room all to himself. He and Miss Iris had talked about it, and she'd said he might have to share it with other students.

Ailey stood in front of the mirror and struggled with his tie. The first two times when he pulled on the ends the knot just dissolved.

"Damn, blasted, no-good, stupid thing." He tried again. The knot stayed together but it didn't look anything like the knots Miss Iris tied.

There was a knock on the door. He walked over to it, the loose ends of the tie dangling. Lucienne!

" 'Allo, Ailee. May I come in?"

No one in Luthersville or Rawling or all of West Virginia ever looked as pretty. She wore a long blue velvet gown with a black velvet choker. An ivory cameo, yellow with age, was centered on the choker. Her auburn hair was piled carelessly atop her head, and a cascade of the excess fell to her shoulders. He would never have guessed that she spent an hour with Mrs. Everade getting ready.

He smiled and stood away from the door.

"That dress is the prettiest I've ever seen, Miss Lucienne."

"Thank you." She blushed and changed the subject. "This room belonged to Antonio Llargas, the Brazilian cellist. He's on tour in Europe."

"He left a book on the cello behind. I've been reading it."

"Are you coming to dinner?" she asked.

He grunted with disgust. "Ah will if I can ever get this fool tie put together. I hate the darn things. I feel like I'm going to be hung."

She giggled. "My father calls them *la guillotine gentille.* I will tie the tie if you like. I do it for my father when I am at home."

Ailey didn't want to admit he couldn't do it himself, but he didn't know what else to do, and he was starved.

"Okay."

She stood close. He closed his eyes. He was so captivated, he couldn't look at her that close.

"There, it is done. Have a look in the mirror."

"Thank you, it looks perfect."

"Ailee?"

He had to look at her. "I don't have many friends here. The others think I have my nose in the air, you know?" She put her finger under her nose and lifted her head. "I am not that way. I have the difficulty with the stranger. I think you and I are special. I want you to be my friend."

"Yes, Miss . . . Lucienne. I will always be your friend." Commitment without reservation.

"*C'est splendide!* Will you take me to dinner?" She smiled radiantly and took his arm.

He wasn't sure what to do, but there was her hand on his arm. That was a fact. He wasn't about to remove it.

The table was almost full. She didn't let go of him even when they walked into the dining room. It embarrassed him, but he would have suffered a lot worse rather than let go.

He was acutely aware that everyone was staring. Mr. and Mrs. Everade smiled as Lucienne led Ailey to their seats. The redheaded boy who played the cello dug his elbow into the boy next to him.

"Do you believe that? Little Miss Ysaÿe and the rebel."

Ailey looked at the red-haired boy coldly, deciding he might have to have a talk with him down among the trees but ignoring him for now.

When it came to food, he was an eleven-year-old. Some of it looked strange. There was a pickled fish that looked like a human brain in a jar he'd seen at the pharmacy in Luthersville.

He'd never heard of a gefilte fish. He tried to imagine what it looked like before it was caught. Some things were so weird, he didn't know what they were called, so he didn't ask.

When they finished eating, the maestro raised his hand for silence. Everyone stopped talking immediately.

"Ladies, gentlemen, I want you to welcome Mr. Ailey Barkwood from West Virginia. He has come to audition for the violin."

There was a light patter of applause.

"I've decided that Mr. Barkwood shall play for us this evening."

Mrs. Everade thought this unnecessarily cruel, too much pressure on a boy his age, but she agreed to go along with it.

Ailey felt a surge of terror, then nausea. Lucienne leaned close and whispered.

"Don't worry. I think he has already decided to accept you, this is just some kind of test."

Ailey looked at her, visibly relieved.

"I don't have my violin, Maestro. I'll go get it." He took a deep breath and stood up.

"No, you will play mine. We'll all go into the library, much better acoustics."

In the library Everade took the case from the piano and held it out to Ailey. The Guarnerius.

When Ailey got close enough to take it, Everade spoke quietly. "Don't worry, Mr. Barkwood. This is like Jesus in wood. It will not let you down."

Violin in his hand, Ailey stopped being a gauche eleven-year-old. The same curious transformation Everade had seen earlier took place.

The library was large with a semivaulted ceiling. The rest of the students and staff were spread around the room in small groups, chatting, as though nothing out of the ordinary was happening.

"What do you intend to play, Mr. Barkwood?" Everade asked.

"The Bach C major sonata. I'm sorry if I don't get all the parts right. I heard it a couple times on my WNEW Saturday. I never could get the sheet music for it, so I'll have to play from memory."

"Do you intend to play all four parts, Mr. Barkwood?" Everade's bushy eyebrows shot up in surprise.

"Yes, Maestro."

"So . . . I'm sure we'd all enjoy the complete work, but perhaps for this evening, one or two would do."

Ailey thought about it.

"I will play the Allegro Assai and the Adagio."

"An interesting selection. Would you mind telling us why you chose those, Mr. Barkwood?" Everade asked.

"I like the Allegro Assai more'n any of them. It's hard to play, but I reckon it's prettier'n any of the others."

"And the Adagio?"

Ailey shook his head. "It's angry and calm at the same time, and it hurts. It's like a scab you know will bleed if you pick at it, but God himself can't keep you away from it."

The maestro nodded. "Some pieces can be like that."

The others talked and laughed among themselves. Ailey stood by the piano. He quickly tuned the violin, then looked around the room. His expression was serious, formal. He waited. Everade said nothing.

The voices died out till only the redheaded boy was left chattering to his friend. Ailey stared at him. The redheaded boy stopped as though Ailey had thrown a switch. Ailey didn't understand the ability to command with a look and couldn't have discussed it coherently. It was the music, of course. It was more important than all of them, and he communicated this without knowing it.

Ailey raised the bow to the violin, paused, and launched into the rapid, cheerful, perpetual-motion melody of the Allegro Assai. His face, normally closed, was open and curiously mobile. The violin on its own wasn't enough to express the joy of making music.

Eyes, jaw, shoulders, moved with the pulse of the music, pushing, coaxing. He demanded that all who listen become a part of the creation. It was his gift, his power.

There were mistakes, but not of tone or interpretation. Notes were added; notes were left out, but from start to finish it was J. S. Bach, rhythmic, passionate, melodic, complex.

The small select group around the library were riveted to the music as easily as he had gathered in three hundred farmers, lumbermen, shop owners, and their families at the Elks hall in Elkins, West Virginia.

With the last note still echoing around the trompe l'oeil ceiling of the old Victorian library, they clapped and whistled like a football crowd after the winning touchdown. Prepared to be exacting, possibly even a little cruel, they could not withhold their excitement.

Ailey held the Guarnerius in front of his body and stared at it. He walked slowly to Everade and handed it to him. The maestro saw the glistening in the boy's eyes and understood. He took the violin and handed Ailey his handkerchief.

"Go on, Mr. Barkwood, have a good blow." He spoke quietly.

Ailey turned his back and wiped his face and his eyes surreptitiously. He took a deep breath and turned back to the other students.

"Ailey Barkwood. I want you stay here and become my newest student. I also want to apologize. I had already decided that I wanted you to stay when I heard you play this afternoon. Someday I'll tell you why I made you wait"—he smiled warmly—"but not tonight."

"Thank you, Maestro. I'll work hard, I promise. I ain't afraid to work. But I better tell you, my fiddle is pretty bad. It was found, I found it. Someone throwed it away in the junk closet of the Luthersville Elementary School. I cain't . . . can't make it sing like that wonderful thing." He pointed to the Guarnerius.

"I understand. Not to worry. We've a dozen good fiddles around here; not as good as this one, perhaps, but adequate for the beginning student, I think." His sly smile took any bite out of "the beginning student."

Ailey glanced shyly toward Lucienne. He wanted to share his triumph with her. Her smile in return lit up the room around him.

"Now, Mr. Barkwood, would you like to finish your program? Are you ready to give us the Adagio, or have you had enough?"

He turned to the other students and staff. "How about you, would you like to hear more of Mr. Barkwood's Bach?"

Their answer was enthusiastic applause.

"There you have it, Mr. Barkwood. Your first encore."

"I'll play it, Maestro, but it's not a very cheerful piece to end on." He looked doubtful. "I know some that's a sight prettier."

"We are all familiar with Mr. Bach. Would you like the sheet music?"

"I'd better not, Maestro, that's a piece needs considerable study. I'll just do the best I can till I learn to do it proper."

"All right." He handed Ailey the violin.

"Has anyone ever killed for one of these, Maestro?" Ailey's question was one part wonder, one part sincere.

The maestro and most of the others laughed.

"Well, Ailey, I don't know it as a fact, but I wouldn't be surprised."

"I'm sorry for havin' such an unchristian thought, but it come to me when I finished the Allegro Assai, and I couldn't stop it."

"I understand. We all do. You go along and show me why."

Ailey stood as before and glanced around at the people seated around the library. This time he didn't have to command their attention or their silence.

Extroverted and filled with joy for the Allegro, Ailey turned inward and became centered as the slow ache of the opening chords were pulled with painful reluctance from the strings.

How does a boy play with the passion and maturity of a man? Everade wondered. *Was I that good?*

He looked around the room at the others and saw that most had their eyes closed, drawn in by the power of the music; captives of their own inevitable response.

It was some moments after he finished before the others responded. Their applause had changed. This time it held respect, the musician's appreciation for genius.

Ailey gave the violin back to Everade reluctantly.

"Someday I will have a violin like that. I don't know how, but I will!"

Chapter 19

Bronxville, New York, Spring 1985

Miss Iris set the form of Ailey Barkwood's daily life with an instruction sheet that covered every imaginable activity. Near the top of the first sheet, written in a neat Spenserian hand, was the command to write her a letter once a week, beneath which an additional command that he must do the same for his uncle Luther.

Ailey knew Luther wouldn't mind if he missed a week or two, but there was no escape. Miss Iris would check. There were further instructions that the letters must be written in a certain form and correctly parsed.

Sitting at the desk in his room, he grumbled. "There is no such thing as total freedom."

Miss Iris's firm hand never strayed far from the reins. He tried to get around her about the letters. Why not one letter to them both, he pleaded. They could read it together, it would save time. It had been a mistake. He received a long lecture on the proper place for efficiency. To help, Miss Iris provided him with another list devoted to all the things a well-written letter should contain.

At twelve there was no time for reflection, consideration of the events of the day. He lived them and they filled every corner of every day. When the day was done it was done, over. The only thing worth contemplating was tomorrow, and as he hadn't gotten there yet, it didn't matter.

He groaned aloud and twisted his hair violently. Lucienne sat cross-legged on his bed, reading a history book. She wore jeans and a Grateful Dead sweatshirt Ailey had given her. She chuckled every time she thought what her father would say if he saw the sweatshirt.

Ailey muttered incongruously. "I hate this century. Where's an amanuensis when you need one?"

"Amanu—who?"

"Amanuensis. You know, a professional letter writer. I read Rudyard Kipling's *Kim* the other day, and when he wanted to write a letter to his friend, Mahbub Ali, the Pathan horse trader, he went to the amanuensis, gave him a few *annas* and got the job done. Wouldn't that be fine! I'll bet there's thousands of boys in New York who'd pay plenty to get a decent letter written, one Miss Iris wouldn't send back corrected like homework."

"Does she really do that?" Lucienne asked.

"She sure did."

"Incroyable!"

"Do you have to write home to your father and mother?"

"But of course. Those letters are easy. I say the same thing every time." She ticked the items off on her fingers. "I am well. The music is good. The maestro says I am improving, that I must work harder on intonation, that's for my father, and can I have some money for a new dress. If I didn't ask for money, they would worry that I was not well. If I want to write a letter to someone who will really listen, be understanding, I write to my aunt Celeste."

"Boy, you're lucky. If I don't write a good letter, Miss Iris calls Mrs. Everade and scolds her. I heard her talking to the maestro. She said Miss Iris made her feel like she was ten years old and forgot to do her homework. She was surprised Miss Iris didn't make her stand in the corner."

"Well, you better hurry up and write the perfect letter."

"Shoot! I know that. You're no help."

Luther sat on the veranda of Miss Iris's house in Luthersville. Each held their letter from Bronxville, New York.

"Hmmph. That boy is twelve years old and he still doesn't know the difference between a colon and a semicolon. What do they teach up there?"

Luther didn't rise to that question. As far as he was concerned, it was a damn sight simpler if you didn't use either one. He cleverly changed the subject, not caring for lectures on the excellence of the English language any better than Ailey did.

"He must be right fond of that little girl, Lucienne. Imagine that, from Paris, France."

Miss Iris laughed. "I know. The last time he mentioned girls he told me they were dumber than a hound. Very poor English, but quite to the point. He went on to say that *I* wasn't dumb, that I didn't ask stupid questions. I'm still not sure if I should be pleased or not."

She read on. "There, he says it again. He is so obstinate, I'm sure it doesn't come from your side of the family. You are one of the most sensible men I know."

"What did he say?"

"Please, don't send any more money. I have plenty. If I get short, I will get a job! And listen to this! What if I was to die of the c-o-l-e-r-a or the b-o-b-o-n-i-c plague? Misspelled cholera and bubonic. Who will take care of my debts?" She rattled the sheets of paper in annoyance. "That boy is stubborn."

"No, Miss Iris. He's just a poor boy raised to think like a man. When you're poor there's some things you hang on to, they keep you from feeling small about yourself."

"But, Luther, I don't want him feeling he isn't as good as those people up there. I don't want him to go without something other children have."

Luther shook his head. "You do what you must, Iris. But remember, that money means something different to Ailey than it does to you. Time could come when what seems like a little problem could get a darn sight bigger."

"Oh, pooh! I don't send that much." She didn't want to talk about it anymore. Miss Iris Bentley didn't understand, and nothing in her background closed the gap between her history and Ailey Barkwood's. She wasn't going to have any of those foreign nabobs looking down on her boy, her Ailey.

"Ailey says he met a nice old man at a park near the school. He says this fella is a rabbi. Isn't that a Jew . . . like a minister?"

"I believe so, Luther."

"You ever know a rabbi?"

"No, I can't say that I have."

Luther stared off across the yard for a moment. "We had a Jew on the 'canal.' He was a good soldier, strange sense of humor. The Japs threw a grenade into his hole, which chewed him up some. I patched him up. He just laughed and shouted that he was already circumcised. I figured he was in shock. Long time before I understood what he was talking about."

Miss Iris listened intently. Luther seldom talked about his experiences in the army, and despite the indelicacy, she was flattered he would tell her.

Miss Iris Bentley had a crush on Martin Luther Cole. It was a source of considerable secret embarrassment, definitely not the sort of thing a woman of forty-five should be thinking about.

Brussels, Belgium, 1881

The lawyer and the doctor stood on the far side of the room, talking in whispers. From time to time they glanced toward the bed where Henri Vieuxtemps lay dying.

"Monsieur le Docteur, I will have another look and see if Maestro Ysayë has arrived. If he does not hurry, I fear it will be too late. I do not like that man, he is rude and arrogant," the lawyer said.

"What can you expect, he spent all those years in France."

"True, but then so did Monsieur Vieuxtemps, and he has never been anything but a gentleman."

The doctor nodded. "Ah, oui. That is nature, monsieur. High position and breeding are no guarantee of gentility. I minister to a vegetable salesman in my district whose manners and temperament put him in the company of kings. Instead, he brings me perfect tomatoes and radishes as payment for his ills. I would gladly serve him for nothing more than the pleasure of his company."

There was a knock at the door.

"Excuse me," the doctor said as he went to the door.

Eugene Ysayë stood in the door, apologetic and contrite.

"Do forgive me, monsieur. I came straightaway when I heard of the maestro's condition," Ysayë said.

"Yes, yes. Well, you better come over and talk to the maestro. He has been asking for you for days."

The doctor left Ysaÿe seated by the bed and walked back to the other side of the room.

"Well, Ysaÿe," Vieuxtemps whispered, "my favorite student, my best student . . . and a Belgian too."

Ysaÿe took the old man's hand in his. "But never did I surpass the maestro."

"You are kind to say so, Eugene, though I fear it is not true. Get the violin from that case, will you? Yes, place it here, where I can see it."

Ysaÿe did as the old man asked.

"I am going to give you this violin, Eugene, but first I will tell you its history. You may have heard of it, it is called the Hercules. A fine man, a Monsieur Diderot, bought it for me when I was nine years old. I have tried to be worthy of it. Sometimes I have succeeded, sometimes I have not. Now, my friend, it is yours. I ask that you pass it along when the time comes, taking equal care to see that it falls into the hands of a master deserving of its greatness."

Vieuxtemps took a breath and closed his eyes. He was very frail, his skin as translucent as the yellowed panes of glass in the windows around the room. He opened his eyes and looked directly into Ysaÿe's eyes. "Will you promise to do as I ask, Eugene?"

Ysaÿe put his hand on the instrument. "Yes, Maestro, I will do as you ask, I could not do otherwise."

Chapter 20

Bronxville, New York, Spring 1986

The maestro was not pleased. His nostrils flared violently. Eyebrows plunged down in a furious V. His hand sliced through the humid summer air.

"Stop! Stop! Stop!"

The maestro pulled his beard so hard, Ailey thought it would come out.

Darn, what did I do now? Ailey wondered.

Everade strode across the room and ripped the sheet music from the stand. He waved it in Ailey's face.

"Read this!" His finger stabbed at the paper. "This is not Jimmy Cash! This is Wolfgang Amadeus Mozart!" He glared furiously. "This is great music, the other is the demented raving of a whiskey-soaked wretch."

Ailey couldn't let that slur go by without response. "Uh, Maestro, Johnny Cash is not a whiskey-soaked whatever. He's a fine singer of country music."

"Be quiet," Everade thundered. "What do you know? Mozart is not hip! You . . . you jazz musician! You will play Mozart as it was written, note for note. Mr. Itzhak Perlman, whose music case you shouldn't carry, plays Mozart note for note. What gives you the right to experiment! Do you understand me, Mr. Barkman?"

"Barkwood," Ailey muttered.

The maestro ignored him. Ailey was in for it. He gritted his teeth and said nothing. It wouldn't do any good.

Outside the cabin, Lucienne sat behind a pine tree and listened to the maestro building to a full head of steam. She worried Ailey would take Everade's tirade seriously, personally, and say something stupid.

Pushed far enough, Ailey had a violent temper. She recalled their one bad argument. She discovered because he loved her, she could hurt in equal measure to that love.

She talked to Rose Everade about it afterward. Mrs. Everade gave her a sound scolding, followed by a lecture on the politics of love. She remembered it clearly.

"You're a silly girl. It's obvious he loves you. At the same time, he's very serious about money."

"But, Madame Everade, it is stupid! I have plenty, and it's only an ice cream! *Incroyable!*"

"Maybe, but it's obviously more than just an ice cream to him. Do you care for him?"

"Of course, more than anything."

"Then listen to me, and remember. It is infinitely easier to hurt someone who cares for you than one who doesn't. If you have a choice, never force the people you care for to make choices needlessly. Give them room to be right for themselves."

In the end Lucienne decided she could put his need before her own. There was one thing she was sure of, she loved Ailey Barkwood with her whole heart.

When the maestro shouted at Ailey, she wanted to stand between them, make him stop. She knew she couldn't. That would just enrage the maestro and embarrass Ailey.

Inside the cabin Ailey waited and the maestro ranted.

Not long now, Ailey thought. He's winding down. When he talks about the sanctity of the master's music, he's coming to the end.

"All right, young man. Remember what I said. I want to hear Mozart played as if he were . . ."

Sitting on that couch, Ailey mimed silently.

". . . sitting on that couch. Will you do that for me?"

"Yes, Maestro."

"Good."

Everade searched around for the sheet music, picked it up, and put it back on the music stand. He opened it to the point where he wanted Ailey to play.

"Start at bar thirty-two . . . allegro."

He set the beat like a conductor. "Remember, this is symphonic. Imagine all the other musicians playing Mozart. You are but one voice among many."

Outside, Lucienne smiled, closed her eyes, and leaned back against the pine. She listened to the liquid purity of the music, now being played note for note, as if Mozart himself were sitting on the couch. She put her hand over her mouth to stifle a giggle.

Everade smiled, shook his head, walked to the window. He saw Lucienne's hair peeking past the tree trunk. *What will become of them?*

With that thought came a picture of Lucienne's father; pompous, arrogant, forever French.

He'd known the man for thirty years. Everade conducted Lucienne's father at the height of his career. Personally, he thought he'd never met a more arrogant son of a bitch in forty years of making music on five continents.

The maestro's thoughts wandered as he listened.

Great gods! Only a year! It isn't possible. He could play with any symphony in the world. He nodded as he listened.

Impeccable tempo, masterful bow, and always the passion. I wonder if he has the Gypsy blood? I must hold him in check. He hates it and I don't blame him. Worse, I must do it for another four years . . . well, maybe three.

He turned and watched the boy closely for a moment.

"Lift your elbow, you're an American, not some mad Russian. Yes, that's better, yes, good."

His thoughts returned to Ailey, now deep in the music.

He's too serious. A man should be serious about his music, but he goes beyond that. Lucienne, another serious one. Together they are . . . mmmm, that would be something.

He watched the tree beneath his window and saw her head peek out and quickly disappear.

The aristocrat and the commoner. He laughed. All the elements of a romance novel. Life imitates art. No, they are far from common, they are the true aristocrats.

When Ailey finished, he looked at the maestro expectantly. Everade looked at Ailey for several moments, nodded, and then smiled, his rage entirely forgotten.

"Better, much better, Ailey. Practice double and triple stops. Scales, my boy, scales. Read the lives of the masters, they all say the same, practice scales. Off you go now, I think someone is waiting for you outside behind that pine tree."

Outside, Lucienne looked around the tree toward the cabin and blushed. He always knew. One couldn't get anything past him. Ailey met her by the tree. They walked toward the back of the property.

"How did he know," she asked. "Did he come over to the window?"

"I don't know. He just spent the last hour shouting at me."

Lucienne took his hand. "Don't worry, he shouts at me, he shouts at everyone."

"I know. I changed only three notes!"

"Sometimes it's just a game. He wants you to know he's paying attention. I've heard the learn-to-do-it-right-before-you-fool-around lecture a thousand times."

Lucienne held his hand possessively. Ailey was too shy to take hers, even after a year.

The path ended at a stone wall near a street that led into the center of Bronxville. Every Thursday they walked to the ice cream shop next to the railroad station. They always had the same argument. Who would pay?

Ailey got a regular allowance from Miss Bentley, and Luther sent money from time to time. Even Mrs. Everade got into the act. It became intolerable. If he sent it back, he'd be ungrateful, rude. If he kept it, his indebtedness increased with no hope of paying it back.

Despite Luther's explanation at the time of the recital in the Elks hall, Ailey couldn't accept taking from people who weren't family.

With Lucienne he compromised, and then only because she would be hurt and could not hide it. He allowed her to pay one week then he paid the next.

Ailey loved Lucienne with the complete devotion of a thirteen-year-old who has neither age nor vice. In his mind he would have gladly thrown himself in front of a truck to save her life. In fact, the idea had a certain dark, romantic appeal.

The problem with being thirteen, and loving a girl more than anything, was how could he show her? Prove it to her?

Lucienne, music, obligation, filled both his dreams and waking fantasies.

Six months earlier they secretly began playing duets. They didn't have the maestro's permission. Music was the only area of their lives where he interfered. He could be tolerant in all others.

In their walks together they discovered an abandoned boathouse at the edge of the pond in the park. After ice cream at the Foremost Shoppe they went to the park and sneaked into the boathouse.

They were unaware they had an audience. Built around the end of the boathouse was a small deck once used to launch rowboats. A bench stretched along the deck. It was the favorite spot of an old man in long robes, a full beard, and a skullcap. Rabbi Sholem Ben Ezra came there for the quiet. A creature of habit, he always brought a paper bag with bread for the ducks.

Over the years the windows had been broken out, even the doors had been removed. He had been a silent witness to their first tryst, as innocent as children in the first garden.

The next time, they heard the bag rattle and were scared. They weren't supposed to be there. There were gangs who used the park for criminal activities.

Ailey crossed the old boathouse and peeked out a broken window right into the old man's face. The rabbi smiled.

"Shalom, bubby. Please, I'm not here. I like the Beethoven. I listen to you play and I have hope." He tossed bread to the ducks. "Every day I see the bad boys and girls. I wonder who will make music when I am dead. I wonder, will there be anybody left to play! Please, go on, I will keep your secret."

Lucienne joined Ailey at the window. "I know you. You're Rabbi Ben Ezra. You're the Everades' rabbi."

"And you are the beautiful and talented Mademoiselle Ysaÿe, from France, *n'est-ce pas?*"

She giggled, *"Oui, Mon Père."*

"Please, please, you should practice. See ..." He pointed to the ducks. They were all lined up in front of the his bench. "They like your music, and so do I."

Ailey and Lucienne looked at each other, eyes expressing a hundred questions. They went back to the music.

Sometimes they shouted at each other. She called him ridiculous things in French, which had he understood he might have been offended. It was so loud, so vehement, the arguments turned to giggling and laughter. Partly out of fear and partly because the arguments were absurd.

It took time, but they learned what many musicians and most people never learn—how to subordinate ego, to become two personalities playing the music as one.

Ailey and Lucienne went back to Beethoven. Within minutes they'd forgotten their audience. They argued, discussed, played parts over and over, absorbed in the power of creation.

As they were packing up to leave, they heard the rabbi's voice from the other side of the wall.

"Play some Schubert next time. I love Schubert."

They didn't know what to say. If anyone at the school found out, they would be in trouble.

They were naive to think no one knew they were going off together to play duets. The maestro knew it after the first time. In her next lesson, Lucienne used fingering that was pure Barkwood.

At temple the next Saturday after the meeting, Rabbi Ben Ezra took Everade aside and told him of the unusual events in the boathouse. The maestro was alarmed, but Rabbi Ben Ezra advised caution with Ailey and Lucienne, that to interfere would be wrong.

"Leave them alone, Maestro. Never in my eighty years have I seen two children more necessary to each other. Wait, watch. What they are is something we could all hope to be."

He held up his hand against Everade's protest. "Not to worry, I'll meet the boy, we'll talk."

Everade discussed it with his wife. Usually he left personal problems to her, but this was potentially more serious. It crossed the boundaries of the children's personal and musical lives.

In the end Everade and Rose came to the same conclusion. It would be more harmful to speak than to let them be. It was difficult. They knew of the dangers outside their small enclave. The park was foreign territory, a meeting place and source of fearful things, unknown things.

Chapter 21

Bronxville, New York, Spring 1986

Ailey got up early on a Sunday morning. He dressed quietly and stole down the stairs to the kitchen. Mrs. Berenson shuffled around in her slippers, making coffee, baking sweet rolls.

"Oh, hello, Ailey. What are you doing up so early?"

"Couldn't sleep, ma'am."

"Neither could I. Do you want some hot chocolate?"

"Yes, please, Mrs. Berenson."

Ailey drank some of his chocolate and got up. "I'm going outside for a while, ma'am. Thanks for the chocolate."

He walked around the side of the main house to a shed where the gardening tools were kept. The need to do something measurable against his keep was strong. He tried cleaning things in the house. That didn't work. The other students laughed at him and the women gently took over. They wouldn't let him pick up a broom, wash a window, or even do the dishes. They treated him with the good humor one gives the not-quite-bright.

Ailey got the rake from the shed and some plastic trash bags. He headed for the front fence. The snow was gone and the debris of winter was exposed. As he raked he put the leaves into the bag. He tried to burn the leaves the previous Autumn and got in trouble. There was a law against it.

Ailey worked along the fence, enjoying the cool air and the activity. He'd been working for fifteen minutes, just getting into the swing of it, when an older boy, Fat Hartmann, cello, came across the lawn in a hurry.

"Ailey, Mrs. Everade wants to see you in the library. Here, I'll take the rake."

Ailey scowled at him and held on to the rake. "Why don't you tell Mrs. Everade I'l be along when I've finished rakin' the yard."

"C'mon, Ailey, Mrs. Everade wants to see you. Don't give me a hard time. You can rake the whole damn town of Bronxville for all I care."

Ailey looked toward the house resentfully. A curtain fell into place. They aren't going to ever let me do anything!

Fat Hartmann, cello, held out his hand for the rake.

The boy wouldn't go away. Ailey had a strong urge to punch that fat boy in his fat stomach.

Ailey threw the rake to the ground and stomped off across the lawn toward the side of the house. Instead of going in, he kept on walking into the pines around the back. He followed a path toward the rear of the property. Fifteen minutes later he trudged through the quiet Sunday-morning streets of Bronxville.

Past the empty stores and closed offices, up by the train station toward the edge of town, till he came to a large building with a dome-shaped roof.

Ailey grumbled and kicked at anything that would move. The sign on the small lawn in front of the building said TEMPLE BETH RISHON L'ETZION. He headed for an alley that went down one side of the building.

Ailey stopped halfway down, unsure if he was supposed to be there on a Sunday morning. Maybe the old man was preparing a sermon. Back in Luthersville, Reverend Ben Thurmond, minister of the Faith and Redemption Baptist Church, liked to practice his sermons an hour before church on a Sunday morning. Sometimes Ailey would go sit under his window and listen. Then during the sermon he smiled, knowing what came next.

He walked on down the alley to a small stoop that led up to the side door of the temple. Six or seven cats arrived before him and milled around, making an awful racket. They banged on the screen door and cried pitifully.

The door opened and Rabbi Ben Ezra appeared in a moth-eaten

robe, slippers from before the Flood, and an ancient shawl over his head and shoulders. He carried two large bowls, a box of cat food, and a bottle of milk. He didn't notice Ailey.

"Be quiet, you hoodlums, you'll wake the dead. You were out all night making *meshugga*. What do you want from me?"

The cats milled around his skinny legs, butting their heads against his shins, rumbling like miniature motorboats.

He filled the bowls, stood up, and rubbed his back. "I'm going to get a table and put the bowls on it. You bums get around better than I do."

Ben Ezra looked around and saw Ailey standing below the steps.

"*Oy gevalt,* another cat has come for breakfast!"

"No, sir, it's just me. I'm sorry I come so early on a Sunday morning an all. I'll come back some other time." Ailey turned to leave.

"Wait, wait, you've come this far. Come in, I'll make tea. Watch your step. Some of these bums are bad-tempered in the morning."

His sitting room was small and made smaller by what looked like a thousand years of memorabilia. Books whose ancient yellow pages were a match for the rabbi's parchment skin. Pictures, paintings, objects Ailey couldn't identify. He looked around curiously, but there was no place to sit.

"Take those books off the couch, put them on the floor. Careful," he chuckled, "they are very old and delicate, like me."

Seizing a chance to make a few dollars, Ailey made him an offer. "If you want, I'll clean this all up, the whole thing ... for ... two"—he looked around again and revised his estimate upward—"three dollars."

The rabbi's sand-dry laugh brought cheer to the small room. "So tell me, Ailey, are you by chance a member of one of the lost tribes of Israel?"

Ailey knew about that from Sunday school. "No, sir. I'm a shoutin' Baptist."

Rabbi Ben Ezra brought two glasses of tea to the couch. "Move that stuff aside, yes, just clear it right off."

Ailey did, and the rabbi put the two glasses on the low table. He sat down beside Ailey with a sigh. The rabbi was as scruffy as an old dog, but Ailey didn't notice or care. The rabbi's eyes contained a century of humanity, patience, and three thousand years of wisdom.

He sipped his tea and sucked on a cube of sugar. "About your offer, I will have to turn you down. My filing system is twenty-five years old, and I haven't the patience to make a new one. But I have other things that need doing around here. By and by we'll talk, maybe make a deal." He sipped more tea noisily.

"So tell me, Mr. Barkwood, are you having trouble with that lovely girl from Paris?"

"No, I don't have trouble with girls. Lucienne is great." He looked around distractedly.

"That's too bad. I know everything there is to know about women."

Ailey looked at him quickly. He knew the old man was teasing him.

"Shoot, you never even been married. You're like one of them Essenes, lives in a cave his whole life, trying to avoid lust and fornication, all that kind of thing. I'll tell you, anyone hangs around women a lot has got to think livin' in a cave's a good idea. 'Course there's exceptions." Ailey couldn't be disloyal.

"Besides, my uncle Luther says no one knows everything about women."

"Ah, well, then it must be true. Is something troubling you, my young friend?"

A wooden clock on a shelf bonged out the hour melodically. "It must be getting close to time for you to sermonize. I didn't mean to take you away from your Sunday work. If you don't mind, maybe I could sit in the back and listen. I miss the Gospel."

"No, no sermon today. Jews have their service on Saturday. We call it Shabat, like your sabbath. You go on and tell me what's on your mind."

Ailey looked at the old rabbi and gave him a shy smile.

"My granddaddy was smart like you, he knowed nothing is ever free. In the hills we pay our debts. I don't think he knew there were folks who don't care if things even out or not."

Rabbi Ben Ezra nodded, acknowledging the truth of it.

"If one of your flock puts money in the plate, he knows your gonna to be around to tell him how Jesus would have done this, that, and the other.''

The rabbi coughed and decided to let Ailey's theological misunderstandings pass. After all, Jesus was an important prophet, that was truth enough.

"If one of yours went astray, you'd read to him from the Book and he'd feel better knowing he hadn't got away with anything. He'd figure he got his money's worth, even if he put only fifty cents in the plate.''

"Yes, what you say makes sense.''

Ailey felt comfortable with the old man and slipped easily back into the vernacular of the hills.

"This morning I got up early and set out to rake up the yard. I ain't given the Everades any cash money since I come up here. I taken salt from their table. I am in debt. It's right I should give them work in equal measure. My granddaddy would be ashamed of me if I didn't.''

Rabbi Ben Ezra nodded, sat back, and closed his eyes. His thoughts wandered. *I taken salt from their table. They live in another time in the hills. Where . . . when is the genesis of that simple phrase.*

Ailey watched the old man, willing to wait. He knew the ways of old men. Grandpa Barkwood had been seventy when Ailey was born. You had to wait when they were thinkin'. They had so many memories, it was like they had to visit each one before they could answer a simple question.

Rabbi Ben Ezra had the clearest picture of an encampment in the desert, of a man, a wanderer, being given shelter and that most precious commodity, salt.

He opened his eyes and smiled at Ailey. "I know exactly what you mean, Ailey Barkwood. Go on, tell me what else happened.''

Ailey felt better already. "Mrs. Everade sent one of the older boys out, had him take my rake. Wouldn't let me do any work. Said I was to come inside and talk to her. So I came here instead. It's always that way. Soon as I try to do a fair day's work, someone stops me.

"They're always sayin' I'm a artist. That's silly. I ain't no artist. I'm not. I'm a student, that's all I am! The maestro is a great man, he knows more about music than I'll ever know. But he's the same way. He does whatever the women tell him.''

"You know the scriptures, Ailey, what you call your Old Testament?''

"Well, sure, some. Not as much as I should, but I know some.''

"Ailey, you are a good boy, and you have a strong sense of what is right and what is wrong. But . . . you are a stranger in a strange land. You haven't been here long enough for this to become your land. Maybe it never will become so. You are a sojourner in this place. Who knows? What can you do?

"When you are in another man's house, you must adjust to his rules, or if his rules are so wrong for you, you must not go there. Are these rules given from malice, you know, to make you miserable, or are they just different? You make allowances for people, because under all the rules they're just like you, and that's more important. Do you understand what I'm sayin?''

"Yes, I do. How do you know all these things, Rabbi?''

"Ahhh . . . well. I haven't always lived here in Bronxville. I was born in Russia. When I came here, everything was different. I was very lonely. I didn't even speak the language. But I learned to become a part of this wonderful country. It wasn't easy.

"So, here's the problem. Some things you have to keep. If you give them up, you aren't you anymore. You must decide what things and still get along. Give those strangers over there a chance, Ailey. I think there is no malice in their hearts.''

"I knew you would know what is right. I'm not sure what to do yet, but I'll sure think on it before I do something dumb.''

Ailey took off on another tangent. "You're getting old, aren't you?''

Rabbi Ben Ezra chuckled. "Well, bubby, I am not a spring chicken, it is true.''

"Old people just up and die. One day they're there, then they're gone. I don't want you to die. Are you feelin' good? Do you eat good? Do you have any trouble with your bowels?''

Ben Ezra laughed so hard, he coughed. He was still chuckling when he answered.

"Are you sure you're not Jewish? No, no, I know. You're a shouting baptist. Don't worry, I'll be around to hear you play at Carneigie Hall. And I'll be sure to eat good.''

Ailey seemed satisfied. "Good. Uh, I know you're not a Baptist, but I'd sure admire to hear you preach sometime. I ain't been to church for quite a while. I miss the Word and the music.''

"We'll see. Maybe we can work something out.''

"You sure you don't want me to clean up? I'll do it for nothin'. It'd be worth it.''

"No, no thank you very much. I'm like a bird. This is my nest. You come over on Thursday, I'll have something for you to do.''

Chapter 22

Paris, France, May 1986

Lucienne said nothing to her mother and father about Ailey for almost a year. But she confided in her aunt Celeste. Her aunt Celeste was a very romantic French woman and Lucienne trusted her to say nothing about her "friend."

In the spring of that year she finally did mention Ailey. She had waited because she knew her mother would feel compelled to tell her father. They did not keep secrets. It was the first letter where she talked about something other than music.

Madame Ysaÿe had read the letter and smiled sadly. She missed her daughter. Lucienne was an only child. She hadn't wanted her to go to America, but Edouard insisted. In that he was very much the French husband. Neither could she fight him on musical grounds. He had been a premier violinist for twenty years, and conductor of one of the finest orchestras in Europe. She, on the other hand, had been a cellist with the Paris Conservatoire, not even a soloist.

Lucienne was an awkward child with no aptitude for anything except music. Over the years she developed an attitude of detachment. Madame Ysaÿe thought it a defense against her father. He could criticize with great skill, but seldom praise.

Gawky, distant, introverted: not happy words to describe a little girl. Now she had a friend, *l' Amércain,* and Lucienne obviously adored him. Would she tell Edouard right away? She didn't know. Usually she withheld nothing, but this was too important.

149

Madame Ysaÿe knew if Edouard heard about it before she told
him, he might bring Lucienne back to Paris. Madame Ysaÿe wanted
her daughter back, but she also knew it would break the girl's heart.

Perhaps she could wait until Lucienne came home for the summer
holidays. She looked at her calendar. It was only three weeks.

Lucienne included photographs of herself and Ailey Barkwood at
a recital given by Maestro Everade's students at Town Hall in New
York City.

Madame Ysaÿe saw what her daughter saw. In the photograph
Ailey was poised to play, leaning forward, staring intently at whatever vision the music held.

He looks . . . so intense, she thought. She had to admit he was a
very good-looking boy in an untamed way. Very American.

There was another photo of the two of them together, holding
hands, taking a bow. Lucienne looked toward the camera, sure of
herself on the stage, and beautiful in her long gown. Ailey looked
at Lucienne. Madame Ysaÿe knew that look. Ailey Barkwood was
captivated.

Lucienne sent the *Times* review by Jack Edwards, the music critic,
in the letter. Madame Ysaÿe read it aloud in strongly accented
English.

I have heard the best and the worst. Surprise is what comes
with a winning lottery ticket. Wednesday evening at Town Hall
I was more than surprised. I heard not one but two fine young
violinists. Maestro Everade has outdone himself. Where does
he get them? First there was Miss Lucienne Ysaÿe from the
distinguished French musical family. Such an elegant style, full
and expressive, what one would expect of a far more seasoned
performer. The Saint-Saëns was especially fine. The second half
of this duo was from another country, perhaps even another
century. With young Ailey Barkwood, one doesn't know where
to begin. Self-taught since the age of four until he came to
study with the maestro a year ago, Barkwood is a talent to be
reckoned with. He played the Bach partitas with a skill and
musicality that was reminiscent of the young Heifitz. He grabs
you, commands you to share in, even be part of a wondrous
creation. I haven't heard such passion, such intensity in many

years. One must go where this young man leads. He gives you no choice.

Madame Ysaÿe sat back, the letter forgotten in her lap. They had described Edouard that way as a young man. She decided for one of the few times in their married life she would not tell her husband about Lucienne's friend.

She could not remember the last time Edouard had a good word for a musician under thirty, and few for those older. Perhaps he would never say anything good about Lucienne's music until she was grown. It made her sad to think that by that time Lucienne might not care what her father said.

Lucienne longed for a kind word from her father and was resigned to never hearing it. Madame Ysaÿe discussed it with him many times. He looked at her as though she were speaking a foreign language.

He was French, thus he was right. He couldn't imagine his family not understanding and agreeing with him. Such can be the nature of Gallic arrogance. Probably when Napoleon announced his intention to invade Russia he ignored the advice of centuries of fools who had made the same mistake.

His idea of Lucienne's progress through life was that she would study and study and then come to the concert stage in her twenties. Then if absolutely necessary, get married in her thirties. The problems of puberty were something that happened to other people's children.

Madame Ysaÿe knew there were difficult days ahead, especially when twentieth-century reality impinged on her husband's nineteenth-century world. She did not look forward to it.

St. Petersburg, Russia, 1908

Stephan Golodkin slipped into the reception room of the Ysaÿe suite. He tried not to shiver, but anticipation, fear, and lingering illness got the better of him. He couldn't remember a time when his health was good.

His fellow musicians at the theater said it was his disposition—a parody of Russian melancholy.

He looked through the well-dressed crowd of the wealthy and noble. Fat, shiny faces, lush with good food, wine, and warmth. Faces that had never known hunger, cold, or disappointment.

Golodkin's attention was on the inner sanctum where the maestro held court with the famous men and women of the Russian music world. He wanted desperately to be there with them, with Maestro Eugene Ysaÿe himself.

Fate and bad luck, not lack of ability prevented Golodkin from being a part of that inner circle of godlike creation, so he thought. He was certain of it. If he could audition for the maestro, all his prayers would be answered.

He refused to consider the idea that he might be mediocre. If he were taught by the maestro, if he possessed a great instrument like those he saw on a table behind the maestro, he could ascend to the heights, know fame even as the maestro knew it. Instead, he was third violin in a third-rate orchestra.

Golodkin's eyes shone with an unhealthy gleam. He could not

153

take his eyes off the great man. His leonine presence dominated the gathering. All eyes turned to the maestro, waiting for their cues, their stage directions. He conducted the play.

Golodkin's hands went to his borrowed threadbare coat. He plucked nervously at the lapels, tried to adjust their tendency to curl. No one paid him any attention. He wanted them to notice him, but was terrified it would be the wrong person.

What about the servants; they would know he didn't belong. ''I am a genius trapped by circumstance,'' *he thought. His father, now dead for many years, said it over and over.*

Golodkin froze. A black-frocked servant with a tray of canapes was headed toward him. He turned away, pretended to be interested in the conversation of two men nearby.

''Sir, may I offer you something?''

Golodkin turned as if surprised, looked at the tray, dismissed it with a regal wave of his hand. ''No, no, I don't care to eat before I play.''

The servant stared at him, looked him up and down insolently, shrugged, and moved on.

Golodkin burned with shame. He knew the look and damned the servant to an eternity of torture for knowing. Golodkin was painfully hungry. When had he not been half starved?

Something was happening. The maestro put on his coat. His voice boomed through the two rooms.

''You're all invited to the Metropole for dinner. My agent, good, generous fellow that he is, has decided to provide dinner. He will no doubt subtract the cost from my fees, but no matter, you've all been splendid and deserve a decent dinner at the very least. If you will join me, I would be delighted.''

Maestro Ysaÿe swept through the anteroom, taking all life with him. Golodkin, half hidden behind a bust of the tsar on a pedestal and the folds of a blue velvet arras, could not move.

His eyes fastened on a tray of sweetbreads a few feet from where he stood. Next to it was a bottle of champagne in a silver bucket.

Still, he could not move. What should he do? If he followed the crowd to the restaurant, they wouldn't let him in. Where were the servants? He listened and heard nothing.

Golodkin took a tentative step toward the tray of food, stopped, and looked around guiltily. Seeing nothing, no one, he darted to the tray and stuffed a handful of sweetbreads into his mouth. He took the bottle of champagne by the neck and drank deeply.

He heard a sound from beyond the door to the suite. His heart beat in triple time. No one appeared and the fright eased.

He approached a violin lying in an open rose-colored-velvet-lined case. It was the one he'd seen earlier in the maestro's sitting room.

There were four violin cases, several bows, stacks of sheet music. Only the one case was open. He felt awe as he looked at the most beautiful thing he'd ever seen.

His hand, independent of his body, reached out and touched the violin. He plucked the G string and then the others in turn. He was transfixed. These were the sounds of the angels. He thought of his own pathetic instrument, its frail, powerless whine. Like himself, it had no strength.

He put one of the bows in the case and closed it. Golodkin stood for a moment with the case in his arms, held more tenderly than a newborn babe.

The impulse to put it down and leave without it came, then passed. Golodkin walked out of the apartments.

Crumbs from the sweetbreads stuck to his sparse beard and cheap coat. A sheen of perspiration covered his forehead and cheeks. Golodkin walked ten miles, all the way to his tiny room on the outskirts of the city.

He sat on the one chair in his tiny room and held the case in his lap. He was confused. The perspiration dried. Color came into his cheeks. He began to relax. A strange euphoria filled his body and mind.

Golodkin was beyond right and wrong, beyond consequence, beyond caring. It was right that he should have this golden violin. With it he would become great, and if he were great, no one would care who he was, or what he had done.

Chapter 23

The train rushed south through a moonless night. Its mechanical song descended mournfully and died quickly in the humid midnight air. A boy sat slumped in the corner seat of the rearmost passenger car. He couldn't see anything through the streaky window.

His thoughts were locked three hours and two hundred and fifty miles behind in Bronxville.

"I can't do it no more, I can't," Ailey whispered for the hundredth time, trying to make right a decision that was surely wrong.

The conductor stopped by Ailey's seat. He asked three times before Ailey heard and gave him his ticket. The conductor was suspicious. What was a thirteen-year-old boy doing on the Atlantic and Southern alone in the middle of the night.

Ailey smiled at the man, tucked the pillow beneath his head, and pretended to go to sleep. The conductor hesitated for a moment, shrugged, and headed back toward the front of the car.

When Ailey was sure he'd left, he opened his eyes and peeked around the seat. Of the many things he was worried about, railroad men were far back on the list. As soon as the conductor left the car, Ailey went back to the pull and tug of his reasons for being on the train. If he hadn't felt guilty, he could have left without a thought, but he did and therein lay the conflict.

I didn't have no choice, he justified to himself. *Why don't they understand? They're so rich, it don't matter. No one listens except*

157

Rabbi Ben Ezra. They talk all the time and never listen. I tried to
tell her, I really did!

He thought of Mrs. Everade smiling her gentle smile as he tried
awkwardly to explain.

"But, Ailey," she had chuckled as if his concerns were silly,
"I've told you a dozen times, we don't want you to work. You are
a gifted artist. Nothing must interfere with that."

He tried, hell, he'd been trying since he went there three years
before. She humored him, said it was enough that he kept the neatest
room in the school. He took it as long as he could, and all the while
the debt of take and never do anything in return became unbearable.

Lucienne had no experience, no history to help her understand.
Her family had been wealthy for generations. No one ever asked her
to do anything except study hard and practice, and she would have
done that without being asked.

In Ailey's world nothing was free, not even friendship. Everything
had to be earned. There was a price. The coin might vary, as his
uncle Luther said, but somewhere, somehow, debts must be paid.

On the train, eaten with worry, Ailey thought of Rabbi Ben Ezra.
He doesn't have to be told how to do things, Ailey thought.

The next time he went to visit Rabbi Ben Ezra the old man had
taken him into the temple and had him clean the pews. All the while
they talked. The rabbi explained about the Torah. He pointed out the
different objects around the room, giving each one a name. Ailey
talked about his dreams and frustrations.

If they would not let him earn his keep, he couldn't stay, and he
couldn't see far enough into the future to imagine a time when he
would have his own money.

He thought about not being able to play the maestro's Guarnerius.
This was immediate pain. Playing it was like being tall, like having
a future without limits. He remembered drawing the bow across its
strings, the sense of power in bringing forth its powerful voice. He
became a genie, able to create beautiful things.

Of Ailey's faults, vanity was not one. He was surprised when
someone said good things about his ability. He was a good violinist,
not great. When he played, he was so much the music, he couldn't
gauge its affect on others.

He finally went to sleep dreaming about the maestro's Guarnerius.

At midnight, as she had for years, Mrs. Berenson prepared for her rounds. In a worn and comfortable robe that had never been stylish, she padded about the kitchen in wooly slippers with furry cats on the toes—a Christmas present from a student. She heated milk and made a cup of hot chocolate. She put it on the sideboard to cool. When her rounds were complete, it would be just right.

On the third floor she opened the door to Ailey's room carefully. He slept lightly. The bed was empty. She frowned and slipped inside his room. He hadn't fallen asleep in the window seat. Still, she wasn't alarmed. Occasionally he would fall asleep in the library over a book. She'd look there after her regular rounds.

Ten minutes later she silently entered the library. A small lamp played faint light over a large chair and the piano. She checked each chair, the couches. No Ailey. She frowned.

She went to the sign-out board in the front hall. Any student going to be out past ten had to put their names on it. She looked at it earlier and his name wasn't there, she would have remembered. She made the rounds again, every room in the big house, her cup of chocolate forgotten.

Slightly ashamed of herself, she even checked Lucienne's room. They were often in each other's rooms, but Ailey was so shy, that problem wasn't likely. Ailey blushed if Lucienne held his hand! After she'd checked everyplace she could think of, she went to Mr. and Mrs. Everade's apartment at the back of the house. She knocked urgently. She repeated it twice before there was a stirring within.

Mrs. Everade came to the door in a robe, her hair up in curlers. "What is it, Louise?" Her voice was hoarse from sleep.

"Ailey's not in the house, Rose! I checked everywhere twice! He's not signed out, and you know how he is about that."

Mrs. Everade frowned, puzzled. It didn't make sense. Ailey was scrupulously careful to obey the rules. They had to keep an eye on some of the older students, not Ailey.

"Oh, surely he's around somewhere. Did you check the library?"

Getting angry, Louise answered stiffly, "I told you, Rose, I'm not senile, I checked everywhere carefully."

"Don't be upset, Louise, please. It just doesn't make sense! Where would he go, and why?'' Mrs. Everade couldn't come to grips with the idea.

''I don't know, Rose. He's an unusual boy. You better wake the maestro. Whether he's gone or not, decisions have to be made. If we don't wake him . . .'' Her eyebrows rose expressively, suggesting a pattern of behavior they both knew too well.

''All right, Louise, you're right. I'll do it now.'' As she disappeared from sight, Mrs. Berenson heard her voice, still puzzled. ''I don't understand, he's so reliable.''

An hour later three worried people sat in the kitchen. By that time all three had checked the house and grounds. They even woke Lucienne. Ailey told her he was going to bed early. That had been at eight-thirty. It took an hour to pacify Lucienne, whose look suggested they were responsible for his being missing.

As they sat in the kitchen, words came, starting and stopping fitfully. Meanwhile, Ailey continued south through the night, asleep. Two hours later he changed trains in Washington, D.C., and headed south and west toward the primal comfort of the mountains. The farther south the train went, the more certain he was he'd made the right decision.

It would be afternoon before he arrived at Luthersville. It was a milk run stopping at every village on the long journey down through the mountains.

It had been a spur of the moment decision. He wondered how the maestro and Mrs. Everade would react. And Lucienne, she would be hurt. More than them, he worried about Miss Iris. But he couldn't think about that.

Ailey decided to go directly to the mountain. Uncle Luther would listen with his man's good sense. Ailey's choice was as much a product of his environment as his age.

As the train drew deeper into the dark hills, he tried to smell the trees beyond the permanently closed windows. Each year he had returned to West Virginia for eight weeks during the summer. It was golden time, spent with Sammy Sue on the farm and evenings in the garden talking to Miss Iris, then with Luther on the mountain. Like the mountain laurel, Ailey needed the sparse earth of the West Virginia hills.

At four in the morning in Bronxville the atmosphere deteriorated to acrimony. Rose Everade's own children were grown and the slender boy from West Virginia had become a natural replacement. The instinct to mother drove all logic before it. The maestro developed the haunted look of a man in a situation he knew he could not win.

She pointed her finger at him like a pistol. "What did you do?" She didn't give him time to answer. "You bully! You're a bully with all the students, and you know it."

He didn't know any such thing, but kept silent.

"I've told you a thousand times to be gentle, and you scoff! Leave the teaching to me, you say. Now he's run away. He could be lying in an alley somewhere, robbed, beaten, God knows what." She began crying.

The maestro pulled at his beard and groaned audibly. "Get a hold of yourself, Rose. Louise, you talk some sense to her, I can't."

He got no sympathy in that direction. Everade waved his hands in frustration and stomped out of the kitchen for the third time. He made up his mind and walked into the front hall. Ailey always came and went to West Virginia by train. He'd call Herman. Herman Saperstein was the night ticket agent. They saw each other every Saturday at temple.

It took five minutes to confirm Ailey's purchase of a ticket to West Virginia earlier that evening. He had boarded the train at ten-thirty. After he hung up the phone he muttered with disgust.

"I ought to let those fool women stew for a couple of hours." He quickly thought better of that. "No, I better not."

He went back to the kitchen and passed along what he'd learned. There was a spate of questions, none of which he could answer.

"Rose, we're going to bed. Ailey won't get to Luthersville until two o'clock this afternoon. We are not going to wake up Miss Bentley and add to the number of people ruining their stomach with worry. He will go to his uncle Luther's on the mountain. When children are upset, they go for the familiar, the safe places. His uncle Luther doesn't have a phone."

Rose started to protest, stopped, and was silent. She nodded slowly. "Yes, Joachim, you're right. I don't like it, but you are right and that's that. I hate the mystery. I feel guilty, and I'm angry because I don't know what to feel guilty for. I feel like it must be my fault. . . ."

Everade walked around the table and hugged his wife. Louise was already on her way out of the kitchen.

"I know the feeling, Rose. I really do. We will find out, but not tomorrow or the next day. We will give him time. I'll call Miss Bentley tomorrow, or the day after, we'll talk, decide what to do."

Chapter 24

Cole's Mountain, West Virginia, September 1986

Suitcase in tow, Ailey caught a ride with a farmer headed for Cole's Mountain. The farmer dropped him at the foot of the road that led into the wilderness. An hour later his arms ached, but he kept on until he was well into the trees. The redolence of pine and cool breezes gave him a second wind.

For the first time since he left he wasn't worried. He stopped occasionally to catch his breath, and once to drink from the stream. He knew if he didn't leave the suitcase behind, he wouldn't make it before dark.

He continued on until he came to an elm whose branches stretched across the narrow dirt road. He pulled the case onto a massive limb near the trunk, then continued up the mountain.

Dark and cool, Cole's Mountain was an enchanted place. The urge to make music was overwhelming. He heard the opening of the "Moldau" clearly in his mind as he'd heard it years before on the porch of his grandfather's farm.

Five hundred yards below the top, Ailey came to a small turnaround where Luther usually parked his truck. It wasn't there. He felt a shiver of doubt and pushed it aside. He had to see Luther, otherwise the trip would be pointless.

Ailey arrived at the top of Cole's Mountain at dusk. In the west the setting sun painted the mountains orange and salmon-pink. The cabin looked empty. There was no smoke coming from the chimney. He tried not to let fear overcome hope.

Ailey saw a small square of paper on the cabin door. As he got closer he saw that it was held in place with a thumb tack. On it he recognized Luther's printing.

At the sawmill.
Back by and by. Luther.

Ailey heaved a sigh of relief. The door had never been locked as long as he could remember. The moon was on the rise when Luther got home. He was covered with a fine coat of sawdust. Weariness made his shoulders sag and his steps slow. He smelled the smoke before he saw it and wondered who'd come to visit.

Inside the cabin he saw a small shape asleep in front of the fire. It had to be Ailey. Who else would go to sleep with a violin case next to his body? He crossed the room silently, picked up the case, and put it on the table away from the fire.

As though the violin were a part of his body, Ailey felt the tug. He woke and watched Luther make a sandwich. It was several moments before he remembered where he was.

"Hello, Uncle Luther."

Luther turned and smiled at Ailey. "Howdy, boy. How y'all doin'?"

"Okay, I guess."

"Got troubles, I imagine. Well, don't worry none. I'll fix super, then we can talk in the morning. Ain't nothing has to be done this very instant."

"Thanks, Uncle Luther. I left my suitcase down the road in that big ole elm."

"It'll be all right there tonight. Can't leave it there too long though. The squirrels chew the handle off for the salt. We'll go on down in the morning and get it. Y'all go to sleep now, we'll talk tomorrow."

Ailey heard the jaybirds before he opened his eyes. He remembered hearing a mockingbird at dusk the night before. This was the natural music of the mountain, familiar, reassuring.

He sat up and stretched. Still in shorts and T-shirt, he walked outside, over the hill to the outdoor john. Luther had built an indoor bathroom for Mrs. Cole shortly after they were married. He explained to Ailey that women were particular about indoor plumbing, and for a man to oppose such notions was not a good idea. The one he built worked fine, but the pipes were so twisted, it sang, groaned, and clanked like an alien monster.

Ailey didn't understand the workings of the female mind, which was one of the reasons he had to talk to his uncle. If he'd asked Luther before he decided to flee the city, Luther would have told him he didn't understand them either, but he knew enough to get along.

Luther came up the back side of the mountain from the spring-house carrying a couple pounds of side meat, some eggs, and a basket of potatoes. He gave Ailey a cheerful wave.

Before he returned to the cabin, Ailey walked around the hill to the spring. A few yards farther down was a small pool at the head of what eventually became Forty Mile Creek. Ailey walked in, stood in the water up to his waist, and reveled in the icy cold.

Ailey liked extremes. He had a child's ability to experience each moment newly. Back at the cabin he dried himself and dressed quickly. His suitcase was there. Uncle Luther had gone down the mountain earlier.

Ailey peeled potatoes in the sink. He'd forgotten the pleasure of doing the simple things that needed doing without someone looking at him like he was weird.

And no shoes! His feet felt alive. He wriggled his toes with pleasure. Ailey began to sing "Rock of Ages," loud! He looked around guiltily, saw Luther by the fireplace smiling, and cut loose again.

Sitting at the worn red oak table, smelling fresh biscuits, eating grits and gravy, Ailey knew what to expect in heaven. He tried to picture Lucienne sitting across from him and couldn't. He wasn't being fair. Maybe she'd be right at home.

He had a startling thought and it made him blush. *Someday I will marry her, and I will bring her here.* He went on daydreaming about her.

I would take her fishing. I bet she'd like that. Wouldn't want to put the worm on, but I'd do that. We'd go swimming in the pond, play music every day.

Luther's voice brought him back to earth.

"Well, boy, why don't you tell me what's going on?"

Ailey slumped in the chair, all the good cheer washed away. "I tried it like you said, I really tried, Uncle Luther. It didn't work, it won't work. They don't let me do anything. They treat everybody like little babies. I swear that Mrs. Berenson would have washed my face if I let her.'' He scowled at the memories.

"Why, there's fellas eighteen, nineteen years old don't lift a finger. I don't mind you send me money from time to time. You're family. Miss Iris, she sends me a hundred dollars every month, and the maestro's wife, Mrs. Everade, she gave me another hundred dollars a while back. Said I should go with the other students into the city, have fun, she said! What could I say? I couldn't say I didn't want it. I tried to tell them a dozen times!''

It all tumbled out so fast, he couldn't keep his thoughts organized. Luther listened patiently. Finally Ailey ran down. He looked at Luther and shrugged. It was an expression too old for a thirteen-year-old.

"I seen it coming, Ailey. I didn't know what to tell you. Money's a peculiar thing. You got too much, you waste it. You got too little, the scarcity makes you crazy. Scarcity and abundance, people fight wars, end up in jail and the crazy house not knowing how to deal with it.

"Folks been living so long on welfare, and others sayin' it's a God-given right, people think everybody wants it that way. Fact is, most people would rather do a decent day's work and be left alone to do it.''

Luther stopped talking and rolled a cigarette. He lit it with a stick from the fire, came back to the table, and sat down.

"What do you want to do, Ailey?''

"I got to earn some cash money. I didn't spend none of that money Mrs. Everade gave me and not much of what Miss Iris sent. I figured I'd go down and ask Wiley Pope again, and I want to go see Uncle George Sumpter in Elkins. He's got a country band, plays parties all over the county. Maybe he could use another musician.''

"That's likely. I seen him a couple months back. He asked about you, seemed to think you might become a good fiddle player.''

Ailey looked puzzled.

"That's right. You ain't never met him. He was at the recital at the Elks hall in Elkins. I got to tell you, Ailey, I don't think much of you working in the sawmill. It's cruel, hard work for man or boy.''

"I know, but I got to do it," Ailey said.

"All right. I'm goin' down to the mill tomorrow. You come along if you've a mind to. Look, boy, this problem ain't going away. Why don't you just get comfortable being home. Git some good mountain air in your lungs. Go fishin' if you want. We'll talk again. It'll come right. No one wants you to feel bad. Other people just don't see things the way we do. They can't help the way they are no more than we can."

The maestro called Miss Bentley a second time a week after Ailey left. The first call had been brief, simply to let her know what happened.

She hid her hurt that Ailey still hadn't called her or come down to see her. Even so, she went to Ailey's defense.

"Mr. Everade, Ailey wouldn't do something like this unless he had a good reason. It may not be a reason you or I would understand, but he'll have thought about it for a long time before he left."

"Miss Bentley, I ... we ... Mrs. Everade and I would really appreciate it if you would find out how he's doing. It's been very difficult not knowing what's going on. Mrs. Everade is worried. We are both very fond of Ailey.

"We waited till now because we thought it important for Ailey to have a chance to settle down where he feels secure. If you could just find out if he's all right, we'd be grateful."

"I'll try, Mr. Everade. I can tell you this much. Ailey is playing in a country band for dances and parties." It came out "pawties."

"Dear God! One of the greatest violinists alive, playing hillbilly music ..."

There was a long pause and heavy breathing while Everade tried to control the urge to shout and curse.

"He'll ruin his bow, he really does have a masterful bow, Miss Bentley." His voice had become plaintive, his confusion evident.

"I'm sorry, Mr. Everade. I just don't know what's gotten into that boy. I will try to find out. I'll go up there and see. Luther is notional, but he cares for the boy, and when need be, he is sensible."

"Thank you, Miss Bentley. Both Mrs. Everade and I, well, you know what I'm trying to say."

"Yes, I do. I'll call as soon as I know anything."

After she hung up she stared at the phone. She had a fair idea of what was wrong. She suspected she was partly responsible.

Miss Bentley spoke aloud. "Well, there's no putting it off, Iris. You better get up that darn mountain. He belongs in New York with Mr. Everade."

She went to her room and changed into her meeting-and-greeting dress. This was a situation that called for hat and gloves. As she went out the front door, Luther's battered truck pulled into the yard. Luther got out of his truck, took off his shapeless felt hat, and walked across the yard.

"Hello, Miss Iris. How y'all doin'?"

"I'm well, Luther." Her voice was cool. "I was just coming out to see you."

Luther had been coming down the mountain once a week to visit with Miss Iris for more than a year. Their relationship had become more affectionate.

"Figured you might. Glad I caught you. It's a long walk up yonder. I wouldn't want you to tire yourself. It gets longer as the years pass. Gonna have to build a house farther down before too long."

"Come in, Luther. I'll make a cup of tea."

She stuck to the pleasantries, weather—unseasonable, local news—bland, until the tea was served. Luther was satisfied to let her set the pace.

"Luther, I just had another call from Mr. Everade in New York. He and Mrs. Everade are worried about Ailey. He waited because he wanted Ailey to have a chance to relax, get over whatever was upsetting him. They know he came here.

"I would like to have heard from Ailey, I really would, Luther," she said plaintively.

"I know, Iris, I know. I told him it weren't polite nor proper, him not going to see you, but he said he just couldn't do it. He was afraid he'd say something to hurt your feelings. He thinks on it all the time. Anyhow, I figured I'd better not wait for him to come on down here."

"Oh, Luther, what did we do wrong?"

"Iris, we didn't do anything wrong. You didn't do anything wrong. Y'all forget, most ways he's still a boy. But his ability makes us expect him to behave like a grown-up man. He did what he did because those folks in New York don't know how to listen. They're so busy talking, it's surprising they hear anything at all."

"It's the money, isn't it, just like before?" she interrupted.

"Yes, ma'am, it's the money. We do what we're taught. I ain't ashamed to say I'd teach him the same. City people, heck, they don't think twice about takin' and takin', never askin' where it comes from. Can't imagine anyone's different than them. . . ."

"But playing in a band, Luther? Good Lord above, when I told Mr. Everade, I thought he'd have a stroke. Do you know what he said? He said that Ailey is one of the finest violinists alive in the world."

"I reckon, never doubted it. Nothing shameful in what he's doin'. Boy's thirteen years old, makes thirty-five dollars a night, might make more if he keeps bringing them in. He makes three fifty an hour at the sawmill on his off days. Let me tell you, Iris, he makes a good deal more than most familys livin' back in the hills."

"The sawmill! You cannot be serious, Luther. You cannot!"

Luther was on the defensive and didn't like it much. "Now, Iris, he ain't the first young fella that's worked for Pope. Wiley pays him a fair wage."

Miss Iris's face was stormy. "That I cannot abide, Mr. Cole. That boy is thirteen years old. There's laws against what he's doing. They are called child labor laws. I cannot believe you allowed that!"

"Iris, there's no need to get angry. A child in these mountains decides when he wants to be a man! What he don't do is ask women folks when it's time. He figures that one out for himself. You want that boy to come down here? Or do you want him to stay up on the mountain? You go to interfering between something he wants and something you want, you shouldn't be surprised if he stays away."

"I can get him out of that mill and you know it, Mr. Martin Luther Cole." Her face was bright with anger. Her mannerly reserve gone.

"Yes, ma'am, you can. That's a fact."

"Oh, Luther, I can't believe you're against me in this, I can't believe it." He voice shook with emotion.

Luther moved his chair close to hers and took her hand. "Now, Iris, don't you get upset. We'll find a way to work this out. I'm not against you, never have been. I'd rather he didn't work at that damn mill. I told him that, but he was determined. He really wants to study up there in New York, but the only way he figures to do it is pay his own way.

"Iris, if you get between him and what he really wants, you'll set him agin you. You want him to go back to New York; I want him to go, even though I hate the place. I had my way, they'd bulldoze the whole dirty city flat and plant trees.

"He wants to go back, Iris. But you got to understand, we don't set the conditions he lives by. I'm askin' you, give it a little time. We aren't the problem. The problem is up there in New York. Now, my guess is, Mr. Everade and his wife are coming down here with fire in their eyes, and I don't think it'll be long. When they do, we'll sit down and talk, and this time, by the Lord, they'll listen, I will see to that."

"Do you really think they'll come?" she asked.

"Yes, ma'am, I do. They are different from us, a lot different, but they care about Ailey. Matter of fact, I'm countin' on that fact."

Chapter 25

"We're going, Joachim. It's been two weeks. I will not sit around wondering what's going on any longer. God knows what he's eating. He's as skinny as a rail. I will not listen to that silly Ysaÿe child weeping and moaning any longer. She looks at me as if I were Lucretia Borgia in the flesh. She threatened me! She says if we won't do anything, she will run away to West Virginia. She and Ailey Barkwood will live in sin, for which I'll be very sorry."

The maestro tipped his head back and laughed.

"You laugh, old man. I doubt she knows what sin is; at least as far as Ailey Barkwood is concerned, I don't think she will ever know. When a girl or woman loves like that, there is no sin. But if she goes down there with that in mind, I imagine before too long the two of them will figure it out."

"All right, Rose, all right. I didn't say I wouldn't go. Why do you keep fighting the war when the battle's already won? I'll call Miss Bentley. We'll pack tonight and leave tomorrow." He sighed wearily. "I'll go see about a flight now."

Everade started to leave and Rose Everade stopped him. "I've got an idea ..." She didn't say anything for a minute, unsure how it would be greeted by her temperamental husband.

"Well, don't keep me in suspense, Rose. I'm a reasonable man. I'm not going to make a fuss."

She struggled not to laugh. "Yes, dear, you certainly are a reasonable man. What I want to do is take Lucienne along."

Everade started to protest, then stopped. He stared at his wife, then smiled. "You're a smart woman, Rose. You make a fuss, then you think. It's one of the reasons I married you."

"Why Joachim, what a sweet thing to say."

"It's the truth. Taking her is brilliant. That boy thinks the sunrise begins when she opens her eyes. If we can't talk sense to him, maybe she can appeal to him on another level."

After the flight, the drive from Wheeling took the better part of an afternoon. As they left the city, the mountains worked their wonder. Beauty pushed their problems aside.

"No matter what happens, Joachim, I'm glad we made this trip. Do you know how many years it's been since we've done anything like this?"

"I remember very well. The children went to your sister's in Israel for the summer, and I had a summer conducting the orchestra in Tanglewood. We lived in that cabin by the lake." They looked at each other with affection. There was sweetness in the memory.

Lucienne watched them silently. She was smart enough to know why she had been brought along. She was determined to tell Ailey as soon as she had a chance, to assure him that whatever he decided was fine with her. If he didn't come back, neither would she.

We won't live in sin, she thought matter-of-factly, we aren't old enough for that, but we will be together.

"There." Mrs. Everade pointed to a sign beside the road. "Only ten more miles to Luthersville. I wonder which of these mountains Mr. Cole lives on? According to Miss Bentley, it's a long way to the top, and we'll have to walk the last mile or so.

"I wonder why we can't all meet at Miss Bentley's house?"

"Miss Bentley said Mr. Cole wanted us to come to the mountain, that I am, after all, Moses." Everade snorted with disgust. "Doesn't sound like a hillbilly to me!"

All of the negotiations had been carried on without Ailey's knowledge. Luther talked to Miss Iris and she decided to go along. When it came to people, he had an uncanny ability to bring them around.

As the Everades and Lucienne drove through the streets of Luthersville, the sense of being in a foreign land grew. This was another country. They did not know the customs, not even the language.

The maestro was annoyed by his uncertainty. He had played and conducted in thirty countries, from one side of the planet to the other. He spoke five languages and got along in several others. But he was not at home in the South.

There were different things at stake. Here there were no theatrical agents to smooth the way. No bellhops, maids, assistants to remove barriers to what he wanted. In Luthersville he had only his wit to solve the problem.

They arrived at Miss Bentley's house in the afternoon. It had been built in another time. Brick and stone and an elegant veranda surrounded by flowering shrubs.

They stayed in the car for several moments and surveyed the house, hesitant to get out and enter a world not their own. Lucienne was first. She looked around, hoping to see Ailey, knowing she wouldn't.

Preconceived notions are dangerous things, and the Everades had more than their share. Rose half expected Miss Bentley to appear on the elegant porch in an antebellum gown like Scarlett O'Hara, flanked by little black boys carrying her parasol and serving mint juleps, whatever that was.

It did not happen that way. Miss Bentley appeared around the side of the house in a simple summer dress, a shawl around her shoulders, carrying a basket of flowers and a small garden shovel. She wore a large hat with a wild bird's feather that Ailey had stuck in the crown.

She put the basket down and came across the lawn to meet them.

"Forgive me for not being here to greet you properly, Mr. and Mrs. Everade, I was working in the garden and lost all track of time. I'm sure you'll think I've become senile, forgetting my manners like this."

She turned to Lucienne. "You must be Ailey's friend, Miss Lucienne. I am very pleased to meet you. He spoke of you often."

Lucienne was delighted and made a small curtsy to Miss Bentley. "Madame."

"You may call me Miss Iris. And if I may, I will call you Miss Lucy. We favor shortening first names here in the South."

Miss Iris called toward the house. "Hannah, Hannah? Come along and give us some help."

She turned back to the Everades. "I've asked my friend to help during your visit. I'm only a fair cook. I wouldn't want you to have a bad opinion of southern cooking."

A large-boned woman in a plain dress came from the house and joined them.

"Hannah, this is Mr. and Mrs. Everade from New York City come to visit for a while. And this is Miss Lucy from France. She is a friend of Ailey's."

Hannah bobbed her head nervously. "I am pleased to meet y'all. If you show me where your bags are at, I'll fetch 'em on into the house." Her accent was so thick, they understood only one word in four.

Mr. and Mrs. Everade looked around the old bedroom, dominated by a grand Civil War four-poster.

The maestro chuckled. "Damn, this place makes me feel like we stepped into a time warp." He took Mrs. Everade into his arms, gave his mustache a twist. "Well, Scarlett, honey, welcome back to Tara," he mimed in what he thought was a southern accent.

She laughed. "This is serious business."

"I suppose."

Everade walked around the room, looked at the pictures, went to the window that overlooked the rose garden.

"This is going to work out, Rose. I have a feeling. It might not be easy, but it will work out."

Miss Bentley was on the other side of the house, getting Lucienne settled.

"Miss Iris, where does Ailey sleep when he stays here?"

"Up on the third floor. There's a big unfinished room up there. It's rough, but you know Ailey, he isn't one for the more feminine comforts."

Lucienne nodded and smiled at Miss Iris.

"You go on up and look around after you get settled in. I left it pretty much the way it was when he was here."

"He should have stayed with you, Miss Iris."

"You are kind to say so, Miss Lucy, but a boy like Ailey will usually go to a man when he's in trouble. It's the way they're raised. Kinfolks, the men are important here in the South."

"Miss Iris, I know why Mr. and Mrs. Everade brought me. They hope if they can't get Ailey to come back, I will help, but I won't. They're very nice, but I won't do that. If he is unhappy in New York, he should not be there." She hesitated before going on.

"Would you tell me if he's angry with me . . . was it something I did?"

"Lord, Miss Lucy, no. That boy thinks the world of you. I understand some of what's wrong, and in a way it involves all of us except Luther, who, it seems, understands Ailey perfectly. Actually they're very much alike."

She helped Lucienne unpack. "We're going up on the mountain tomorrow. Until then we wait. Ailey's uncle Luther is an unusual man. He's old-fashioned, very true. He won't talk about it until we're all there." She chuckled. "He said he isn't of a mind to explain things twice. But don't you worry, I trust Luther. It will be all right. We'll have dinner at seven-thirty this evening. Wear a nice dress."

The rented station wagon moved slowly up the dirt road through the trees. The station wagon was a mistake. Everade had dented a fender and there were strange noises coming from underneath, where he'd scraped over a small boulder.

The car swayed and dipped. "Someone should have told me we were going on safari," Everade growled.

"Oh, no, Mr. Everade," Miss Bentley said with a straight face, "this road is in fine shape."

"Right." He gritted his teeth as the front end dove into a ditch washed out during the last rainstorm. "It must be a special skill, like driving in snow." He winced as something scraped along the bottom of the car.

"Perhaps you're right. Not much farther." Miss Bentley turned around to face Lucienne in the backseat with Mrs. Everade. "How are you doing, Miss Lucy?"

"Fine, Miss Bentley. It's so beautiful. I see why Ailey wanted to come home. I wish we had a Jeep. I have seen them on the TV. They look like fun."

"That's because you have thirteen-year-old kidneys." Mrs. Everade winced as the car hit another rock.

They finally reached the turnaround and parked next to Luther's truck.

"We won't bring water," Miss Bentley said. "There's a nice stream halfway up. Don't hurry now, there's time, and it's really not that far."

It was an odd group following the well-beaten path up through the trees. They were quickly surrounded by forest, immersed in the sounds and smells. Squirrels chattered, birds sang, and the wind, ever present, accompanied. It was a symphony that had provided inspiration to more than one composer.

By the time they reached the brook, Mr. and Mrs. Everade were gasping for breath. Lucienne walked around, looking at everything, eyes bright with anticipation.

Miss Bentley couldn't resist a gentle dig. "I don't suppose there's much chance for exercise in Bronxville. It's a pity. A good walk adds zest to living, don't you think?" Miss Iris took inordinate pride in her strength.

Everade made a rough sound in place of what he'd like to have said. Mrs. Everade just gasped, not ready for talk of any kind.

Miss Bentley waved a hand at their surroundings with genuine appreciation.

"Try to see these hills as Daniel Boone and the first settlers saw them one hundred and fifty years ago. There's not much difference today. Luther Cole is a direct descendant of the men who settled this country."

Lucienne, who had been listening, came over and stood beside Miss Bentley. "Please, Miss Iris, go on. I love your stories. You must be a wonderful teacher."

"Lord have mercy, child, I don't know about that. It's true. I have always liked teaching, and this area is filled with history. These mountains breed strong men and brave women. Simple, so people believe, but I don't think so." She scooped water from the brook and put it on the back of her neck.

"Poorly educated, that is true, but not simple. They were, still are, naturally devout, loyal far beyond the average, and independent. They have little use for governments, yet more than their share have given their lives for this country in times of trouble."

She paused and took another drink from the stream. Mr. and Mrs. Everade looked much better. The were listening carefully. They realized Miss Bentley's impromptu speech was more than the idle chatter of a spinster schoolteacher.

"Did you know that Mr. Martin Luther Cole was awarded the Congressional Medal of Honor by the president of the United States Harry S. Truman?" She spoke to Lucienne. "The Medal of Honor is the highest award for valor given in the United States of America."

"Why, if he wore all his medals, from two wars, it would take hours to tell how he got them. Many of them were for saving other men's lives. Yes, indeed. He is a man who cares deeply about others."

"You admire him a great deal, don't you, Miss Bentley," Mrs. Everade said.

More than that, Miss Iris Bentley, you're in love with Mr. Martin Luther Cole.

Miss Iris laughed self-consciously. "I do indeed, Mrs. Everade. I don't always agree with him, but I always listen to him. He is a wise man, a man to be respected."

"Come along now, I'm getting hungry," Miss Iris said.

It took them another half hour to walk the last five hundred yards. It was still late morning when they reached the top of Cole's Mountain, West Virginia.

Mrs. Everade was exhausted and had to be helped to the bench in front of the cabin. There was no one there to meet them, but Luther told Miss Iris he might be off hunting, for them to make themselves to home.

Miss Iris went inside and returned with a washcloth and cold water. She wiped Mrs. Everade's face carefully and placed the cloth around the back of her neck.

"You rest for a moment, Mrs. Everade. When you've caught your breath, I'll take you inside. You can lie down and have a nice nap."

Rose Everade started to protest.

"You do like I say, Mrs. Everade. I've seen heat exhaustion before. You'll feel much better after you've slept. I'm sorry I wasn't more considerate. I'm used to the hills. It was thoughtless of me to act as though you were also."

Mrs. Everade smiled wanly. "Don't be silly. I was determined to come up here, and I'm glad I did." She looked around. Mr. Everade hovered at her side, rubbing her hands worriedly. "This is a magnificent setting. I can see why Ailey came here."

Everade stood. "Come along now, Rose, you do like Miss Bentley said. We'll take you inside. You have a nap."

Rose Everade stood slowly, looking better. "I will, but you must promise to wake me before the sun sets. I want to see the sunset."

"Don't you worry, Mrs. Everade, I'll wake you in plenty of time," Miss Bentley said.

After Mrs. Everade was settled in the bedroom, they gathered around the red oak table and Miss Iris made them lunch.

"Where is Mr. Cole?" Everade asked.

"He said he might go hunting. He should be back anytime. He also thought he might go to the pond, get a couple catfish for supper. You might like to go along, Miss Lucy."

"I . . . that would be fine, Miss Iris."

She laughed. "You're dying to know where Ailey is, I know. Well, he won't be home till seven. He's working down at the mill."

The maestro's head came around with a jerk.

"The mill!"

"Now, Mr. Everade, don't you worry about that. We'll not be talking trouble or business until Mr. Cole gets back, and then not until he decides."

"But, great gods . . ."

Miss Iris gave him a look. "Not until Mr. Cole gets back."

The maestro struggled and finally gave up.

"You eat some of this sweet potato pie. I'm told it's very good for the choler."

"Choler?"

"Yes, choler."

There was a chuckle from the bedroom. Mrs. Everade wasn't asleep yet.

Everade's nostrils flared violently, signaling an imminent explosion.

"What is choler?" Lucienne asked.

"Bad temper." Miss Iris smiled so sweetly, Everade's protest died before it was born.

St. Petersburg, Russia, 1908

Golodkin woke slowly. Even though it was summer, he was cold. He dreamed about living in the South of France, or Mexico, anywhere there was warmth.

But he wasn't in the South of France, he was in St. Petersburg, and he had done something terrible. He knew it the moment he woke up. He turned his head to one side and there it was, right where he'd left it the night before, on the chair next to the bed.

The case was closed, but it didn't matter, he could see the violin within as though the case were transparent. He sat up too quickly and felt a deep throbbing pain in his forehead. He rubbed his temples and squeezed his eyes shut, willing the pain to go away. It did not.

"What am I going to do? I can't take it back, they'll throw me in prison. I'll be sent to Siberia. They'll make me cut trees for the railroad. I'll never play the violin again."

He knew what he had to do, but he couldn't take the first step. "If I stay, I'll always be Golodkin, third violin in the worst orchestra in St. Petersburg." The truth of it sank in like a shaft of light in a dark room.

"I must go away, far away and make myself a new life."

The final decision came from nowhere. It was fully formed and right. He would go to America. There a man could start a new life. It didn't matter what he'd been in any former life. It didn't matter what religion or what language one spoke. They said America was

179

big, like Russia, and there were no secret police. Naiveté is not restricted by nationality.

He thought about it for a long time. How to get there. First by Europe, which he quickly discarded. They would be looking for him there. Someone might see the violin and recognize it. In the end he decided on the unthinkable. He would cross Russia to the east. No one would believe he'd go that way. To the east there was nothing but thousands of miles of empty land.

No matter, he would take the railroad. He would go all the way to Vladivostok and from there he could get a ship to America.

Golodkin took the case in his hands and held it tenderly. It was his now. It should always have been his. He deserved it. No one, not even the great Ysaÿe himself, deserved to have four such fine violins.

Golodkin opened the case and held the violin in his hands. It was so beautiful he could scarcely believe it was real. He looked more closely. Through the curled, S-shaped opening in the top he saw a bit of parchment glued to the back of the instrument. He held it close to his face and read what was written on the paper. He read aloud, slowly.

"ANTONIUS STRADIVARIUS CREMONA." Golodkin groaned.

"Dear God, I am doomed. It is a Stradivarius."

Chapter 26

Miss Bentley was sitting on the bench in front of the cabin when Luther appeared out of the forest. He carried a tom turkey by the neck, and a rifle rested on his shoulder. Miss Bentley smiled at an unbidden thought. Though she would never admit it to anyone else, even under torture. She thought him the handsomest man she'd ever seen.

He tossed the turkey on the ground and leaned his rifle against the cabin.

"Afternoon, Iris. How y'all doin'."

"Mr. Cole. Very well, thank you. I made some lemonade. Would you like a glass?"

"Don't mind if I do, Iris."

Miss Iris went into the cabin. Luther spoke to her through the open door.

"Had to walk five miles down the crick to find that bird. Was a time I could have got one down there in the oak grove." Luther rolled a smoke, lit it with a kitchen match.

"You bring them folks from New York?"

"Yes, Luther, I did. Mr. Everade fell asleep in the chair in your room and Mrs. Everade is taking a nap. The girl, Lucienne, took a walk down by the creek. Mr. Everade was very upset when I mentioned that Ailey was at the mill."

"Hmmm. Does the girl know she was brung here to get Ailey to go back there?"

"She does. She's smart. She told me right off if he's not happy in New York he should stay here." Miss Bentley chuckled. "If he does stay, you're going to have another guest whether you want one or not."

"Who might that be?"

"Miss Lucy herself."

"Well, I'll be, might be nice. Like to have had a daughter."

"Now, Luther, we agreed it would be better for Ailey to go back and continue his studies."

"I know, but ain't nothing been decided yet."

Miss Iris came out with a pitcher of lemonade and several glasses. After Luther had a glass he got up. "I think I'll wander on down to the spring and see that little girl. She's likely to fall in, then Ailey would be after me."

Luther headed off in the direction of the spring. He found Lucienne a hundred yards downhill by the stream. She had her shoes off, bent over, looking in the water. Luther stood in the shade of a pine and watched.

Lucienne splashed her feet in the cold water. She looked right at Luther and didn't see him until he stepped forward. She gasped, eyes wide.

"Pardon me, miss, didn't mean to frighten you."

"You didn't frighten me, monsieur. It's so quiet, it is hard to believe anyone lives here."

"That's true. It's one of the reasons I come up here. I'm Luther Cole, Ailey's uncle. I'm going down to the pond, catch a catfish. You want to come along?"

"Yes, I would like that, Mr. Cole. Ailey wanted to take me. I wish he were here," she said wistfully.

"He'll be along this evenin'. You want to wait and go with him tomorrow?"

She hesitated.

"Why don't you do that. I reckon it's something Ailey wanted to show you. A gal ought to experience new things with her beau. makes nice memories."

She smiled sunnily. "Do you always know the right thing to do? Ailey says you do."

"I'm his uncle, he's supposed to think that. 'Course, he ain't learned I'm same as anybody else. Be easier if he never did, but he will. One the first things you learn when you grow up is folks ain't neither as bad nor as good as you thought they was."

"I think Ailey is right about you."

"I'll be back in a few hours. Don't wander into the forest too far till you know your way around."

"Mr. Cole, I'll bet Mr. Everade has never been fishing in his whole life. He might like to go."

Luther nodded, gave her a keen look, smiled at the ploy. He turned and disappeared in the forest as silently as he came.

Smart girl, Luther thought.

Mr. Everade was awake, stirring the fire beneath a coffeepot. He stood up and looked at Luther carefully, impressed. Luther seemed to fill the room both in size and presence. This man was what? Not the enemy, but he had influence over Ailey.

Luther smiled, walked over with his hand out. "Howdy, I'm Luther Cole. Call me Luther."

"Joachim Everade. You may call me Joachim." They shook hands.

"Y'all makin' coffee?"

"Yes."

"Good. I going down to Blair's Pond. Figured to get a catfish or two for supper. You ever been fishin', Joachim?"

He tried to remember. "Wait, I went with my father when I was a little boy, more than fifty years ago."

Luther put coffee in a thermos. "It's a mile and a half down yonder. Pretty steep in a couple places." There was no doubt or challenge in Luther's voice. He stated it as a fact.

"As long as I don't have to run, I'll be all right."

"Fine."

Luther put a couple of apples in the pocket of his jacket.

"I like to smoke a cigar, Luther. Is it all right if I bring some along?"

"Sure, favor 'em myself from time to time." He got poles and a canvas bag from the corner and handed one of the poles to Everade. After he got the thermos in the bag they left.

He stopped outside for a moment. "We're going on down't the pond for a couple hours, Iris."

"That's good. You bring back six or seven decent catfish and I'll clean them. You bring back less, you clean them."

Luther smiled at Everade. "Sounds fair, what do you think?"

"I think we better catch seven. I've never cleaned a fish. I'd probably slice my fingers off."

As they moved down through the forest, Luther made no effort to make conversation.

Everade's mind was busy, trying to think of a good way to bring up the subject.

Luther stopped suddenly. One moment he was moving, the next instant he was motionless, his hand held up, signaling Everade to stop.

Everade was mystified. There wasn't anything to see except forest. He started to move again. Luther chopped his hand down abruptly. Again Everade stopped.

Luther stared at a thicket of laurel and small pine. He wasn't tense, so Everade didn't worry. He began to perceive a shape different from the forest. As his eyes scanned the branches of the pine, he stopped. He realized he was looking into the eyes of an animal.

With that he became aware of the shape of the animal. A deer stepped out in front of them, turned, and ran into the forest.

Everade let out a breath. "Damn, that was something. Would he have stayed there if we hadn't stopped?"

"Likely. Come here, and I'll show you why."

Luther walked into the thicket. He parted the branches carefully. Everade looked over his shoulder down into a bed that had been hollowed out of the brush. In it a fawn lay very still.

"It's beautiful."

"Umm . . . it is that. If you don't listen long enough, you won't hear. If you don't watch real careful, you won't see. Could be you might miss something important."

Luther headed on down the mountain. "C'mon, let's catch some fish."

Everade followed down the mountain.

Old fox. We aren't going to catch fish, we're going to catch a New Yorker named Everade!

He chuckled to himself. *Well, I better pay attention, I think I just entered Martin Luther Cole's cracker barrel school of philosophy.*

"Luther, I want to talk about Ailey. My wife and I are very concerned, and we need to know what's going on."

"Plenty of time for that. Best just enjoy the day. We're goin' fishin'. Fishin's better if you just free up your thoughts. That old Englishman, Izaak Walton, said a day fishin' was like a day added to your life. I figure he knew what he was talkin' about."

"But—"

"Not now, later on will do."

They approached the pond through the cattails just as Ailey did when he came. Luther led them along the shore to a large moss-covered rock. He baited up and had his line in the water in a few moments. It took Everade a while to get the hang of it. Luther left him to it, offering no advice or help.

Luther wedged his pole between two rocks, sat back, and rolled a cigarette.

"Rough-looking tobacco, you grow that around here?" Everade asked.

"Yep. Grow it on my daddy's farm. I don't, but a friend of mine does. I been leasin' him the acres for . . . must be thirty years now. Miss Iris thinks it's a nasty habit." Luther laughed. "Mind you, she don't say nothin', she's a lady through and through. My wife, before she passed, tried to get me to quit, said it were turning my lungs to coal dust. Funny thing was, she liked a small glass of whiskey before bed, claimed it was good for her arteries."

Everade took out a cigar, rolled it between his fingers with appreciation. He bit off the end and lit it carefully.

"Rose is the same way. I have to take a walk when I want to smoke. She says it makes the house smell like a pool hall. Me, I never noticed."

He puffed on the cigar with satisfaction. "I hope when I go it's not from cancer. A nice embolism would do. If it's cancer, I'll take a lot of hard talk about these cigars on the other side."

Luther got some action on his rod and pulled in a nice fish.

"Well, that's one step closer to us not havin' to clean no fish."

Luther rebaited his hook and tossed it out into the pond. "First time I seen the boy"—he turned to Everade—"Ailey was right over there. He was fishin' and singing at the top of his lungs. When he's happy he likes to sing loud. He sings good, but loud. Probably scared half the deer off the mountain.

"Anyhow, he weren't payin' attention to his line and a big ole catfish took the bait and headed thataway with no intention to stop this side of Tennessee. Surprised the boy and took his pole right on into the water. Ailey jumped right in after it. Lordy, it was a sight.

"Anyhow, I seen he was stuck in the mud and come on over to pull him out. Even then he wouldn't no ways let go of that pole."

Luther took a drag on his homemade, ground it out with his fingers, and tore the remainder into small pieces.

"His daddy and granddaddy were both good men but stubborn. They set their mind to something, took powerful persuasion to change it."

"I thought we weren't going to talk about Ailey."

"Aren't. Talking about stubbornness. Ailey just come along for the tellin'."

Everade laughed, less inclined to challenge. Fishing moves to a different clock and didn't incline him to be argumentative. They had six catfish and two more by four in the afternoon.

Everade gave up trying to get what he wanted. It was the sort of afternoon when things that seemed important lose their significance.

"I haven't had an afternoon as easy as this in a long while," Everade said. "It probably has added a day to my life. What time does Ailey come home?"

"He'll be along about seven."

"Seems like a long day. What time does he leave in the morning?"

"Six."

They walked up the mountain slowly. Everade was deeply disturbed by the idea of a thirteen-year-old boy working from dawn till night, but didn't know what to say.

"That seems like a long day for a twelve-year-old boy."

"It is," Luther said. "It's a long day for a grown man. If you want to know, I don't like it much, but it ain't my business to interfere."

Luther stopped for a moment while Everade caught his breath.

"Joachim, I'll tell you something, and you'd do well to listen. Life is hard in these hills. It ain't bad, but it is hard. Everybody has to do his part. Cain't be nobody just coming along for the ride. Men, women, boys, and girls, everybody does his share."

Everade made to say something, and Luther stopped him. "I know you got things to say, and we'll hear them. Let's wait till we get home."

Luther helped Iris make supper while Everade and his wife sat on the bench in front of the house and watched the sun set.

"I wish we could come back here when there weren't any problems. I get tired of the students," Rose Everade said. "I know I shouldn't, but I do. Twenty prima donnas, all thinking the world revolves around them. Smell the honeysuckle? This air is wonderful."

"I know what you mean, Rose. Are you all right? You had me worried this afternoon."

"I'm fine, Joachim. Dr. Samuels has been telling me to get out, get more exercise, for years. I guess I should have listened. I have a feeling, a good feeling. This will all work out. Ailey will come back to New York, though God knows I can understand why he'd rather be here."

Everade told her about their encounter with the deer, and Luther's roundabout attempts to teach.

Miss Iris called out from the kitchen. "Supper's on."

Lucienne came around from the back of the house. "Mr. Cole, did you know there's a big, brown furry animal living in your woodpile?"

"That there's Ben, the raccoon. Ailey named him after the preacher, Reverend Ben Thurmond down at the Faith and Redemption Baptist Church. According to Ailey, they got the same kinda hair on their face."

"He wasn't afraid of me at all. He came right up and took pieces of apple out of my hand."

"I'm glad of that. Means you're a good person, Miss Lucy. Animals know who's safe and who isn't. They know what's in the heart of a person."

When the meal was done, Luther got up and began to put the

dishes away. "Give me a hand with this, Joachim. The women done cooked a fine meal, it'd be fair if we cleaned up."

"I'll help, Mr. Cole. I didn't do any cooking," Lucienne said.

"I thought all French people were supposed to be good cooks?" Luther said.

"We have a cook at home. I've never learned how."

"Woman ought to be able to cook for a man, Miss Lucy. A man admires that in a woman."

"I will learn."

"Now then, Mr. Everade, Mrs. Everade. I've got some things to say. You too, Iris. I want you to listen without being so busy plannin' what you're goin' to say you don't hear what's being said. Ailey says you folks talk a lot, but you don't listen.

"This here ain't no debate. There's no need to be figurin' on how to argue with what I say. I'm goin' to tell you how things is with Ailey."

The maestro started to get up. "Y'all set a spell, Joachim."

Luther rolled a cigarette, looked at Miss Iris, changed his mind, and put it on the table. He looked at the women, then at Everade.

"The boy's been with you for two years now. During that time he's tried to tell you how he feels about doin' his share. You haven't been listenin'. One way or another he's been working since he was four, even if all that meant was sweepin' the floor or bringin' wood for the stove.

"That boy was raised proper. He ain't never had no servant, and I doubt he ever will. He's been raised to pay his way, by work or cash money.

"Every time he tried to do something for his keep, y'all treat him like a baby, like he's not very bright wantin' to help. That has got to stop. And people makin' fun of him 'cause he wants to work his passage through life. The reason he's here, workin', is to earn cash money to give to you, Mr. and Mrs. Everade.

"You feed him and you give him a room. You teach him what he most wants to learn. What does he do in return? Nothin'. Y'all tell him he's a great artist, he's not supposed to do nothin' except exist."

He looked at each of them in turn. "No way he'll ever believe that. He could be the best in the world and he won't believe that.

He'll still know and want to do his share. He might go back there
with you, but it will have to be on his terms."

Everade couldn't stand it any longer. "But he is one of the greatest
violinists I've ever heard!"

"Never thought he wasn't. But it don't matter. You ain't dealing
with the whole man. There's more to his life than music. Y'all better
get used to that idea."

"What if he hurt himself? What if he hurt his hands?" Mrs. Everade asked.

"If he did, which ain't likely, he'd have to heal like anybody else.
But like I said, it ain't likely. His family were powerful men. They
were long-lived, good stamina. His granddaddy died in his eighties.
He could do a good day's work up till he died."

"You make us sound like insensitive fools, Mr. Cole, like we
didn't have any feeling for what Ailey needs."

"Didn't intend that at all, Mrs. Everade. Meant for you to understand that Ailey was raised different, that you got to pay some attention to that fact. It's up to you. You got to do what you thinks right."

Lucienne got up and walked away from the table. Luther knew
she was angry.

"Miss Lucy, y'all got something on your mind, why don't you
say it. Ain't no one excluded from this talk."

She looked at the Everades accusingly. "I do not see what's the
problem. Ailey wants to work. It is important to him. Why not let
him do what he wants to do?"

Luther was silent. The question wasn't for him.

There was a scraping outside the door and the sound of footsteps.
All attention turned to the door. Lucienne ran to the door and opened
it. Ailey banged sawdust from his clothes.

"Ailee, *mon cher*." She threw her arms around his neck and
kissed his cheek.

He struggled to untangle her. 'Hey, take it easy. I'm all dirty.
Hang on a second."

"I do not care."

They walked into the room. Lucienne clung to his arm possessively, ready to do battle with anyone who opposed him.

He smiled tentatively at Miss Bentley. "Hello, Miss Iris. I'm real
sorry I didn't come by to visit, I've been real busy."

Everade and his wife stared at Ailey as though he were an apparition from a bad dream. His face and hair were full of sawdust. His rough clothes were worn and patched.

He was obviously very tired and had dark circles under his eyes.

"Miss Lucy, why don't you make Ailey a mug of hot tea. Put some of that honey in it?" Luther said.

He turned to Ailey. "You hungry, boy?"

"I am, Uncle Luther."

Lucienne smiled and practically ran to make the tea.

"Come on in, boy, we got company."

Ailey walked over close to the fireplace. Everade was looking at Ailey's hands fixedly. His mouth moved but no sound came. He stood abruptly and walked over to Ailey. Ailey cringed as though the maestro were going to hit him.

Everade took Ailey's arm and held his hand up to the light, where he could see. Ailey's hands were covered with dirt. There were several large splinters in the palm and cuts that hadn't healed from previous days.

Without letting go of Ailey's hand, he turned on Luther. His face was red with anger.

"You knew about this? This is what thirteen-year-old boys do in these hills? This is the price of pride?" The last is shouted.

"Stop. They aren't your hands. They ain't mine. They're his."

Everade roared with anger and pain. "Wrong! Not true! They belong to the world!"

There was a long silence. Everyone in the room was frozen by Everade's passion and anger. He dropped Ailey's hand and stomped out of the cabin.

Mrs. Everade and Miss Iris took Ailey to the sink and soaked his hands in a pan of hot water and Epsom salts. They sat him down at the table and carefully began removing the splinters.

Lucienne hovered close by, wincing each time they removed another splinter.

Miss Iris, who had seen every kind of cut and bruise, was having a hard time. She knew if she wept, the girl would too, and the whole thing would turn into an emotional mess.

"Don't you wear gloves, Ailey?" Miss Iris asked.

"Shore. But mine got so worn out, they wouldn't stay on my

hands." He looked toward his uncle Luther, his eyes full of apologies.

"I'm sorry, Uncle Luther, I didn't mean for all this trouble to come on your house."

"Don't be. You are family. Children don't bring trouble to a house, they bring life and whatever happens along the way." He put chicken and catfish on a plate. "You want some biscuits 'n honey?"

"Yes, sir. Thanks."

"Luther, shouldn't you go out and say something to Mr. Everade?" Miss Iris said.

"I will in a bit. He ain't in no mood to be talked to right now."

A half hour later Everade came back into the cabin. Ailey was finishing the last of his supper, talking in whispers to Lucienne. The two women were sitting on the couch by the fire, deep in their own thoughts. Luther stood in front of the fireplace, smoking.

Everade cleared his throat. "I'm sorry I shouted. I've never seen anything that upset me more. Ailey, I'd feel the same if someone wantonly destroyed my Guarnerius. When there is only one of a thing, it should be, it must be, preserved."

Mrs. Everade got up and stood by her husband. "Rose, we better understand what's going on here. I don't ever want to see anything like this again! Not ever!"

Luther nodded. "All right. Mr. and Mrs. Everade, Miss Lucy, y'all can stay up here this evenin'. They's plenty of room. We'll talk some more tomorrow mornin'. Ailey, y'all stay home tomorrow." It was a command.

"All right, Uncle Luther."

"You two can bundle or Ailey can sleep out here by the fire, whichever suits."

Miss Iris was shocked. "Luther!"

"Now, Iris, my aunt Sara used that bundling board, her and Uncle Henry. They never come to no trouble till they was married."

Lucienne's eyes shone with excitement. Ailey spoke up in a hurry. "I'll sleep out here, Uncle Luther."

Lucienne was obviously disappointed.

"Iris, why don't you show the guests to the big room in the back."

Later Luther and Miss Iris walked down the path to the road. Luther carried a lantern. Miss Iris took Luther's hand.

"Luther, what was all that business about a bundling board. Shame on you."

Luther laughed cheerfully. "I just wanted to see you blush, Iris. You look mighty pretty when you blush. You're right though, you and me never used that board."

"Luther Cole! They will hear you!" Miss Iris held her hand over her mouth to keep from laughing. "You are a sweet-talker and a tease, Martin Luther Cole. I never would have believed it."

The light bobbed down through the trees, and their voices faded gently into the darkness.

In the morning Mr. and Mrs. Everade woke late. The cabin was so still, they could hear a branch driven by small breezes scrape the roof.

"I haven't slept this well in twenty years." Rose Everade sighed and stretched. She reached over to a small table beside the bed and looked at her watch.

"My God, it's almost nine o'clock in the morning."

"Rose, I don't care what time it is. As bad as this mess is, I slept well. I caught catfish yesterday, smoked three cigars, and enjoyed every one of them."

He put his arms around his wife and hugged her. "Must be something in the air."

Rose giggled and snuggled closer. "I don't know about the air, which is wonderful, but we should come here more often."

Rose came into the big room by the fireplace. There were two notes on the table. She read the one from Luther first. She laughed out loud.

> Going courting. Miss Iris is taking me to lunch and a movie show in Elkins. Eggs and vegetables in the root cellar, meat in the smokehouse. See the map. Be back this evening.

There was an arrow pointing to a map drawn on the bottom of the paper. The second note was from Ailey.

> Lucienne and I have gone fishing at Blair's Pond. Be back this afternoon. Ailey.

"Well, it looks like we've been deserted, Joachim."

"What's that?"

"Come out here, there's something I want you to see," Rose said. Everade walked into the room, hair awry, unshaven. "What is it?"

"Read these."

He read the notes and laughed. "Well, I don't know what's going on. I came up here to raise hell and I end up having a vacation. Hell, everybody's on vacation!"

He reread Ailey's note. "I'm not sure I like this."

"Oh, don't be silly. They're just thirteen years old. It's better he goes fishing than back to that mill."

"That is a fact. But, just remember, Rose, she's French, and she wants that boy for her own."

"You should listen to yourself, old man, you sound like a father."

"Hmmmph, somebody better. I want them making music together, not romance."

"Oo-la-la. I'm not going to put that nasty thing on the hook." Lucienne looked at the wiggling worm with fear and loathing. "Doesn't that hurt the worm?"

"I don't know, I doubt it. Anyhow, Uncle Luther says God made worms so man can fish. He says fishin' is important to a man's disposition, and Uncle Luther knows just about everything that's important to know."

He threw her line out into the middle of the pond. "There, that ought to do 'er." He baited up his own line and tossed it in the water.

"Ailey, are you coming back to New York?"

"I don't know yet. Maybe, maybe not."

"If you don't come back, I'm going to stay here with you. Do you think your uncle would mind? I can get a job."

Ailey just looked at her, not knowing whether to laugh or take her seriously. He decided to err on the side of caution.

"What kind of job you gonna look for?"

"I don't know, maybe I could teach violin, or maybe I could get a job in the eelbeely band you play in. What do you think?"

"Uh . . . I don't know. I'd sure hate for you to not to be able to study. Besides, I don't think your father would let you stay."

"You don't want me to stay?" She pouted, undecided whether tears were required.

"Darn, I didn't say that. I'd be happy for you to stay here. I just think there's not much chance."

"Well, you might be surprised."

I sure would. Her father would probably send the police, Ailey thought.

"Hey, you got a bite, see your bobber jumpin'. Hold on, wait a little, don't pull it in yet." The line didn't move for a few moments. "Shoot, I guess he lost interest."

Lucienne decided to try another tack. "Ailey . . ." Her voice was as sweet as a spring flower.

"Uh-oh . . . Ailey thought.

"Do you like me, you know, as a girlfriend?"

" 'Course I do. I ain't no womanizing phy-landerer."

"Where do you get these words? Half the time I don't know what you are talking about."

"Oh, I been reading a lot since I came down here. Uncle Luther, he likes to read all the time."

"What I want to know is am I your girlfriend? I don't mean just friend, I mean . . . like sweetheart," Lucienne asked.

"Yes, Lucienne, you are."

She smiled with satisfaction. "I'm glad. I love you more than anyone in the whole world, and it would be terrible if you did not love me."

"Well, I do, so there's nothing to worry about."

Lucienne slid over next to Ailey and put her face against his chest. Ailey was uncomfortable, but he made no effort to make her move.

"When we're old enough we will be married."

"I don't think your father's goin' to want you carryin' on with no poor folks from the hills," Ailey said doubtfully.

"Don't you worry about that. Besides, it won't matter. When we're eighteen we can do what we want. He can go . . . fish!"

They were all gathered at the cabin by dusk. Everyone was nervous except Luther. His certainty was a rock against which seas of emotion had no effect.

The maestro was the first to break the silence. "Ailey, Rose and I have talked about everything. We want you to understand we didn't mean to make things hard for you. Like most people, we had gotten used to doing things one way, and just couldn't see the problem. We do understand now, and we'll do whatever we can to make it possible for you to stay and study.''

Rose Everade interrupted. ''And not just to get you to stay. We forgot that people have different ways, and we have to do the things that will put you at ease with your conscience. Do you understand what we're trying to say?''

''Yes, ma'am, I do. I will try to make things work.'' He turned to Everade. ''I miss my lessons, and I miss the Guarnerius most of all.''

Everade heaved a dramatic sigh. ''Thank God. If I saw one more splinter . . . well, I don't think my heart could stand it. Ailey, I know you want to work, but would it be okay if you do things that don't put splinters in your hands?''

''I reckon.''

Rose Everade sat back and looked around the big room, the shelves of books, the stone walls, the great fireplace.

''Mr. Cole, I hope we haven't made ourselves unwelcome here. I haven't felt so peaceful in years. This is a perfectly wonderful place. Just thinking about coming back would please me.''

''Ma'am, just because people have some trouble don't mean they got to stop seeing each other. I know all about that. Y'all come back when you've a mind to. You'd be most welcome.''

St. Petersburg, Russia, 1908

There was pandemonium at the hotel when Ysaÿe found the Hercules missing. The maestro raged. He physically threw a servant through the open door into the hall beyond.

Ysaÿe could not admit the Hercules was gone because of his own carelessness. He could not forget his promise to his old master, Henri Vieuxtemps.

He blamed Russian servants, Russian hotels, the people of St. Petersburg, the country of Russia itself. But he had not said the words he knew to be true.

"It was my fault."

He was the maestro, and could never be wrong, he would never say them. Never in his whole life. As the years passed and the story became embellished, it would always be those foul Russian peasants, in that never-to-be-forgotten city, in that never-to-be-forgiven country.

Chapter 27

Bronxville, New York, Spring 1988

Lucienne burst into Ailey's room. Ailey looked up, annoyed. His anger evaporated when he saw her.

"What's the matter?"

"The maestro is in a great rage. He has broken that cheap glass vase in the library. How do you suppose he knows never to break the expensive one? He wants to see you *immediatement!* What is it? What have you done?"

"I haven't done anything."

"Well, you better go down right now, before he has the heart attack."

Ailey left the room muttering, Lucienne right behind.

"He must have heard about the fiddle competition. One more week, that's all I needed. I'd be on vacation. Well, I'm going to do it, I don't care what he says."

"What are you talking about, Ailey? I don't understand."

"C'mon, you might as well find out. Everybody else has."

Ailey entered the library like a soldier stepping into a mine field. The maestro was pacing up and down furiously. He didn't see Ailey and Lucienne in the door.

"Maestro, you wanted to see me?" Ailey said.

The maestro turned to Ailey and strode across the room. "You, you miscreant out of hell! You hillbilly hacker. You bluegrass bum! You . . . jazz musician!" The last was the worst accusation he could imagine.

199

Ailey tried not to laugh. He whispered an aside to Lucienne, who was edging away.

"Alliteration."

Everade took a poster off the piano and unrolled it about six inches from Ailey's face. The poster proclaimed the Tenth Annual Bluegrass Festival in Wheeling, West Virginia. Near the bottom was an announcement that there would be a fiddle competition, first prize three thousand dollars, second, fifteen hundred.

"Look at this, Miss Ysayë, look!" His big finger stabbed at a picture of a man holding a fiddle in the crook of his arm.

"See how this single-digit dwarf is holding his instrument? Like a machine gun on his hip. This clodhopping, moonshine-swilling dolt thinks he is Jerry Dillinger."

"John Dillinger," Ailey and Lucienne whispered simultaneously.

He threw the poster on the floor and was about to stomp on it, when Ailey darted forward and picked it up.

"I'm sorry, Maestro, that there is mine."

"I know whose it is. Do you think I don't know! Who do you suppose is entered in this ... this competition, Miss Ysayë?" His voice dripping sarcasm.

"Ohhhh ..." She turned to Ailey excitedly. "Wow, Ailey, *incroyable!* Superb! Did you enter?" She looked at the poster again. "Oh, that's not fair, I'll be in Paris. I want to be there. I want to hear you play."

"Miss Ysayë." Everade's voice was filled with sadness. "Not you too? Surely you see this is madness. Sure you see that this idiot, Barkman, will ruin his bow, acquire every kind of barbarian habit?"

"Not all fiddlers hold their fiddles that way, Maestro."

"You be quiet, you ... you ..."

Ailey finished for him. "Jazz musician."

"Jazz musician," the maestro shouted.

Everade sat down in the nearest chair. He rubbed his temples dramatically and wrung his hands.

"I have failed. My first failure. My very first ..."

"Don't be sad, sir. I'm not your first. You told Tommy Schwarzchild he was your first failure just last week, so I must be your second failure."

"Hah! Very funny, Mr. Bergman, very funny. You mock your teacher. This is a terrible thing, terrible."

"Barkwood," Ailey murmured.

"Please don't worry, sir. I will practice everything you taught me all summer long. This is a chance for me to make some real cash money. I need that money. Besides, it's a lot better than working in Wiley Pope's sawmill."

It was a telling blow. Visions of Ailey's hands when he came back to Luther's cabin after working all day in the sawmill still haunted the maestro.

The maestro sighed hugely. "That's a cruel way to manipulate a tired old man who's just trying to be sure decent music doesn't die in America. My boy, I would almost be willing to give you the three thousand dollars if you don't play in that fool contest."

Lucienne giggled. "I'd take him up on that offer before he changes his mind, Ailey."

"You, you should be on my side. Forget that, it wasn't a serious offer." Another long sigh. "How sharper than a serpent's tooth . . . you, you ungrateful child."

"Sir, it'd be three thousand dollars, and I talked to the fella who runs the contest. He said they record the best. I could make some money from that too. I'd be able to buy a decent violin. I'm real tired of being the only person in the whole school who doesn't have his own instrument."

"Do you not like to play the Guarnerius?"

"Of course I do. But, sir, it just isn't the same as having your own."

"You think I don't understand. Well, maybe you're right. For me the only thing is the music, the making of great music. How you get there doesn't matter as long as nothing gets in the way of the artist being able to create. Ailey, I can't stop you. But you've come so far. I want nothing to interfere with what I am sure you may one day become."

"Don't worry, Maestro, I will be back here in the fall ready to work hard and learn everything I can. This won't slow things down a bit. They're going to put the competition on television. You and Mrs. Everade could watch."

"What! Watch! Would I intentionally set my body on fire like some mad Asian monk?"

"Well, I want to win that contest," Ailey said. "That money's real important to me."

Everade nodded, defeated. He waved his hand for them to go. "All right, go now, practice real music every day so you won't forget." He bowed his head as though Ailey were headed for death row.

As Ailey and Lucienne left the library, the maestro talked to himself.

"Why? I ask you? I should have gone into my father's business. I'd be a millionaire, have a house in Southampton, hobnob with the Rockefellas . . ."

Ailey closed the door carefully. He looked at Lucienne and grinned, shook his hand expressively. They left the house and headed for the cabins at the rear of the property.

Lucienne was very quiet. Ailey was too excited to notice.

Back in the house, Everade shook his head in disgust, Mrs. Everade entered the library, saw her husband, and laughed.

"Not you too, Rose?"

"I'm sorry, dear. But you look so woebegone."

"It is my fate to be defeated by eccentric hillbilly musicians. It is not fair. I am getting old. I should be reaping the rewards of a life of hard work."

"Yes, dear."

He looked at her, feigning anger. "I don't think you understand the situation at all."

"Yes, dear."

"Yes, dear, yes, dear. I suppose you think I should just let him go off to play with that gathering of incompetents, ruin all the good work he's done here?"

"Yes, dear." She couldn't hold back a smile. "When does he play, do you remember the date?"

"Yes . . . no . . . why would I want to remember that!"

"I was just asking. Some of the students wanted to know so they could watch. I understand it's going to be on the TV."

"Ah . . . Rose, you're not asking for the students. Tell the truth, you want to know so you can watch," Everade said with disgust.

"Well, Joachim, he is our student. Even if it's not Carneigie Hall, we should be in his corner. I have an idea, no, you wouldn't like it."

"You always do that! Now I'll have to drag it out of you. C'mon, for the sake of Pete, tell me. I've had enough trouble this morning without you starting on me."

She looked at him, all innocence. "It's really simple. If you want to be sure he doesn't acquire any bad habits, why don't you go down there with him, besides"—she chuckled—"you might find it educational. You're a terrible snob."

"Snob, is it! Me! You know that isn't true. Why, I'm the most egalitarian person I know."

"I didn't mean personally. I mean musically."

"Hmmph, all that wandering around in the hills of West Virginia has done something to your mind, Rose. Go to Wheeling? Madness. They probably don't even have a four-star hotel!"

"I told you you wouldn't like the idea, so there's no need to shout."

"I'm not shouting!"

"Yes, dear."

"Arrrggh." Everade stomped out of the room.

Chapter 28

Bronxville, New York, Summer 1988

The maestro wandered, as if by accident, into the library of his home in Bronxville, New York, for the fifth time in a period of ten minutes.

The library was already full of students. His wife, Rose, was settled on the couch directly in front of the TV. She didn't care what he thought, she intended to watch Ailey play, and win.

Everade walked out again, muttering about lazy students, the quality of music in the world, how things used to be in the old days. He stood outside the door, pretending that he didn't want to see Ailey play.

He was in the kitchen making tea when he heard a shout from the library. He dropped the teabags and hurried toward the library, dignity and complaints forgotten.

In the library he went directly to the TV and turned the sound up.

"Joachim," Rose said, "what are you doing?"

"I'm watching this damn thing, that's what I'm doing," he said defiantly.

Everyone, including his wife, laughed.

"Disrespectful bums. I should send you all home. Maybe you can get jobs in some roadhouse bebop band. What's going on, has he played yet?"

"No, dear, but he's going to be interviewed after the commercial."

"Really, why are they doing that?"

"Oh, I imagine because he's your student," she said sweetly.

"Well of course." That, at least, was something he could understand.

The television switched to a studio shot. Ailey, in jeans, open shirt, and sport coat, sat beside the interviewer and looked straight into the camera. He was very serious, as usual.

"Mr. Barkwood, you are how old?"

"I'm fifteen, sir."

The interviewer looked at his notes. "It says here you've been playing since you were four years old. It also says you are a student of Maestro Joachim Everade. He's the classics. This is a long way from Bach and Beethoven, wouldn't you say?"

"No, sir, not that far. If you listen to folk music, you will hear a lot of Bach and other composers' melodies that have come across the years. I reckon I know this music as well as anyone. I was raised on it over in Luthersville."

"How does your teacher feel about your playing in a country fiddlin' contest?"

"I think he'd prefer me to be studying Beethoven and Mozart."

"Oh, you mean he doesn't like country music."

"How could I mean that if I didn't say that? I meant what I said, which was he'd prefer me to be playing Beethoven and Mozart. Maestro Everade is one of the greatest musicians and teachers of this century, and he don't have no trouble telling people what he thinks. If you want to know what he thinks of country fiddlin', you should give him a call. I sure don't do his thinkin' for him."

The interviewer stuttered and fumbled with his notes, taken aback by Ailey's vehemence.

"Hah! Did you hear that!" the maestro shouted. "By God, damned fool interviewers, looking for something controversial, worse than lawyers."

He looked around fiercely, daring anyone to dispute him. "That's a good boy. He will play rings around those hillbilly heathens, you wait!"

"You mean you're going to stay to hear him play?" Rose said innocently.

"Hmmmph ... don't you start on me again, Rose. He is my student. I'd better see what mistakes he makes. I probably should have let him have the Guarnerius. Boy can't do much if everybody has a better instrument.''

It was a half hour before the contestants actually began performing. The backup band was made up of fine musicians and soon had the old Edwardian room rocking with a handclapping, high-spirited audience.

It was evening before the contestants were narrowed down to a sprightly old man in bib overalls and a check shirt, the sentimental favorite, and Ailey, the brilliant newcomer.

The students discussed their chances like the aficionados they surely weren't. But they knew music and thought Ailey had a chance.

"He's so serious, Joachim. If he'd just smile once in a while, act like he was having fun,'' Rose said.

"You're right. It's fine for Beethoven, for real music. People expect a person to approach the masters with some decorum, but with this music he needs some showmanship. He should watch Bernstein conduct—there's a man who can have fun with any kind of music. He will have to pull out all the stops if he's going to win.''

Ailey played the final piece with a skill the likes of which probably hadn't been heard in the hills for fifty years, but aside from an instant cheering section of young girls in their teens, the bulk of the crowd was behind the old man, who told country jokes with real wit and was a fine fiddler.

In the end the old man won, but by such a small margin, he told the audience he should have given half the prize money to Ailey.

The maestro and Rose had spotted Luther and Miss Iris in the crowd as the camera panned around. The maestro had second thoughts about being there, but it was too late.

"He was very gracious with that man, but I know he is deeply disappointed about losing,'' Rose said.

"I'll send a telegram congratulating him and say some nice things, which I doubt he'll believe.''

One of the other students said it wasn't so bad, that he'd won fifteen hundred dollars for second place.

"Hmmm . . . maybe, but that boy likes to win. He's won every competition he's entered,'' Everade said.

"Well, don't worry, dear, in a few years he'll be making a lot more than fifteen hundred dollars just for one concert.''

Chapter 29

Bronxville, New York, Spring 1989

From outside, the Everade school appeared serene, elegant, stable. Strollers passing by heard snatches of music as they had for many years and were comforted by this famous monument to musical excellence.

What did people think as they walked on the granite, paving-block sidewalk? Perhaps they wished that their lives had such high purpose, such peaceful intentions.

They would have been as wrong about what went on in the Everade house as Rose Everade had been about Miss Iris Bentley's antebellum mansion in Luthersville.

Back in the pines behind the school, in the rearmost cabin, there was trouble of the most common, most prosaic variety. Ailey and Lucienne sat on the worn couch. She sat at one end and Ailey sat at the other.

Lucienne, arms folded across her recently arrived and much-longed-for bosom, was stubborn-angry. She would not look at Ailey or answer his pleas. He should know what was wrong. How could he be so insensitive?

Ailey's expression ranged from frustration to fury.

Lucienne, seeing she was about to lose control, spoke first.

"Ailee, Miss Bentley would let me stay with her, you know she would."

"Sure, but . . ."

"Why wiz zee but?" As Lucienne became angry, her accent thickened. "You don't want to be wiz me, why don't you admit it?"

"Judas priest! Did I say that? I did not say that. There are a dozen reasons for you to go back to Paris this summer. That is not one of them."

"You do not love me ..." She injected a pitiful sob of pure heartbreak, just like Mimi in the opera. "You have nevair said eet, nevair. You do not hold my hand. You do not kiss me! We have not made love!" She sobbed theatrically.

Ailey's mouth opened and closed silently like a fish brought to the sand. Finally he found his voice. "But, but ... it's ... we can't. I've never met your parents! Your father would shoot me!"

Lucienne's expression changed from despair to impatience. "Oh, Ailee, we don't shoot the man in France unless the husband finds the woman's lover in bed. Then"—she shrugged—"sometimes the lover is shot, but its all right, everyone understands."

As much as Ailey understood, Lucienne could have been speaking Swahili. He saw the gap between them widening, and became afraid.

They were sixteen, and dangerous chemistries were at work. He slid across the couch and put his arm around her. He took her hand in his. She remained tense, unresponsive. She hadn't extracted all the drama the moment demanded.

"Lucienne,"—he embraced her tenderly—"you are the only girl, you know that. You will always be my girl." He leaned forward and kissed her cheek chastely.

The effort to remain aloof was more than Lucienne could maintain. She threw her arms around his neck and kissed him thoroughly, on the lips. She had been practicing the moment in her mind for years.

Knowing little about the subject, Ailey was more spectator than participant.

When they finally came up for a breath, Lucienne smiled at him radiantly. "Oh, Ailee, I know you care only for me. I didn't mean that about making love. We can't do that for a while, probably two or three years." She was very practical. "You don't mind, do you?"

"Uhhh ... yes, I mean, no, that's okay with me." He was visibly relieved.

"Ailey, I'm sorry. I am miserable when we are apart. Perhaps if my parents were more fun, more lighthearted, it wouldn't be so bad.

My father will question me about my music. He will criticize everything. He will contradict everything the maestro has taught me, yet
it was he who insisted I study here. *Ma foi!* I will never understand them.

"I am so angry with you." She did not look angry. "I wanted to
be there with you in West Virginia, when you played in the fiddle
contest. If I had been there, you would have won." She laughed.

"Oo-la-la . . . if Papa knew you were in such a contest, he would
forbid me to ever associate with you. He already told me that you
wouldn't be good for my career. I don't know what that means, and
I don't care."

"Well, I can't do anything about that, but I don't want to stir up
no trouble where it don't need stirring. I'd rather get along."

In the distance they heard someone shouting. "Ailey, Lucienne
. . . where are you?"

Timmy, the redheaded cello player, slammed through the screen
door and skidded to a stop.

"The maestro wants you"—he took a breath—"both of you
right now!"

"What's wrong?" Lucienne asked.

"I'm not telling, you'll see." He was smug with his secret.

Ailey got up and moved on Tim threateningly. "Oh, I think you'll
tell me."

Tim skipped out the door, laughing. "No, I won't. You better
come quick, the maestro's in an uproar."

Ailey looked at Lucienne. They started back through the pines
toward the main building. Outside the cabin Ailey took her hand
impulsively. She forgot all about the maestro. She put her arms
around his neck and they embraced under the pines. Ailey was getting the hang of it, and decided it wasn't that bad.

Tim ran back to the house and into the library.

"I told them what you said, Maestro. They're down in the
pines, kissing."

"You young twit! I don't give a damn if they're dancing the
hoochee-koochee."

When they arrived, Everade was pacing up and down in a state
of high excitement.

"Well, finally. Is it too much to ask for you two to untangle long enough to answer a small request from your teacher?'' He waved his arms theatrically. ''Don't bother to answer. You haven't brains enough between you to answer a simple question.''

He continued pacing. ''Hormones!'' he shouted. ''I hate hormones!''

Ailey and Lucienne moved closer together, tried desperately not to laugh. Whatever it was couldn't be too bad. He never shouted when he was really angry.

''You aren't going to ask me what's wrong? Why I asked you to come here?''

''No, *Monsieur l' Empereur,*'' Lucienne said.

''Hah! Now my students make fun of me. In the old days things were different, very different. When I was a boy, the teacher was a god!''

''You're right, your holiness.'' Lucienne bowed her head and made a sign of the cross.

Everade looked at Lucienne myopically over the top of his reading glasses.

''Hmmph, very funny.''

The maestro took two letters from the piano and handed one to Ailey and one to Lucienne.

''I also received a letter,'' he said.

Ailey looked at the letter. There was a crest in the left-hand corner and the postage was foreign.

Lucienne realized what they were first. ''The Queen Elizabeth Competition!'' She tore her letter open, took one look, and threw her hands up with delight.

''*Incroyable!* Ailee, we are in.''

Ailey opened his letter nervously. ''You're right. This is fantastic. I cannot believe it! We both made it. Miss Iris will be very happy.''

Ailey walked over to the maestro and held out his hand very formally. When they shook, Ailey bowed, acknowledging Everade's part in their success.

Ailey understood the need for the grand gesture. Everade was deeply touched.

Everade's voice shook. ''I am very pleased for you, my boy. You deserve it, you both deserve it.''

Lucienne hugged the maestro. He turned away and blew his nose with great force. When he had regained his composure, he turned back to them. "Did either of you notice the date?" Everade asked.

Ailey and Lucienne looked at their letters again. "September twenty-fourth!" Lucienne said with dismay. "It's too soon."

"Yes. There isn't much time." Everade began pacing again. "There is much to do, an impossible amount, but you will do it, of course you will. We must decide what you are to play. You must learn how to handle the judges. This isn't for the United States, like the North American Competition. This is for the whole world. This is the big time.

"If you win, even place in the top three, you will be offered concert tours. You will get to play with orchestras all over the world.

"This is wonderful." He took a great breath, clapped his hands together with a bang. "There are two great competitions for the violin. The Queen Elizabeth and the Tchaikovsky in Moscow."

Ailey couldn't resist a dig at the maestro. "You reckon they'll mind if I hold my fiddle under my arm like a machine gun?"

"You do and I'll whip you with the bow. And I want you back here a week early."

They both nodded.

"Good, good. Again, I am very proud of you. You will take Europe by storm. Mr. Barkwood, if you come back from the hills holding you violin under your arm like a machine gun . . ."

"But, Maestro, it's really more comfortable that way," Ailey laughed.

Chapter 30

Cole's Mountain, West Virginia, Summer 1989

Trains had carried Ailey to every great event in his life. This time it was not just another summer vacation. This was a turning point. He was more aware than a boy of sixteen should be that winning could mean independence, financial freedom.

He wanted to win, not so much for the prestige as for the rewards it would bring. He sensed the contradiction.

This time he had news for his family, the best possible news. For Miss Iris it was vindication, complete rightness, the capstone of a dream.

Too much to think about. Over the years the maestro carefully placed Ailey and Lucienne in different competitions. They played in recitals all over the United States, both to growing acclaim but avoiding competition against each other. How did she feel about competing? They stepped around the subject, wary as two cats meeting for the first time. Lucienne was fiercely competitive, he knew that. He didn't mind, he understood it.

A year before they had read James Clavell's *Shōgun* together, and for weeks had gone around the school saying *Karma, neh?* every time something seemed incomprehensible. Ailey smiled as the phrase passed through his thoughts.

Uncle Luther. Ailey smiled as the train sped south. Luther would not make a fuss, but he'd be proud. Ailey knew that, and in his heart he wanted that. Luther was as close to a father as he'd ever have.

And Ailey had a boy's dreams of pleasing his father, of making him proud.

Ailey wanted to play an all-Bach program. The maestro was opposed, violently. That argument wasn't over. Ailey knew it would continue. He didn't mind. He'd already decided to give a little, slowly.

Ailey wasn't aware of how much he'd changed. Almost six feet tall, rail-thin, black hair to his shoulders. His arresting looks had fascinated young girls at every recital and competition. His clothes had acquired style under the tutelage of Miss Iris and Lucienne's European eye. These days, dressed in tan slacks, a button-down broadcloth shirt, and blazer, he looked more like a Princeton undergraduate.

A powder-gray mist clung to the sides of the valleys and hollows as the train neared the small town of Luthersville. To an outsider it might have been depressing. Those who lived their lives in the mountains adjusted to the rhythm of a briefer sojourn with the sun. When it came, the hills and forests would be awash in beauty, a beauty more appreciated because of its brief visit.

Miss Iris, wrapped in a long coat and shawl, paced the worn planks of the Luthersville depot. The train, whose whistle she'd been hearing for five minutes, appeared out of the trees, swaying and clattering on the poorly maintained track.

When the train stopped and the passengers descended, she looked right at Ailey, then away. She looked for someone four inches shorter. As he walked toward her, she realized the tall, handsome boy was Ailey.

He allowed her to hug him, which was a big change for Ailey.

"You've gotten so tall, Ailey. You'll give me a crick in the neck. I'm so glad your here."

They walked to her car after he found his luggage.

Miss Iris smiled. "It makes me laugh every time I think about what the maestro said when he found out you were playing in that contest over in Wheeling last summer."

Ailey grinned and retold the story. "Oh, Miss Iris, he had a tantrum that lasted an hour. He broke a vase—the cheap one—a music stand, and he pulled hair from his beard. It was quite a sight."

"You don't mean it. He pulled hair from that lovely beard?" She laughed with Ailey. "He must have been furious."

"I reckon. Between you and I, Miss Iris, it don't mean anything. If he's really mad, he gets as cold as Forty Mile Creek in the winter. One time I sneaked out of the house to play at a party.

"I didn't tell him, and I forgot to sign the sign-out sheet. Well, I figured he'd say no anyway. Boy, I don't ever want to see him like that again."

"What was he so upset about? It sounds like a very nice thing to do."

"Yes'm, I suppose. But there must have been forty gang members there. They're a rough bunch."

"Ailey, you don't mean it."

"Oh, sure, it's true. Anyway, the maestro wasn't very understanding. I even played with a Latin band. The music is wonderful. It was just like a party in the hills, except the people don't speak the same language. Everybody was real nice, very respectful. And the girls were beautiful."

"What did Lucienne think about that?"

"Oh, well, I didn't tell her about the girls, though she must have asked eight or ten times at least."

Miss Iris looked at Ailey curiously, and frowned. "Ailey, is there something? Is there some news you haven't told me?"

"How do you do that? How come you always know? I mean, I used to take cookies and things, and I know you couldn't hear me. Still, you knew every darn time."

"Hmmph . . . Ailey, boys and girls have been trying to hide things from me for many years. I've had lots of practice."

"Well, you're right as usual. Lucienne and I have been selected to participate in the Queen Elizabeth Competition in Brussels, Belgium, in September."

He handed her the letter. He'd kept it handy in the pocket of his jacket. It was wrinkled and had a jam stain in one corner. He'd taken it out twenty times to read, still unable to believe his good fortune.

She sighed and smiled a smile all for herself. "I knew it. I always knew. You had the mark of greatness when you were a little boy playing in your grandfather's old barn.

"I know what this contest means. I do not worry that you will win or lose. You will have greatness."

Ailey shrugged. "I'll have to practice all summer, more than I ever have before."

"Yes, of course you will. September. My, my that doesn't seem very long, does it?"

"No, ma'am, it sure doesn't."

Miss Iris paused as if unsure about speaking something that was on her mind. "Ailey, would you mind awfully if I came to Europe? I mean, it is public, isn't it?"

"Yes, ma'am. It'll be in the Royal Opera House. I'd be proud to have you there, but I think it must be terrible expensive."

"Oh, Ailey, I'm an old woman with nothing to spend my money on, and I've got rather a lot of it, thanks to my daddy. There's nothing in this world I want more than to be there and hear you play in front of all those people."

Hours later, slouched on the big divan in Miss Iris's living room, Ailey could barely keep his eyes open. He'd had to answer a barrage of questions from Miss Iris.

"Your uncle Luther will be so proud of you. Of course he won't say so," she said wryly.

"You better go on to bed now, you'll fall asleep in that chair."

"I think I will, I'm pooped."

He walked over to her, embraced her, and kissed her cheek as if it were the natural thing to do. Then he smiled and left the room. Ailey didn't understand what was important.

She stared after him for a long time. He had never kissed her willingly in all the years he had stayed at her house. She felt recognition. She felt like a mother.

Miss Iris stayed up for a long time after Ailey went to bed. She had an album, kept since Ailey came to stay with her. She faithfully collected every picture, newspaper clipping, and review ever written about him. She fell asleep in her chair, the album open in her lap.

Miss Iris drove the old Ford like a soldier at attention. She negotiated the road to Cole's Mountain with familiarity. Ailey was impressed.

"Miss Iris, how do you know your way up here so well?"

"Oh, I've been coming up to see Luther every week for two years."

When she realized what she'd said, she blushed, and Ailey laughed.

"Well, I'll be, is he your beau, Miss Iris?"

Miss Iris was still blushing. "You hush, Ailey Barkwood. I declare, those New Yorkers have taken all your manners. You better behave. You're not so big I can't take a switch to your britches."

"I'm sorry, Miss Iris. If I'd known he was your beau, I wouldn't have said anything, honest."

Miss Iris couldn't resist his teasing, and laughed. She liked being teased about a man. It wasn't something that had happened very often in her life.

"You keep it up, Ailey Barkwood, I'll have Mr. Cole tan your hide."

Ailey grew silent among the trees, happy to be there, where the spirit was strong. Ailey adjusted his pace to Miss Iris's as they walked through the forest. Luther had been talking about building a house lower down, but Ailey figured it was just talk. The cabin where he'd lived most of his life was native soil and he'd not be at ease elsewhere.

Ailey carried a small suitcase with a few changes of clothes, his violin case, and a great deal of music. It was a violin he'd borrowed from the maestro, nowhere near as fine as the Guarnerius, but a hundred times better than the one he'd found in the Luthersville elementary school.

Ailey wondered if the maestro would let him play the Guarnerius in the competition. Lucienne had a beautiful Amati and another fine instrument as a second.

Halfway across the clearing in front of the cabin, Miss Iris called out to Luther.

"Hello the house. You have company, Luther."

Luther opened the door with an easy smile on his face.

"Hello, Ailey. Whooeee, you have grown some since I saw you last. Don't reckon I can call you boy no more." He shook Ailey's hand, put his arm around Ailey's shoulder.

"See there, Iris, another couple inches, he'll be as tall as me."

He turned to Iris, put his big hands around her arms, leaned down, and kissed her. Miss Iris blushed as pink as the climbing rosebush alongside the cabin.

Ailey grinned. "Well, it ain't no secret now, Miss Iris. I'd say Uncle Luther was your beau for sure."

"Luther, I think you better take this smart-talking jaybird in hand."

"Iris, I ain't ashamed of the fact I'm sweet on you," Luther said.

"There, see, I reckon you're going to have to find that switch yourself, Miss Iris. Shoot, you could do worse, ma'am. There ain't many men in these hills got their own mountain. There's folks down below think Luther's got a gold mine up here and that's why he don't go to town very often."

Luther chuckled. "Well, I guess I've been over every inch of these hills. Can't say that I've ever seen any gold. There's a nice seam of coal north of here near the state road. I think that's on my property, but I ain't anxious to have no one diggin' for it."

"When you an' Miss Iris getting married?" Ailey tried to keep a straight face.

"Well, now, boy, that's something to think about."

"I not staying out here all day while you two stand around making fun of an old woman." She went into the cabin.

"No man in his right mind will ever call you old, Miss Iris," Luther called out.

They could hear her laughing in the kitchen. "Well, that's better, you've gone from teasing to sweet-talk. I'm going to cook something, make some coffee. Only way to get you two to stop is fix something to eat."

Ailey and Luther sat on the bench in front of the cabin, Ailey sighed with satisfaction, looked around the clearing.

"They ought to build symphony halls in places like this, Uncle Luther, make it out of glass so's people could have the trees and sunsets, mountains and music, all at the same time."

"Sounds like a fine idea, Ailey. When I'm gone, why don't you do that."

That sat in companionable silence while Luther rolled a cigarette. Once Luther had it lit, he turned to Ailey. He had a curious expression on his face.

"Somethin' on your mind, boy. You look full to burstin'."

"Miss Iris said the same thing."

"Well, boy, you live out here, you have time to study things. I'd say you have something on your mind, and if I had to guess, I'd say it was something exciting."

"Lucienne and I have been selected to play in one of the most important competitions for the violin in the world." Ailey handed Luther his letter of invitation. "It's called the Queen Elizabeth Competition. It's in Brussels, Belgium. Next to the Tchaikovsky Competition in Russia, it's the most important. If I do well, my chances of going on tour are excellent. There'd be recordings, and a real chance to make a good livin'."

Luther nodded, read the letter again. "Damn, Brussels Belgium, think of that. Don't they have no competitions in the United States?"

"Sure, Lucienne and I have been winning them all over, like that one in Chicago, but this is for the whole world. Nowadays when a soloist goes on tour he might play in fifteen or twenty different countries."

"Well, I'm proud of you, Ailey. Almost makes me wish I got out and around more so I could brag a little. The maestro must be some pleased, might make up for you going to Wheeling, playin' in that fiddle contest."

"Mmmm . . . He was. I'm going to have to work harder than ever all summer."

"Lucienne must be happy. You said her father's a famous musician, violin player?"

"He's a conductor now. It's kinda sad. She said he never says anything good about her music." Ailey paused for a moment. "Uh, Luther, I got to talk to you about her. She isn't a little girl no more, and she's . . . well, she's my girl, and I sure do love her, but things could get out of hand. If you know what I mean."

"I do know."

"I worry about her and I being in the same competition. She really likes bein' the best. I don't blame her none, so do I. Still, I don't want to have any trouble over that."

"You got some things to think about, Ailey. It'll keep for now. We've got all summer to think on it. We'll talk again soon. Right now, I'm hungry. Let's go inside and see what that beautiful woman from the flatlands has cooked up."

*　　*　　*

After midnight, full dark on Cole's Mountain. In the fireplace the embers glowed. Ailey had gone to bed in the back room two hours earlier, and Miss Iris had returned to Luthersville. She wouldn't stay when Ailey was there. She said it wasn't proper.

Luther waited. He meant to talk with God. One didn't just up and start gabbin'. A man had to be in the right frame of mind. He got up and walked outside, across the clearing into the trees. Once there, he sat on a rock.

He remembered with perfect clarity the terrible years of war and wondered why it still hurt so bad.

"Lord, you'd think after all these years, I wouldn't have to see them things no more. I wish I'd been better, seems like I been sorry long enough."

The trees sighed and the whippoorwill that lived near the spring sang a sorrowful coda.

"It is time, Lord. You showed me before, but I couldn't see the day. I kept faith like I said I would. We will put beauty back into the world. The boy shall have the violin, and he will go forth and do your work."

Luther got up slowly and walked back across the clearing to the cabin. Inside, he went to a cabinet and took the violin case out. He brought it over to the old red oak table, opened the case, and held the golden Stradivarius near his chest.

NOVOSIBIRSK, RUSSIA, 1908

Golodkin hated the train. It was hot and it smelled. He sold every-thing he could to that Armenian thief in St. Petersburg. He pleaded with the man for a better price, whined about his old mother in Georgia who was dying. The lies came easily. It hadn't helped.

Three old women in babushkas and rough leather boots cooked over a brazier at the rear of the car. The smoke and smell of rancid oil made him nauseated.

He tied a length of rope around the violin case and around his wrist. He was desperately afraid someone would steal his violin while he slept.

Three soldiers in the tattered uniforms of some local militia, smell-ing of potato brandy, asked him to play so they could sing. For a moment he thought they were going to force him.

He shouted at them to leave him alone, he was ill. He told them he was in mourning for his mother. They cursed him, called him a stupid Balt for his coldness. A real Russian played when he was sad, then he would feel better.

Half asleep, between life and dreams, he created a beautiful home in New York City, America. Then someone shook him awake. He was terrified. An old man in uniform stood in front of him with his hand held out.

Golodkin clutched the violin to his chest so hard, his knuckles turned white.

223

"Never," he screamed, "I'll never give it up!"

"Here, you silly fool, I only want your damn ticket."

The soldiers laughed and made circling motions near their foreheads. "He's mad as a Cossack. Better be careful, old man, he'll bite you and give you rabies."

Golodkin stared at the old man blankly.

"Come on, young fella, just give me your ticket so I can get on with my job."

It finally dawned on Golodkin what the man wanted. He fumbled in his coat, found his ticket, and gave it to the conductor.

"Sorry," Golodkin muttered.

One of the old women whispered to her friend just loud enough for Golodkin to hear.

"That man acts more like a thief than a thief."

Chapter 31

Paris, France, Summer 1989

Dinner at the Ysayë house was no different than Lucienne remembered. One dressed as one was told. Appeared at the correct hour, and had little to say. She couldn't talk freely to her mother. If she brought up some subject that was on the disapproved list, her father would break in and let his displeasure be known.

Alternately he would discourse on subjects in which she had no interest. Unlike his countrymen Voltaire and Montaigne, who delivered their aphorisms with wit and charm, the elder Ysayë went on at length about such banalities as the Paris railway system. Why a musician of his stature should care about such things was a mystery his family wasn't likely to uncover.

No matter how incomprehensible parents are to their children, they still have the capacity to surprise when they show some odd bit of humanity.

Lucienne expected her father to say little about her selection to the Queen Elizabeth, or, failing that, to criticize her selection of music. But he did neither. He seemed genuinely pleased that she had been selected and said she must select her own music.

He did go on at length about how to prepare and win such a competition, and she listened. He had vast experience. He won the Tchaikovsky when he was twenty.

"This boy, this rustic violinist I've been reading about, he was also selected."

"Yes, Papa."

"You are friends with him, no?"

"Yes, Papa."

"You must believe me when I tell you how important the people you know are in this business. I don't see how associating with some backwoods cowboy can possibly help your career."

"He's not a cowboy, Papa. He is a violinist. Maestro Everade thinks he may become the greatest violinist in the world."

"How can you say this. I don't understand. You are to be in competition with this ... this ... bumpkin. You must believe you will win. You must know you will win."

"I didn't say I couldn't win. I will of course do my best. I want to win. However, it will be up to the judges."

"Listen, *ma chère,* I know you care for this boy. But now is the time for your music. To succeed, you must put everything else aside, be ruthless with your emotions, and concentrate all your talent on your instrument. In years to come there will be time for love, some-day, even marriage. With someone suitable to your position in life, of course."

"Yes, Papa."

Eugene Ysaÿe looked at his daughter, one eyebrow raised. He shrugged. He knew she would do what she wanted as soon as she was away from him.

"If you win, you will be offered a world tour with the greatest symphonies in the world. Have you thought about that?"

"I have, Papa."

"Do you want to do that?"

"Yes. Ailey ... my friend and I have talked about it often. We, Ailey and I, are writing music. He has already completed two sonatas and several shorter pieces. I had hoped you might look at them and give us your opinion."

"Really? Why do you say *us* if he wrote them?"

"Because I wrote some of them, and part of one of the sonatas."

"Really, well, I am impressed. Yes, by all means leave them with me. When I have time." He did not tell her that in his mind he had already rejected the idea. Not for the reasons she thought.

Her father couldn't bear the idea that she might have written something mediocre, done something that would not make him proud. The fact that he had never told her he was proud went unnoticed.

He imagined people should know what he felt, that he shouldn't have to tell them.

"When I think of you on that stage in Brussels, I think of your great-grandfather, my namesake.

"If the Hercules hadn't been stolen by those filthy Bolsheviks, you would be playing it before those judges. Did you know Menuhin said he saw it in Berlin after the war? I've asked myself a thousand times what might have happened to it. I dream about it, that it is in someone's closet, that they find it and return it to us."

Mother and daughter sighed. They had heard the story so many times, they could repeat it from memory.

Lucienne tuned out his voice and thought about Ailey and the last time they had been together. She was getting ready to return to Paris. He brought flowers to her room. They had kissed and petted for an hour. They had finally stopped by mutual consent. The consequences frightened Ailey more than they did Lucienne. He knew instinctively the change that would make in their lives and wasn't ready. She would have given herself to him then.

In her heart she doubted they could wait three years. He had written a double violin concerto and given it to her as a present, swearing they would play it together on all the stages of Europe.

She would not show this one to her father. Across the top Ailey had written: To the only girl I will ever love, Ailey Barkwood.

Chapter 32

Cole's Mountain, West Virginia, Summer 1989

Ailey woke to the sound of birds. A squirrel made a racket on the windowsill. He wanted to go back to sleep, but the squirrel wouldn't quit.

He dressed quietly in jeans and a sweatshirt with a picture of the maestro on the front. He and Lucienne took a picture of the maestro in the East Village in Manhattan. There, a man had taken the picture and made a transfer which he put on sweatshirts for the both of them. They had him print underneath; World's crankiest genius: Antoine Joachim Everade.

The maestro laughed uproariously, saying he wanted one just like theirs. It had been a happy day. One of many during the past year.

Ailey walked across big room over to the fireplace. Luther was cooking sidemeat, eggs, and grits.

"Welcome home, Ailey. How y'all doin'?"

"I am right where I want to be, Uncle Luther. This is as good as it gets."

"Set the table for three. Miss Iris ought to be here anytime. When you got that done, why don't you walk down the trail and meet her, in case she's toting something. Woman thinks she's twenty-five years old."

"All right, Uncle Luther, are you and Miss Iris gonna get married?"

"Well, boy, I don't know. I give it some thought from time to

229

time. We might. We been keepin' company for nearly three years. I admire her considerable, but we ain't exactly runnin' in the same social circles. What do you think about it?''

"I think it'd be great. You and her are my two favorite people in the world."

Ailey met Miss Iris coming across the clearing.

" 'Morning, Miss Iris. You look prettier than a rosebud in the sunlight."

She laughed. "Where did you learn such sweet-talking ways."

"Oh, I was just askin' Uncle Luther if you and he were gonna get married, and here you are looking so pretty an' all, I see where he might be inclined."

"Ailey Barkwood! You hush, he might hear you. What did he say,'' she half whispered.

"For someone who isn't interested—"

"I think I will take a switch to you."

"He said he'd been thinkin' on it a lot. He probably can't imagine why a beautiful person like yourself would want marry an old hillbilly like him."

"Ailey, you're making this up. You should be ashamed."

"I'm not, I swear. If I was you, Miss Iris, I'd marry him. Folks say he's got a gold mine up here, and he isn't really that old."

"All I can say is it's a good thing we have you back home. Your manners need improvement."

After breakfast they sat around the table and talked about Ailey's year. What he'd seen and what he'd done.

Luther got up and went to the cabinet. He got the violin case and brought it to the table. Ailey was immensely curious, but he waited.

Luther's hands lingered on the case, unwilling to break the connection. "Ailey, I've thought about giving this to you many times over the years. Each time I held off, knowing the time had not come. Now it has. I've had this fiddle more than thirty years. The fact that it's here, at this very moment, is a small miracle.

"I found this in the wall of a Korean farmhouse during the war. It was December 1951. It were a terrible hard year. Don't make no sense my even being here alive to tell you this story. I believe the hand of God was present.

"So I brung it back, and I have kept it and preserved it as I was intended to do until the time came to pass it on to the person meant to have it.

"That person is you, Ailey Barkwood. Some men say the universe is an accident. I've read the philosophers fore and back. I don't believe it, boy, not for a minute. What seems like a coincidence gets started somewhere. Problem is, men are so far removed from the causes, they think the effects are just a roll of the dice. Time is the burden that shortens our sight. Too much or too little, never just enough."

He pushed the case toward Ailey. "I once thought if I kept this thing, if I preserved it, I would be forgiven the terrible things I done and didn't do. It ain't happened yet, but maybe it will."

Ailey opened the case and looked at the golden perfection of what he knew was a very old, very valuable instrument. He looked at it carefully. When he looked through the holes in the top he saw what so many others had seen before him.

He read aloud: "Antonius Stradivarius Cremona."

Chapter 33

Bronxville, New York, August 1989

Ailey was asleep when the train pulled into the Bronxville station. Even in sleep his hands held the violin case in a sure grip.

A young woman sat across from Ailey. She traveled with her baby daughter to visit her husband in prison in Upstate New York. She reached over and shook Ailey gently. "C'mon, wake up now. We're at your gittin'-off place."

Ailey woke with a start. He was confused for an instant. It was a long way back from the place of his dream. He'd been on the stage of the Royal Opera House in Brussels, Belgium, waiting to begin. The conductor, who looked a lot like the maestro, kept asking questions about his music, his teacher, his violin.

"Thanks," he said hoarsely.

He smiled at the baby, who stared back, so solemn, as if she knew life wasn't going to offer her many chances for laughter.

"I hope everything works out for you, ma'am, I truly do."

"Thank you kindly, Ailey Barkwood. Y'all go on over there and show those Europeans how a West Virginia boy gets the job done, heah?"

"I will surely try to do that, ma'am."

When he got off the train, no one was waiting at the station. Lucienne would arrive later that evening from Paris. They were both coming back two weeks early, as arranged with the maestro.

Ailey had the one carryall plus his regular violin and music case.

He'd put the Stradivarius into the larger bag surrounded by his clothes. He decided to walk. It was a heavy load, but he didn't want to spend three dollars on a taxi.

Ailey had money. He'd received a seven-hundred-and-thirty-dollar royalty check. It was from a recording company, the one that recorded the contest in Wheeling.

He debated over whether to go to the school or to see Rabbi Ben Ezra first. The weight of his luggage made the decision for him. He'd go straight to the school. He could visit his friend the next day.

Late summer in Bronxville was like West Virginia, and not much cooler. The trees were still lush and green, and the heavy air foretold thunderstorms during the night.

He was sweating by the time he reached the school. Mrs. Berenson met him at the front door with a big hug, which he accepted with good humor. She helped him carry his things up the three flights over his protest, chattering about ordinary things.

Somewhere among all the talk, Ailey thought she might have asked him questions, but she never waited for an answer. She filled in the blanks with whatever answers she found more acceptable.

A curious phenomenon that made a queer kind of sense. Her answers were better than anything others might provide, and she never had to worry about hearing anything she didn't like.

It took Ailey four years to realize that New Yorkers as a group were genetically, socially, and temperamentally incapable of listening to anyone except themselves. If he was willing to scream at the top of his lungs like a fishmonger selling crab cakes, someone might listen. But it wasn't genuine. They were just waiting until they could reassert their own opinions.

Ailey couldn't do it. He couldn't even entertain the idea of doing it.

Ailey had a notion that he'd have a better chance of communicating in New York if he took out an ad in the *New York Times*. People in the Everade household and Bronxville liked their truth from the newspaper better than an actual flesh-and-blood person.

As far as he could tell, they judged their entire world on what they read in the newspaper and heard on TV. He personally thought it pretty dumb. But he had the advantage, or disadvantage, of being raised by his uncle Luther, Miss Iris Bentley, and Sammy Sue. All of whom, for a variety of reasons, trusted nothing they read in the newspapers. Newspapers were written by people from the city. The city meant government, and government meant liars. In their own way, Ailey's people were as judgmental as the peculiar tribe called New Yorkers.

When Ailey had finished unpacking, he took the Stradivarius out and went looking for the maestro. There were several new faces around the school. Many professionals and beginners came in for the summer. The professionals came to the maestro to brush up their technique and to get help adding new pieces to their repertoire.

A young man, a few years older than Ailey, stopped him in the hall on his way downstairs.

"You're Ailey Barkwood." It was a statement, not a question. "I was in Chicago, The North America, got bounced out in the preliminaries. I stayed for the finals. I told my friends if you didn't win it, the panel was mad. I'm glad you did. You are very good.

"If you're going to be here for a while, I'd like to spend an hour or two with you, learn how you get through the double and triple stops so smooth, so crisp." He shook his head with wonder.

"You can charge a regular master's fee if you like. It'd be worth it."

Ailey was too surprised to do anything but nod. He was also very flattered, first because he was recognized and then that anyone would consider his technique worthy of emulation.

"Would you think about it, please? I'd really appreciate it."

"Sure, I'll do that."

Ailey continued down the hallway, still caught up in the strange meeting and the idea of being a teacher.

He found the maestro on the back patio with Mrs. Everade.

Rose Everade hugged Ailey as if he'd been away for years. "We're so glad you're back. Ailey, you're getting as handsome as a movie star. Lucienne will have to keep you close."

Ailey blushed. "I don't reckon she's got anything to worry about."

"Enough, Rose. Mr. Barkman's got more important things on his mind than romance and Hollywood."

"Barkwood, sir," Ailey murmured, not in the least annoyed.

The maestro gave him a sly smile. "Right, Barkwood it is. Sit, boy, sit. You want coffee . . . tea?"

"Tea would be fine, sir." He started to get up.

"Stay seated, Ailey, I'll get it," Rose Everade said.

"So, Ailey, did you work hard this summer?"

"Just like you said, six hours a day, most often more than that."

"Good, good. Do you still insist on the Bach?"

"Yes, for the finals. Maybe some other pieces during the early round." Ailey put the case on the table. He wanted the maestro to ask about it so he could show him.

Everade looked at the case curiously. "What have you got there, Ailey. That case is over a hundred years old, more maybe. They stopped making that kind around the turn of the century."

Ailey opened the case.

The maestro didn't reach for the violin for a moment. Rose came to look over his shoulder.

"Ailey, it's beautiful!"

Everade held up his hand for silence. The look he gave Ailey was part puzzlement, part amazement.

"It's a Stradivarius, isn't it?"

"Yes, Maestro."

The maestro let out a breath and nodded. "Yes, it had to be. The Maestro of Cremona made his signature as plain as . . . well, I'd know it anywhere."

He looked up at Ailey, then at the violin.

"May I?"

Ailey was startled, then he remembered, he always asked if he wanted to touch the maestro's Guarnerius. It was a professional courtesy.

Ailey bowed slightly. "Yes, of course, Maestro."

Everade lifted the violin from its bed of rose velvet. He looked at it slowly, thoroughly, absorbing it in its entirety. He looked at it with all his senses, physical and aesthetic. Finally he looked down into the body of the instrument. He sighed hugely.

"My God! My God, as if he made it this year. Look here, Rose, down here. Read what it says on the parchment, there, on the inside."

Rose Everade put on the glasses that hung from a chain around her neck. She peered into the violin and read each word separately.

"Antonius . . . Stradivarius . . . Cremona . . . oh, Ailey this is incredible, wonderful! I'm so happy for you. I know how much you've wanted your own violin.''

Everade put the violin back in its case. He shook his head with wonder. "It hasn't been played in a long time. These strings, they aren't even made anymore. We must take it to Jacques Français in Manhattan right away. You'll need a modern bridge, decent strings, and you must insure it immediately.''

"Yes, sir. Would it be possible for you to go with me? I'm not sure I know what to tell them.''

"Yes, that would be best. I'm dying of curiosity, but I'm not sure I'll be able to believe. So, tell me, Ailey, how do you come to have this beautiful thing?''

"I don't blame you, Maestro. I still have trouble believin' it's mine, how it came to be mine.''

He looked at Mrs. Everade and smiled. "But it sure enough is. My uncle Luther gave it to me this summer when he heard I was playin' in a competition in Europe.'' Ailey smiled at the memory.

"He said the Lord told him it was time, and I believe him. He's had it since the winter of 1951. He found it in the wall of a destroyed farmhouse in Korea during the war. He said the Lord intended him to preserve it until it was time to pass it on.''

The maestro stood up and pulled at his beard absentmindedly.

"Amazing, I knew he was involved somehow. It's like him to be a part of this thing's history. In the wall of a farmhouse . . . I'll bet he didn't even know it was a Stradivarius, or if he did, he didn't care.''

"No, sir, that wouldn't matter to him, sir.''

"How did it get there?''

"He doesn't know, Maestro, I asked him. He was wounded, near dead when he found it. I think it was only important that he preserve it, at least that's what he said.''

Everade turned to his wife. "Martin Luther Cole, mountain mystic. We must go down there and visit again soon. There is more to that man than meets the eye.''

He closed the case. "Practice, Mr. Barkman.'' He smiled, "Mrs. Everade and I have work to do. We'll get started with your program tomorrow. Lucienne will be arriving in a few hours. Mrs. Berenson has something in the kitchen if you're hungry.''

Ailey took the violin and left. In his room he lay on the bed. He thought about the things he had to do. He wanted to wait for Lucienne, but the excitement of being back and the long trip from West Virginia caught up with him all at once and he went to sleep.

When Lucienne arrived, everybody had gone to bed except Mrs. Berenson, who never seemed to sleep. They had a cup of hot chocolate together, then Lucienne went up to her room. She had a bath, then changed into a thin cotton nightshift and robe.

She didn't go to sleep. She had been thinking about Ailey for six weeks and had to see him before she went to sleep. She slipped silently down the hall to his room.

When she went in his room he didn't wake up. He was still stretched out in his clothes.

She whispered his name. "Ailey . . ."

He smiled in his sleep, and she knew she loved him so much she would die if anything ever came between them. She took off her robe and sat down on the bed beside him slowly, took his hand to her face, and kissed it. She lay down beside him carefully, afraid to wake him, yet wishing him to be awake.

She snuggled close, wanting to feel her body against his. She knew it was dangerous. Lucienne had had long talks about sex and love with her aunt Celeste.

Aunt Celeste had told her to go slow, that boys grew different from women and her Ailey came from an old-fashioned world where sex was a very serious thing. They would both be seventeen in a month.

She eased one leg over his and snuggled closer. She shivered with the intensity of her feeling, totally aware of her body and of his. She wanted to lie on top of him and press down, feel him, touch him.

She flushed in the darkness and felt heat.

He woke slowly and his arms went around her naturally. "Lucienne," he whispered.

She rolled on top of Ailey and hugged him fiercely. It was a few moments before he realized she wasn't wearing anything under the shift. She kissed his face, his neck, and whispered endearments in French.

Ailey slipped out from under her and sat up. He held her in his arms lightly. Her breath came in little gasps, and she tried to get closer.

"Ailey, please, I want you to. Don't you want me too?"

"Of course I do."

She took his hand and put it on her breast over her heart. Ailey bit his lip in the dark. He wasn't as backward as she thought, but this was not the time. He did not take his hand from where she placed it, but he did not caress her either.

"Lucienne, we can't do this, not here in this house. It isn't right."

She was frustrated and ashamed. "You think I am bad . . ." she started to say, and tried to pull away.

Ailey wouldn't let her go. "No, I don't, I never have and I never will. You are the only girl I care about, will ever care about, so it won't do no good your bein' mad at me.

"C'mon, put your robe on. Let's sneak downstairs, I'll make you a cup of tea."

Lucienne stood up, her head down, unable to look into Ailey's face. She stamped her foot in anger. He put the robe around her, at the same time taking her in his arms.

She could not resist him. "You make me very angry, Ailey Barkwood. You make me feel like a little girl. It's not fair, I am older than you."

She took his hand and followed him out the door. "Ailey . . ." she whispered, "weren't you impressed with my . . . figure?"

"Y'all better quit, I could change my mind."

She giggled mischievously. *"C'est splendide.* You didn't answer my question."

"Yes, dammit, I was impressed."

"Mmmm . . . That's good." She was reminded that Napoleon said a great many things about patience.

Mrs. Berenson was in the kitchen, reading what Rose Everade called one of those trashy novels.

She looked up, raised her eyebrows. "Hello, Lucienne."

Lucienne gave her a hug. "We're going to have some tea."

"What have you two been up to?"

Lucienne blushed and looked away, pretending not to hear.

"You two better not be fooling around. The maestro would send you packing, competition or no competition."

"We haven't been fooling around, Mrs. Berenson," Ailey said.

"Hmmph . . ." She went back to her novel.

"Wait here, Lucienne, I've got something I want to show you."
Ailey dashed out of the kitchen and ran up the three flights of stairs
to his room.

When he came back he put the violin case on the table in front
of Lucienne.

"Ohhh . . . you got a new violin! That's wonderful!" She frowned
when she looked at the case. "Where did you get this case? *C"est
très ancien.* May I look?"

"Sure, that's why I brought it down."

She opened the case and hissed with surprise. She knew how
much money Ailey had, practically to the dollar. "But, Ailey, this
is expensive, this is very old?"

"It's a Stradivarius, Lucienne. My uncle Luther gave it to me."

"*Incroyable!* Tell me, tell me everything."

"Well, you know Uncle Luther was a soldier in the war in
Korea. . . ." Ailey went on to tell her the story.

Even as she listened she felt a hollow sensation in the pit of her
stomach. She heard her father's voice as if he were there next to her. "A
perfect golden orange . . . tuning pegs, a buttery yellow, quite unusual. I
think the Maestro of Cremona was experimenting . . ."

Ailey went on about how Luther had preserved the violin all these
years after rescuing it from the wall of the old farmhouse.

"May I pick it up?"

"Don't be silly, of course you can. I would give it to you if you
didn't already have the Amati."

She looked up at him and saw he meant it. "Oh, Ailey, no. You
don't give something like this away."

She looked at it closely, becoming more certain with each passing moment.

I will always know it . . . someday it will turn up.

"How will you know, Papa?" she always asked.

*You remove the A string tuning peg. The name Ysaÿe is scratched
onto the side near the inner end.*

She loosened the peg slowly. It came out easily, as the string was
loose, without tension. When it was out far enough to see, she
stopped.

What am I to do?

She bent over the violin and looked closely at the peg. Ailey was going on, completely enthralled by the story and his remarkable good fortune.

It was there as clear as the day her great-grandfather made his mark on the violin Hercules. She let out her breath and put it back in the case.

She tried to join Ailey in his excitement. She did not want to spoil his moment with her own indecision.

Lucienne sat on her bed for an hour. It was an impossible situation. She knew without doubt what she'd seen in the kitchen was, had been, a part of her family, a part of her heritage, for nearly a century.

What should she do? What could she do? She loved her father. She didn't like him, she couldn't like him, but she couldn't ignore all the years he searched and dreamed. *He is my family.*

What would her father do? He would want it, of course, but it wouldn't even exist if Ailey's uncle Luther hadn't found it and preserved it.

Of course Ailey will keep it, she thought, *there's nothing Father can do about that.*

At least her father would know it wasn't lost forever. The internal argument went on for a long time before she made up her mind. It was nine A.M. in Paris, her father would just be getting up. She left her room, closed the door silently. Lucienne shook her head in anger. Why was she sneaking, she wasn't doing anything wrong.

She tiptoed down the three flights of stairs, carefully avoiding the squeaky risers out of habit.

The telephone seemed terribly loud in the quiet of the night. She looked around guiltily. Mrs. Berenson came padding out of the darkness, stopped, and gave a small gasp.

Lucienne jumped and turned on the old woman angrily.

"Why don't you say something? Can't I make the telephone call in privacy?"

Mrs. Berenson puffed with annoyance. "Hmmph ... well, I'm sure I don't care who you call, Miss Ysaÿe." She left the front hall muttering.

"Typically French ... rude ..." She continued to mutter as her voice faded out.

Lucienne had to hang up and start over again. This wasn't going the way she wanted at all. She always got along with Mrs. Berenson.

She dialed the number again, biting her upper lip with concentration. It rang for a long time before anyone answered.

"*Ici Ysaÿe.*"

"Papa ... Lucienne."

"What's the matter, *chérie,* are you all right?"

"Yes, Papa, I'm fine."

"But, it must be ... what, three in the morning over there?"

"Yes, Papa. It is important. Something remarkable has happened. The Hercules has been found ..."

"What!"

"The Hercules."

"All right, I must be calm. My God, after all these years. Tell me from the beginning to the end, everything."

"My friend, Ailey Barkwood's uncle Luther found it during the Korean War."

Her father interrupted many times before she was finished.

"What are you going to do, Papa? It would still be in that wall, or destroyed, if he hadn't found it and taken care of it."

"Yes, of course." He sounded distracted. Lucienne knew her father was thinking as fast as he could.

"Well, you better go to bed, Lucienne, you need your sleep. Don't worry, I'll think about what must be done."

"*Oui, Papa.* Bye-bye."

Filled with unease, she hung up the telephone.

"I had to do it," she said softly. "I had to do it. . . ."

Irkutsk, Eastern Russia, 1909

Irkutsk lies near the edge of the great northern permafrost, along-side Lake Baikal, the largest fresh water lake in Russia, and, indeed, the world. It was the only city of any size in hundreds of miles.

Twenty miles north of Irkutsk one disappeared into the taika, the great Russian forest.

The woman cutting firewood stood in front of a tree stump and swung the ax like a man. She was in her twenties and looked ten years older. It was not an easy place to live.

She wore rough hand-made boots, kulacks, and a bearskin jacket, fur side out. Her head was wrapped in a coarse woolen shawl. The original colors of her clothing had faded to a dull brown, almost no color at all.

She stopped for a moment and looked toward the cabin. A ruddy complexion, deep black eyes, and high-shelving cheekbones attested to Yakut Indian blood not far back along the genetic trail.

As she looked toward the cabin, her face became not beautiful, but pretty. Her attention on the cabin was so intense, it could be felt physically. Whatever held her was the focus of her world.

The air in the forest was still, crystalline, and patches of snow lay on the ground.

The cabin had been built in front of a pile of granite boulders, extending out from a natural cave formed by the rock. One room and part of another if you included the cave.

A pretty melody, simple, Russian, replaced the stiffness. It started and stopped as though the maker was uncertain where it wanted to go, couldn't remember what came next.

The woman stopped and listened intently, her face wreathed in a radiant smile. It was obvious she didn't care about the quality. The music itself was enough.

Inside the cabin, Nikolai Golodkin, in threadbare clothing and a six-month growth of beard, sat on a hand-made chair and stared at the violin in his hand. Its perfection was not at odds with the mean surroundings. It would have been just as remarkable in a palace. He wiped it carefully, then put it back in the case.

Golodkin whimpered and descended into apathy.

He had been in Irkutsk for five months. He'd almost been picked up by the local militia, but he was certain they were the secret police disguised as local militia. He'd been playing in a tavern that catered to timber cutters. He noticed a man better dressed than the others watching him curiously.

Seized by paranoia, Golodkin was sure the man's gaze was fixed on the violin. When the tavern closed, he gathered his pathetic collection of belongings and fled out of the city into the forest. He was freezing when the woman found him and half carried, half dragged him to her cabin. It took him a month before he recovered enough to understand where he was. She bathed and fed Golodkin and cared for him like a child. She whispered over him.

"Now you are in Sonia's heart."

He asked for a map and she brought it. It wasn't possible, but he asked anyway. He desperately needed the map. It took two weeks and four perfect sable furs, but she returned with as good a map as existed at the time.

He didn't explain why he wanted the map. It was enough that he wanted it. Before he came she lived in the cabin with her half-wit brother, a trapper, gone three weeks out of four, only he and the animals knew where.

Yet he always returned with a large pack of furs which Sonia sold at the government trading post at the edge of town.

Golodkin tacked the map to the wall of the cabin. He sat in front of it and stared at it for hours. His mad eyes darted back and forth between Irkutsk and Vladivostok, just there, on the coast of the Sea of Japan.

Such a tiny distance, three inches on the map. Yet a terrible wedge of the unknown, Mongolia, intervened. Names and places he'd never heard of, could not pronounce. On the map it looked as if one could just step over Mongolia and finally reach the ocean and freedom. Freedom from Russia, from the secret police who lurked in every corner of his broken mind.

But Golodkin wasn't a giant. He could not take that step. The train, the great Trans-Siberian Railroad went east around the horn of Mongolia, buried like an evil claw in the belly of Russia, and on to Vladivostok.

He could not take the train. They would have been warned. They would be looking for him! Golodkin tried over and over to explain to the woman that he had to get to Vladivostok, his very existence depended on it. She understood, but pretended she didn't.

It wasn't that he was kind to her, or gentle. Most of the time he didn't even know she was there. Though she had moved him into her bed as soon as he was healthy, he seldom gave her what she wanted, what she needed. Love perhaps. Connection to another life surely.

He was there. She could think, wherever she was; I am not alone. He is in Sonia's heart. It was enough.

She knew where he wanted to go. She even knew how he could get across the strange country to the south. The market for furs in China, Korea, even the Japans, was insatiable. And she knew a man who trekked into the interior of those places. He had even crossed to the coast to trade.

It was the fall of 1909 before she decided to tell him. The transformation was miraculous. The light came back to his eyes. He began to eat, fix his clothes, gather things for the journey.

She arranged for him to become a member of the caravan as a baggage handler. Golodkin didn't care if he had to shovel the dung of all the horses in China. He would finally be on his way to that golden promise beyond the ocean.

Kriskin Rossievitch, the leader of the caravan, came to visit Sonia and collect her furs. Part of what he paid for the pelts included his promise to take her man on the journey and care for him.

He was a giant, hard as the trees that surrounded Sonia's cabin. Privately he doubted this man from the city would last. It was a long, dangerous journey. But he had been paid in prime pelts. And if Golodkin didn't last, well, too bad. He would lie a little and tell her, her man had reached Vladivostok. He'd tell her whatever she wanted to hear. She was, after all, a source of prime pelts.

In late September 1909 Golodkin disappeared from Sonia's heart into a life much stranger. He didn't know when they crossed into Mongolia, as that happened at night. It did not matter. Each hour, each day, he was closer to the ocean.

Chapter 34

Ailey woke early. The first thing he did was look toward his small desk. The Stradivarius was there. He had an overwhelming urge to tell all the school of his good fortune. But first he would visit Rabbi Ben Ezra.

He took a quick shower, dressed in a hurry, gathered up music and the violin. Downstairs he stopped in the kitchen for a sweet roll.

"Good morning, Mrs. Berenson."

"Good morning to you, Ailey. It nice to have someone with manners back in the house, unlike some people around here."

Not knowing what to say, he smiled and nodded. "I'm going to town to visit Rabbi Ben Ezra."

"I don't know what you see in the scruffy old man. Besides," she chuckled, "he's about as far from a Baptist as you can get."

"Oh, that don't matter. He's a good old man. He's like my grandfather, he listens to every word you say, and he's smart. May I have a sweet roll?"

"Of course, Ailey. Here"—she put a half dozen in a bag—"take some along to the rabbi. He's a grouch until he eats, and he likes my sweet rolls."

"Thank you, Mrs. Berenson."

"Your entirely welcome, Mr. Barkwood."

Ailey ran most of the way to the temple. He knew the old rabbi's habits and wanted to get there before Ben Ezra began to read. Once immersed in his books, he didn't like to be bothered.

As he walked down the alley he knew he was on time. There were half a dozen cats milling around the porch, mewling and pushing at the screen door.

Ailey waited for the inevitable.

The door swung open and the rabbi stood behind the screen, talking to the cats.

"Get away, bums. Stop scratching my screen. What do you think this is, a circus?" He opened the screen door and scuttled onto the porch. The purrs and cries of the cats became more insistent.

"So wait a moment. Am I a young man? It takes time to pour milk. Hey, get out of the bowl, you gonif."

When he finished putting out the cat food and milk, he stood up slowly and rubbed his back.

"Well . . . aren't you going to say thank you? That wasn't easy. I should be a Catholic priest with lots of young boys in white dresses as servants."

He looked up and saw Ailey standing beside the building.

"So, welcome back, Ailey Barkwood, my favorite cat come for breakfast. What's in the bag?"

"Mrs. Berenson's sweet rolls."

"Ahh, that's good. That woman talks too much, but her cooking is a gift from the gods." His small sly smile made Ailey feel good.

"That wasn't a theological judgment, Mr. Barkwood."

"Well, I'm sure glad of that. I can't be associating with no heathen idolators. Reverend Ben Thurmond don't approve of idol worship."

"Hmmph . . . well, good for him. I don't think much of it myself. Come along, I'll make some breakfast. I've never known you to refuse food."

"You're right, Rabbi, that wouldn't be Christian."

Ailey followed Rabbi Ben Ezra's chuckles inside the manse.

They sat at the small table in the kitchen, drinking tea and talking about God. Ailey liked to talk about religion with the rabbi. Ailey cleaned off the table and washed the dishes.

"What's this." Rabbi Ben Ezra pointed to the old violin case.

"I thought you'd never ask."

"Oh, I saw it when you came in. I knew you were dying to tell me about it. I wanted to see if you could last till after we ate. The disciplined mind has patience. You can tell me now."

Ailey went on as though he hadn't heard. "You know I've been writing music. I've finished two sonatas."

"All right, all right, I didn't say I had patience."

Ailey laughed.

"Shameful to make fun of a poor, helpless old rabbi."

"You're old, Rabbi Ben Ezra, that's a fact. But you ain't helpless. Go ahead, open up the case."

The rabbi opened the case, sat back, and looked at the violin for a long time.

"So, Ailey, this is marvelous. This beautiful thing has come a long distance to find its way to my table." He touched the case reverently. "I think many great artists have held this."

"It's a Stradivarius, Rabbi, a real one. The maestro and I are taking it to the luthier, Jacques Fraṇais, down in Manhattan, to restore it. I'll be able to play it in the competition in Brussels in September."

"That's wonderful. I would like very much to hear you play this wonderful thing."

Ailey reached over and touched the old rabbi's hand shyly. "I've written a violin sonata and I've dedicated it to you. I hope y'all don't mind. I call it 'Sonata Sholem Ben Ezra.' "

The rabbi looked up at Ailey, Baptist and violinist from West Virginia. "You shouldn't have done that. You should dedicate such music to your teacher or your girlfriend."

Ailey took a dozen sheets of music held together with a paper clip from his case and put it in front of the old man. At the top it said *Sonata Sholem Ben Ezra.* Beneath that it said *For Rabbi Ben Ezra, my friend, with love. Ailey Parkman Barkwood, 1989.*

The rabbi rubbed the sheets of paper with his wrinkled fingers. He got up and wandered to the sink.

"I'll make a fresh pot of tea."

Ailey smiled to himself. "He likes it."

Mrs. Berenson heard the doorbell from the kitchen. She looked at the clock over the sink; 9:30. She frowned, got up, walked toward the front of the house. She met Mrs. Everade in the hall.

"I'll get it, Louise."

She walked to the front hall and opened the door. Two men in three piece suits with briefcases stood side by side on the steps.

"Gentlemen, how can I help you?"

They brought out cards. The taller of the two, a thin man with a premature bald spot, introduced himself. "I'm Mr. Caswell, this is my associate, Mr. Haverford. We're with the firm of Caswell, Caswell, and Ostermeyer. We'd like to see Mr. Ailey Barkwood, please."

Rose Everade looked at the cards, then at the two men.

What in the world do lawyers, high-priced ones at that, want with Ailey? she wondered.

"Come in, gentlemen." She stepped aside until they were in the front hall. "Wait here, please, I'll get my husband."

"Oh, that won't be necessary, Mrs. Everade. We just need to see Mr. Barkwood for a few moments."

She gave them "the look." "You'll see the maestro, then perhaps Mr. Barkwood."

She left, headed for the rear of the house. The two men looked at each knowingly.

Ailey took the steps to the front of the house two at a time. He fumbled with the door for a moment, then entered the front hall.

Caswell, on a hunch, asked, "Are you Ailey Barkwood?"

"I sure am," he said, smiling cheerfully.

Haverford opened his briefcase and removed some papers. Caswell looked at Ailey coolly. He stepped closer.

"Is that the Stradivarius?"

Ailey stopped smiling, but he was still polite.

"Yes, it is."

"Would you mind very much if I looked at it for a moment?"

Still unsuspecting, Ailey put down his music case. Caswell put out his hand to take it. Ailey just looked at his hand until he withdrew it. Ailey didn't intend to let go of his violin for strangers.

Still caught in the euphoria of the moment, he didn't think of asking how the man knew he had a Stradivarius. Ailey opened the case and held it out for them to look at. The two men stepped closer and examined it.

"Are you from the insurance company," Ailey asked.

"Ummm . . ." Mr. Caswell made a noncommittal sound. "Would you mind observing the A string tuning peg closely, Mr. Barkwood? It won't take a moment."

Ailey hesitated.

"If you just wind it out a bit, you'll see a name scratched into the side of the peg."

Ailey was curious about anything having to do with his violin. He sat down on the floor, put the case down next to him, and removed the peg carefully. He looked at it for a moment, then he looked at it more closely.

"I'll be darned . . ." he said. "It says E. Ysaÿe."

He looked up at Mr. Caswell suspiciously, put the violin back in the case, closed it, and stood up. He didn't know what to think, but the situation had become threatening.

"What did it say, Mr. Barkwood?"

"E. Ysaÿe."

"That's correct, Mr. Barkwood. I'm going to have to ask you to give that instrument to me. It is the rightful property of Mr. Eugene Ysaÿe of Paris, France."

He took the papers from his partner. "I have here an injunction that authorizes me to take legal possession of the Stradivarius violin known as Hercules until proper ownership can be established."

He tried to present the papers to Ailey, who looked at him as if he were a madman.

"You're plumb crazy, mister, this violin is mine. It was given to me by my uncle Luther."

Caswell stepped forward and took hold of the case.

"Come, come, Mr. Barkwood, we represent the law. This can all be settled without trouble. These papers give me the legal right to take possession of the violin."

Ailey tried to pull the violin away from Caswell. "Hey, let go, you don't have no right to do anything. You're crazy!" Ailey shouted.

Caswell twisted the violin case from Ailey's hand and stepped back. Ailey was stunned. Fear and disbelief overwhelmed him. In that instant, rage replaced a lifetime of good manners. He ran at Caswell and hit him in the face as hard as he could, then grabbed for the case.

Caswell, a graduate of Yale Law School, and who made two hundred thousand dollars a year, reverted to the playground. He did the unthinkable and reacted. Still trying to fend Ailey off, he shouted at

Ailey to knock it off, and when he wouldn't punched Ailey viciously below the heart, knocking him to the floor.

In the midst of these incredible events the maestro and Mrs. Everade rushed into the front hall, followed by Lucienne and several other students.

The maestro charged across the hall between Caswell and Ailey.

"What in God's name do you think you're doing!" he shouted in Caswell's face.

Lucienne rushed over to Ailey and stopped dead when she saw the expression on his face. He wept with frustration, pain, and rage. The look was bitterness and betrayal.

"No, no, Ailee, I did not want this, I swear to you, I did not know, I swear it."

Ailey turned his back on her, still holding his stomach, trying to get his breath.

She turned and ran from the hall, sobbing.

"Joachim, call the police right now. I intend to see this ... this brute imprisoned for assaulting a child."

Haverford held up his hand and spoke in a loud voice. "Please, let's just calm down, everyone. This is all an unfortunate accident."

"Accident!" she screamed. "Accident, you Nazi bastard. I'll see you and this other thug in jail. When grown men beat up children, it is no accident!"

It was another ten minutes before the noise level dropped to a point where anyone could hear.

Mrs. Everade wanted blood and the maestro was trying to find out what was going on.

"All right, all of you out of here. Remember exactly what you saw, your testimony will be needed when these criminals go to trial. You, Timmy, take Ailey with you."

Ailey struggled to his feet and headed for Caswell again. He was still holding his stomach. "I ain't going anywhere. That man stole my violin. I ain't leaving until I get it back."

Caswell handed the papers to the maestro. "I'm really sorry this happened. The boy struck me and I lost my temper. I am sorry for that, but the papers speak for themselves."

Everade got between Ailey and the lawyer. "Hold it, Ailey. There isn't going to be any more violence in this house.'' He turned back to the lawyer.

"And you, Mr. Sleazy Lawyer, your apology is not accepted. Rose, now, dammit, Rose, don't argue, call Stan Raman and tell him I need him right now.''

"Joachim . . .''

"Now, Rose. Call him and tell him what I told you.''

Everade read the lawyers' papers. "Ailey, I'm sorry, there's nothing I can do right now. We have to let them take the violin, but they won't keep it, I promise you that. When the judge hears about this, these two will be in jail.''

Caswell started to speak. "You shut up,'' the maestro roared, "and get out of my house! The next time I see you will be in court, and it won't be about this violin.''

The two lawyers left quickly, Caswell still holding the violin in his arms.

"Maestro, please,'' Ailey pleaded, "you can't let him have it, you can't!''

"Ailey, I can't stop them now, but I will, I promise you.'' He saw Ailey holding his hand. "What is it, what happened to your hand.''

Ailey looked down at his hand for the first time. "It don't matter now.'' He turned and ran from the hall.

The maestro looked around wildly. "Dear God, how could this happen?''

Ailey ran through the house, out the back door, and down through the pines. He ran fast, as though speed alone might wash away the horror of the moment from his mind.

He was halfway through town before he realized where he was. He stopped again, trying to catch his breath. He saw the train station nearby and ran into the waiting room.

On the far side of the room were three pay telephones. He ran to the nearest one, got out change, and dialed the operator. It was the first thing Miss Iris had taught him when she knew he was going to New York City.

"Operator, how may I help you.''

"Operator, I want to place a person-to-person call to West Virginia.''

Ailey waited for a long time. Finally Miss Iris answered the phone.

"This is Iris Bentley speaking."

"Miss Iris, this is Ailey"—his voice shook with grief—"they stole my violin. They come to the school and stole it."

"Ailey, please slow down and tell me exactly what happened."

"You got to tell Uncle Luther, he'll know what to do. Promise me you'll tell Luther."

"I will, Ailey. I promise. Now, you must promise me to be calm, let us do what we can. I'm sure Mr. Everade is going to do everything he can, and so will we. Do you have someplace you can go where . . . where it's quiet?"

Ailey was silent. "I can't go back there. I can't never see her again."

"I know how you feel right now."

"I'll go see the rabbi. He knows about everything, like Uncle Luther."

"All right. Ailey, try to be patient. I'm going up the mountain right now."

Rose Everade came back into the front hall, where the maestro pondered what to do, what they could do.

"God, Rose, what a mess. When is Raman going to be here?"

"He said he'd be here in a half hour. We handled this very badly." She shook her head sadly. "You tell Raman everything, and get the students who saw that man strike Ailey to tell him what they saw. No matter what happens, I will see that man punished. I'm going to talk to that girl. She's at the heart of this."

"Rose, gently, I'm sure she didn't want any of this to happen. I've got to find Ailey, we have to get his hand looked at."

Ailey trudged the last few yards to the temple slowly. He was in doubt about everything. All the things that mattered were upside down, all the things he depended on had turned out to be false. What if the rabbi didn't want to be bothered?

He knocked on the door timidly. No one answered. He knocked again; still there was no answer. He started to turn away in despair, and heard the door open behind him.

It was Rabbi Ben Ezra.

"Here, Ailey, what's the matter? Come here."

Ailey walked toward the old man, practically stumbling with weariness and relief that the rabbi was there.

"They stole it, Rabbi Ben Ezra . . ."

"Come along inside, come along." He led Ailey to the couch. "Sit, boy, sit. No, don't tell me anything yet. We'll have some tea, settle down a little, then we'll talk."

In a few moments he came out with a pot of tea. "What's this?" He picked up Ailey's hand. "You've been in a fight. Such foolishness."

Ailey started to get up. "No, just sit, drink your tea. I've dealt with this sort of thing many times." He talked from the kitchen. "I'll heat some water, I've got some salts around here somewhere . . ."

Ailey heard the clatter of a pan, cupboards being opened and closed. "Ahh, I knew it, here we are. We'll give your hand a good soak."

He brought a tin basin. The water was steaming. He poured crystals in the water and stirred them around with his finger. "Come on, give me your hand, we're going to put it in the water. It will hurt a bit at first, then it'll feel much better."

Ailey put his hand in the water and hissed. He grunted and kept his hand in the water. The pain was distracting; it kept him from thinking about things that were worse than what might be wrong with his hand.

He leaned forward and held his head with his good hand. "Rabbi, I must have done something awful bad for this to have happened, but I can't think what it is."

"Well, we'll get around to that. First we'll deal with your body, then we'll see to the soul. You keep rubbing your ribs, what's the matter?"

"That man punched me right here. Darn, I wish I'da known how to fight better. He knocked me right off my feet. It hurt fierce, I could barely breathe."

"Open your shirt, let's take a look."

Ailey unbuttoned his shirt with his good hand and lifted up his T-shirt. There was a big dark-colored bruise right over his ribs.

"Well, you've been hit hard. I'm going to feel around a bit, see if anything's broke. It'll probably hurt. Are you up to it?"

"Sure, go ahead."

Rabbi Ben Ezra probed Ailey's ribs gently. "Well, it doesn't feel like anything's broken. If it still hurts in the morning, we'll go to Dr. Goodman, he can give you an X ray."

He pulled Ailey's hand out of the water. "Well, my boy, you must have hit that fellow pretty hard."

"I did, as hard as I could. It didn't do any good, he took my Stradivarius anyway."

"Here, you put your hand back in the water, just hold it there. I'm going to get a cold cloth for your ribs."

"I'm real sorry to be bothering you this way."

"What? Don't be silly, who else should you come to? I'm your minister." He chuckled. "I suspect your Reverend Ben Thurmond would approve."

Ailey didn't look up.

"So, Ailey, tell me what happened, slowly, calmly, from the beginning. Please, leave nothing out. I want to know what everyone did, what they said. Be precise."

"I came back to the school from visiting you. The maestro . . ."

Rabbi Ben Ezra, grunted an acknowledgment and asked questions every so often. Sometimes he had Ailey go back over a particular point.

"She betrayed me, Rabbi. How could she do that? She must have called her father last night."

"All right, I understand how you feel. We'll talk about that part of it later. Now go on with the story."

". . . and the two lawyers left with the Stradivarius. The maestro said he would do everything he could. I left and came here."

"Well, that's quite a story, quite a tangled web we weave when first we practice to deceive . . . That's Shakespeare."

"What can I do?" Ailey asked desperately.

"For now we do nothing. In a while I will go see the Everades. I will also talk to the girl, Lucienne, and everyone else. You must do what is going to be most difficult for now, be patient. Do not give up, my boy, it isn't like you. You have a lot of people who want to help. What we must do is be sure this doesn't get into the courts. That is the place of greatest danger, the place of least justice."

"I will try, Rabbi."

"You stretch out on the couch. It's comfortable. I've slept on it many times. I'm going to call the school, let them know where you are." He left the room and came back in a moment with blankets and a pillow.

"Here, stretch out now, that's it. You like that pillow? I like it, it's very comfortable." He tucked the blankets around Ailey. "There, rest, my boy, rest. Things will look different soon enough."

Ailey held out his good hand to Rabbi Ben Ezra. The rabbi took his hand.

"You will help, won't you?"

"Yes, bubby, I will help. Rest now."

Chapter 35

Luthersville, West Virginia, August 1989

Miss Iris didn't go to the mountain immediately. She sat quietly at a table in the kitchen that looked out at the garden in the rear of the house. Then she called the Everade household and asked for Mrs. Everade.

The two women talked for some time, then Miss Iris went to her car and drove to Cole's Mountain. Outwardly calm, Miss Iris was furious. When she asked if she could speak to Ailey, Rose Everade said she didn't know where he was, that she thought he went to see Rabbi Ben Ezra at the temple.

What Miss Iris did know was that Ailey had been physically hurt and no one at the school had looked after him.

She rushed up the trail to Luther's cabin too fast and arrived at the edge of the clearing with a sharp pain in her chest that frightened her.

Luther, who had somehow known she was coming up the trail, strode across the clearing to her side. He eased her to the ground and went back to the cabin for a jug of water. She tried to speak, and Luther shook his head no.

"Just rest a moment, Iris. What're you a-doin' runnin' up the mountain? You ain't twenty years old."

Miss Iris gave him an angry look.

"Don't give me that look, Iris. I ain't had but two lady friends in my whole life, you bein' the second. I'd like to keep you around."

"Well, that surprises me, Luther, you only having had two lady friends, as much as you get around me with sweet talk."

"Do you want to get up now?"

"Yes." She put out her hand and Luther lifted her to her feet.

He put his arms around her and held her. She hung on tight, thinking how desperate life would be if she didn't have his strong arms to hold her.

"Mmm, Miss Iris, this is much better. I'm prepared to do more than sweet-talk you if you're in the mood."

She blushed and hugged him closer. "Oh, Luther, almost any other time I'd keep you awake till the sun came up, but we've got trouble."

"All right, let's go to the cabin. I'll make you a cup of tea and we'll see what's to be done."

"They hit him?"

"Yes, Luther, they did."

"These were growed men?"

"Yes, I imagine they were, a man doesn't usually get out of law school until his mid-twenties. Then the lawyers left the house with his violin. Luther, he sounded so beaten. Those people have broken his heart."

She couldn't hold it in any longer, and wept. Miss Iris's tears disturbed Luther more than he let on. She was the most self-contained woman he knew. Luther was grim. He held her hands and tried to comfort her.

"Now, Iris, don't cry. My fault for lettin' him go up there among those people. They are strangers and they have took what weren't theirs to take."

He patted her hands and looked away. "I promise you he will have it back, and those that have hurt him will know the pain of retribution."

"Luther, it isn't the violin, it's what they've done to his spirit. I don't care about that old violin."

"I do, Iris, and so does he."

"All right, Luther. I don't want those people getting away with manhandling my boy."

"They won't, Iris, believe me, they won't."

Miss Iris, as decent and cultured a woman as any raised in the South, knew the source of her anger. Her instinct was to protect her boy, and it overpowered everything else.

"You stay here tonight, Iris. We'll go down in the morning and catch the afternoon train. I didn't ever want to go to that place, but the time has come. You call them folks tomorrow and tell them we're on our way, and they better have both the violin and Ailey to hand, or I will read to them from the book. You tell them that way, Iris. I want to be sure they understand."

"I will, Luther. Luther, I want to sleep in with you tonight if you don't mind."

"I don't mind, Iris."

The maestro sat in a wing chair, his feet up on a leather-covered ottoman, looking out the window. He couldn't see much except shadows from the streetlights around in front of the house.

Rose Everade sat up in their bed, pretending to read a magazine. They hadn't said much for an hour, yet neither was ready for sleep.

"What will he do, Joachim?" she asked.

"Who ... oh, Luther." The maestro shook his head more from worry than doubt. "Just what he said, I imagine. What I'd do if Ailey were my boy. I'll tell you one thing, Rose, if I were that lawyer, I'd leave town and I wouldn't leave a forwarding address."

"I have no pity for him," Rose said. "I hope Luther catches up with him. He'll think twice before he ever does something like that again."

Joachim pulled at his beard nervously. "I'm worried about Rabbi Ben Ezra, that is a very hard old man, and he's very fond of Ailey. You see him as your rabbi, I see him as a survivor of the camps. I think you better have some answers for him, because he will certainly ask a lot of questions."

"I think you're wrong about Rabbi Ben Ezra," she said. "If we had saints, he'd be one. He will be our greatest ally in this mess."

Rose Everade riffled the pages of her magazine while she thought about what she wanted to say. "You haven't called Ysaÿe?"

"I know, Rose. All I have to do is think about that man and I feel my blood pressure rise. Mrs. Berenson overheard Lucienne calling Paris. She said Lucienne screamed at him, said she would never,

never speak to him again, would never look on his face again if he did not have the Stradivarius returned immediately. Mrs. Berenson said it was much more effective in French.''

''Her . . . stupid child, if she loved the boy, how could she do that? She must have known how her father would react.''

''Rose, that is a mother's reaction. Ailey is not your son. You do not decide what girl is good for him or isn't. She is in her room now, miserable, desolate. She has committed a crime against her love. Even you must know that she loves Ailey. She made a bad decision, probably out of duty. That she regrets her decision cannot be in doubt.''

''Hmmph, wailing and moaning, she did not get punched by that horrid man, nothing was stolen from her.''

The maestro knew a dead end when he saw one. Getting his wife to change her mind about Lucienne was about as likely as him becoming a jazz musician.

''Well, you're going to have to call Ysaÿe. I think Lucienne should go back to Paris until this is all sorted out.''

''No, Rose, I won't do that. I'll call him, that is something I have to do, but I won't send Lucienne back. What we must do is get Ysaÿe to come here. As long as he sits over there in Paris, arrogant, self-righteous, untouched by any of this, there can be no resolution.''

The maestro rubbed his face and eyes, then yawned hugely. ''God, I'm tired. You know, Rose, Ysaÿe is like the president of a corporation, an accountant, one of those fellows who's never seen a worker and decides it would be better business to let a few thousand employees go. The assassin mentality. They stand off at long distance and blow people up. It's . . . it's target practice.

''They never see a ruined life, for them there is no blood and gore. Ysaÿe must be made to feel what he's done. He's got to see the bodies before he'll stop.''

''Hmmm . . . yes, you're right about him. I remember him when we were in Germany, Munich. Such a cold fish, arrogant. Well, dear, it'll take an act of God to get him over here.''

Everade nodded to himself. ''Yes, that's exactly what it will take.''

''Come along, Ailey. It's like the dentist, the sooner you get started, the sooner it'll be done. How are your ribs, do you still have pain?''

"It's not bad. They're sore, but I don't think anything's broken"—he flexed the fingers in his right hand—"but my hand is stiff."

"Well, we'll soak it again a little later. Meanwhile keep exercising it even if it hurts."

"Why don't I just wait for you here?"

"Don't be silly, bubby."

He held the door open until Ailey went outside. It was a gray day with rain threatening. Rabbi Ben Ezra took small steps, and Ailey had to adjust his pace.

"Look around, Ailey. Every day in God's world is a good day. Everywhere there is something good to see. A tree, still making shade. See, over there, the ice cream shop is still open. You are alive, boy. Many people on this planet would consider that enough."

"I'll try. You sound like my uncle Luther."

They walked for a while quietly. "He'll come, you know," Ailey said.

"Who?"

"My uncle Luther. I called him. He has an old-fashioned view of justice. He really is a mountain man. He would never get a lawyer to settle something he could settle his own way."

"What are you saying, he will make trouble, physical?"

"I don't know for sure. He might. He'll certainly want to deal with the man that beat me. If it'd been a boy my own age he wouldn't have said nothing, he'd expect me to take care of that on my own. But for a grown man to do that and walk away? He won't like that at all. My uncle Luther is very fair."

"Well, I'll talk with him when he gets here. I'm sure we can reason together."

When they arrived at the front of the school, Ailey disappeared around the side of the old three-story stone house with a wave of his hand.

The maestro came to the door.

"Rabbi, I'm glad you're here. We need your help."

"Blessings on this house. So, good, I'll give it a try. Let's go to the library. You can tell me what happened."

They met Mrs. Berenson in the hall. "Ahhh . . ." Rabbi Ben Ezra said, "the greatest cook in the western hemisphere."

She raised her eyebrows skeptically. "Rabbi Ben Ezra, you're too old for that kind of talk."

"A man is never too old to say pretty things to a beautiful woman."

"I better bring you something to eat, a glass of tea, maybe that will put a stop to your foolishness."

"That I would like very much, Mrs. Berenson."

The rabbi eased into a comfortable position in one of the large chairs. "Now, young man, bring your chair over here, close to mine."

Everade did as he was asked.

"I want you to tell me everything that happened. Start before the unfortunate day you let lawyers in your house. You realize you should never have let them take it?"

"Forgive me, Rabbi. Of course, I am an idiot for letting them get away with Ailey's violin. After it happened she burned my ears for two hours. I won't even tell you some of the things she said. I haven't heard that kind of language since the time she caught me with that soprano from the Met." He held his head, trying to shut out the memory.

"All right, Joachim, we leave punishment to God. He will know what to do. It is enough that you know. So begin where I told you. I want to hear everything, every detail, what everyone said. Don't leave anything out."

"Well, well, well . . . so, it will be interesting to meet this Martin Luther from the hills, he sounds like a real mensch. Right now I must go to the men's, my kidneys are twice as old as I am. Then I will call this great one in Paris. He's a Jew, isn't he, Joachim?"

"Yes, he is of the faith."

"Good. Him I know how to handle. When I'm done with him I'll talk to the girl, Lucienne. Stay close by, Joachim, I will need your help with this. Make sure your lawyer stops those men from shipping the Stradivarius to France."

"I have already done that, Rabbi."

Rabbi Ben Ezra got up and left the room.

Chapter 36

Bronxville, New York, August 1989

Ben Ezra sat in the library. The phone looked too large in his frail hands.

"Who am I speaking to please? Mrs. Ysayë . . . ahhh, this is good. I am Rabbi Sholem Ben Ezra."

The rabbi listened for a moment.

"Yes, yes, I know. Yes, it's true one of the lawyers beat the boy and took the violin. Of course she's upset. She's caught between the two most important men in her life, her father and her first love, and in their lives, probably their only love."

The rabbi listened patiently.

"What do you mean, how do I know! I've seen every kind of love in more than ninety years, the sacred and the profane. I have seen the two of them together. They are the twins of each other's souls. She will choose Ailey Barkwood, believe me, Mrs. Ysayë. Yes, of course I'll do everything I can, but he must come here to New York, and he must come now."

The rabbi nodded, made noises of agreement.

"It will do no good to cry, madame. Please, now bring him to the phone." The rabbi sat back in the chair and muttered. "Hurry up, will you, this phone is heavy and my kidneys are a thousand years old.

"Yes, hello, Mr. Ysayë? Good. I am Rabbi Sholem Ben Ezra."

Ysayë talked so loud, the rabbi held the phone away from his ear and winced.

"You don't have to shout, the phone works quite well, and speak English or Yiddish, if you know how."

The maestro, who stood in the doorway to the hall, could hear Ysayë quite clearly.

"I don't know Yiddish, why should I know Yiddish?" Ysayë shouted.

"Yes, of course, why should you? You will listen to me now, Ysayë," he said in a commanding voice.

"You will for the good of your soul and the happiness of your daughter come to New York on the next flight. No more thugs beating children, no more destroying dreams. Your daughter loves this boy, remember that!"

The rabbi hung up the phone with a bang.

"Well, Ben Ezra, you old fraud, you handled that wonderfully. So, God will surely forgive a little exaggeration in a good cause. He will come, he is not a criminal, he is just a fool and a Frenchman."

The rabbi rubbed his legs, then stood up. "You can come out now, Joachim."

Joachim had been hanging around the door to the library. The maestro came into the library sheepishly.

"I told you to stay close, not in my back pocket," Ben Ezra said.

"I'm sorry, Rabbi."

"Don't be. You go get the girl and bring her here. What time does the man from the hills arrive?"

"Miss Iris, I mean Miss Bentley, she was the boy's teacher, told me they would arrive at four this afternoon."

"Good . . . good. I will talk to the girl and the other students who witnessed what happened with the lawyers. Also have Rose call Mrs. Ysayë. She is to tell Mr. Ysayë she does not want to talk to him if he answers. Tell her to work on the wife. He will not have peace until he comes here and sees the mess he has created."

Everade looked at the rabbi and shook his head.

"Are you of the Italian Jewish tribe, the Macchiavelli branch, by any chance? I would not want to be on your bad side, Rabbi."

"Shoosh . . . I don't have a bad side. However, sometimes one must do things a certain way to ensure the proper outcome. Now, go, do what I say."

*   *   *

Lucienne sat in the same chair where the maestro sat an hour before. Her head hung in shame.

Rabbi Ben Ezra drank tea and munched on a sweet roll. Mrs. Berenson, who growled and scolded him, had been careful to see that he got the best rolls and anything else he wanted to eat.

"You are a foolish girl, Miss Lucienne Rosamond Ysaÿe." She wept inconsolably.

He reached out, took her chin, and lifted her head. "Now, don't blubber, it isn't pretty. You should have told Ailey the moment you knew. When you love someone, you don't hold back."

She looked miserable and lost. Her eyes were swollen with tears. She clutched his hand desperately. "I would do anything to get the Stradivarius back to Ailey. I never should have told my father, never!"

"All right, I know. You were caught in the oldest trap there is. Not to worry. Go to your room and get cleaned up. Your sweetheart, my Gentile friend from West Virginia, will never forgive you if you look like a witch."

Lucienne tried to smile. She kissed his hand. "I know you can fix it. Ailey says you know everything. He says next to his uncle Luther, you're the smartest man in the world."

"Mmm . . . well, he's inclined to exaggerate a little."

When Lucienne left, Mrs. Everade entered the library with a tray. She put a fresh pot of tea on the side table and several sandwiches.

"So, Rose . . . I thought you had better sense. You let those men into your house even when you knew they wanted to see Ailey, and now you're blaming your husband and Miss Ysaÿe.

"That is unfair. This is a Jewish household. Do I need to tell you who's really in charge here? The people who live in this house aren't shopkeepers."

He poured tea and picked up one of the sandwiches. "Ahh, tongue and fresh onions, very good. Mmmm. These are musicians, Rose. Not ordinary musicians, but special, arrogant, not of the world. Yes, they are all these things. It is no small thing that you make it possible for them to create."

When he started she looked cross, ready to protest. By the time he finished, she was near tears.

"I'm sorry, I'm sorry, Rabbi."

"Yes, that is good, but you should tell that to Miss Ysaÿe, and Joachim. He will worry himself into the grave with this thing if you let him. Now you must help me straighten this mess out. I have an angry man from the hills of West Virginia coming here this afternoon. I don't want him talking to anybody until I've put him in the proper frame of mind."

"Yes, Rabbi Ben Ezra, I will do whatever you ask."

At four in the afternoon Ailey and Mr. Everade were standing on the platform of the train station. Both were tired and careworn.

It was another hour before the train arrived. Luther got off the train followed by Miss Iris Bentley. He wore dungarees, a white shirt, and a brown sport coat she'd helped him pick out a few years earlier. He stood very straight. Luther's hair was long and very gray beneath a worn fedora.

Ailey ran to meet him. Luther put his arms around the skinny boy, now almost as tall as his uncle.

"Y'all take it easy, boy, everything will be okay. I will see to it."

They walked over to Mr. Everade. He was hard-eyed and taciturn. Miss Iris greeted him. "Hello, Mr. Everade."

"Miss Iris." He bent over her hand gallantly. "I am truly sorry for all the trouble."

"I know."

The ride back to the school was silent and tense. The only new piece of information was that Eugene Ysaÿe had decided to come to New York.

Ailey walked up to the house behind the maestro and Miss Iris. "Uncle Luther, my friend, Rabbi Sholem Ben Ezra, came here to help. He's going to try to fix things, will you talk to him?"

"I don't need help, boy, I know what to do."

"It's all right, he's a wonderful man, and he's been very good to me." Ailey paused. "And he doesn't lie, Uncle Luther." Ailey's voice was filled with bitterness.

"All right, boy, if you think I should talk to this man, I will."

Ailey led him into the library. Rabbi Ben Ezra, looking very small in a large wing chair, was dozing, his head buried in his beard on his chest.

Ailey cleared his throat. "Harrumph . . . Rabbi Ben Ezra?"

The rabbi woke and looked at Ailey and Luther for a moment, then he smiled, clear, guileless.

"Ahhh ... Mr. Cole, good. Ailey, you run along, I'll find you later."

Ailey smiled with satisfaction and left.

The two men looked at each other curiously. "Sit here, please, Mr. Cole." The rabbi pointed to a chair directly in front of his.

Luther did not move toward the chair.

"Not to worry, Mr. Cole. It is true, I am a Hebrew priest, but I haven't bitten a Gentile in forty years, and he was a Nazi, so it doesn't count."

Luther sat, doubtful, wary. Rabbi Ben Ezra sat directly in front of Luther and pulled his chair close, which made Luther uncomfortable.

"So, Mr. Martin Luther Cole, what should have been a wonderful time for Ailey, for everyone, has become an unhappy mess. I have spoken to everyone except yourself and Mr. Ysaÿe. He will arrive late this evening. I will speak to him also."

Rabbi Ben Ezra looked directly at Luther, his heart open to the man from the hills of West Virginia.

"He will speak to me the truth, all of it, and so will you, Mr. Cole, for it is in your nature to do so, and I think you have the need. Now, tell me about the war, both wars. Tell me about the violin, how you found it, what it meant to you, everything."

Luther looked at the tiny rabbi and sensed that in all his strangeness there was also simplicity and integrity.

This man likes Ailey. He cares what happens. Luther sighed deeply. *Lord, I will tell him all that I know and believe,* and receiving no instructions to the contrary, he began to tell Rabbi Ben Ezra about the terrible years of the war.

"I were too young, and the war took my youth, pretty near all of it. But my family has always gone when we was called, sometimes before we was called."

The telling went on for a long time as he related everything, the horror of his two wars, the terrible days leading up to the moment when he found the violin.

He could not help but relive those fearful moments; loss piled on loss, his own perceived failures, and the long years of healing that followed, the hope for a final absolution that never came.

He told Rabbi Ben Ezra what the violin meant to him, of his stewardship, his need to preserve something beautiful out of the ugliness.

He told of his long communion with God as he tried to decide what to do. In the telling of these terrible and wonderful things, the tears came to his eyes freely, for in the end he had never been able to forgive himself for the death of his men, and worse, that he, less deserving, had lived.

When he had finished, Rabbi Ben Ezra put his hands on Luther's knees and leaned forward.

"Yes, yes, I know of that thing. It was that way in the camps. When God takes those you love, men, women, children . . . far more deserving of life than you . . . why should you live?

"It seems a monstrous joke. One's faith in his God is put to a terrible test. We are alike unto Job, bewildered . . ."

He took a breath and sat back.

"God may forgive you, you think, but how do you forgive yourself? So we atone, we choose different ways, but we try to atone." He leaned forward again. "Come, give me your hands."

Luther did.

"You are a good man, and I thank you for giving me a full and honest account. If it means anything at all, I forgive you, Martin Luther Cole."

Luther smiled shyly at the old rabbi. "It does, and I thank you."

"Good, let's sit for a while, catch our breath. It has been a long journey, very long."

They sat together in silence for a half hour.

"Now I must go back to the temple. I will return in the morning and talk with Ysayë. One thing, if you talk to Ailey, tell him not to be so hard on Miss Ysayë. She is heartbroken. She did only what she thought was her duty to her family. You more than most understand duty. For some strange reason she loves that stiff-necked boy."

Luther nodded. "I will do that."

The maestro was in the front hall, waiting for Rabbi Ben Ezra.

"Rabbi. What are we going to do?"

"You? Have supper. Teach your students to make great music. Spread some cheer. I will talk to Lucienne's father at eight in the morning. Stop worrying, there's a way out of his mess. You have everybody here at one o'clock tomorrow afternoon.''

Ailey sat on his bed and Luther sat in the only chair in the room. Music could still be heard around the house, though it seemed more subdued.

"You were right, boy, he's quite a man. You know, he read to me from the Book.'' Luther smiled wearily. "We talked about things I didn't even think would get said.''

"He's smart and he knows how things should be done. He's old and kinda small, but he's tough.''

"I know. Now you tell me something. You care for that pretty red-haired girl whose been in her room cryin' her eyes out since this mess started?''

Ailey stood up abruptly, all the bitterness and hurt back.

"She should of told me, Uncle Luther. She should have! I would have tried to do what's right.''

"You didn't answer my question, Ailey. Ain't like you to squirm around when I ask you a question.''

"Yes, I care. She's the nicest girl I ever met. Least she was. Heck, I didn't ever figure to want another.''

"Well, it's a fact she made a mistake. Good thing she has a beau that never made one himself.'' Luther got up. "I'm goin' along to the hotel now, Miss Iris will be wondering where I am. Think I might just get a good night's sleep for a change.'' He hesitated. "You think on it, boy. Faithfulness in hard times is right up there with duty and honor, even forgiveness. Might be you could use a little yourself. She's not perfect, Ailey. Be careful about punishment, boy. It's a drink that only gets more bitter with time.''

Luther left the room. Ailey looked after him. Then he sat on the bed and stared at his swollen knuckles.

Chapter 37

They were all there in the library except Rabbi Ben Ezra, who had been there in the morning, waiting for Ysaÿe. He never showed up for his meeting with the Rabbi, and after waiting an hour Everade drove the rabbi back to the temple. Ysaÿe didn't arrive until noon. What was surprising was that Ysaÿe had sent the Stradivarius, Hercules, ahead to Everade.

The open case lay on a small table in the middle of the room. In it Hercules lay in Renaissance splendor.

It was a tense, emotional group. Lucienne sat in one corner, her head bowed. Every few moments she glanced at Ailey longingly.

Ailey was a closed fist of anxiety.

Luther, in a twenty-year-old blue serge suit and dark tie, looked at Ysaÿe coldly. It was a measuring look, part curious, part hostile.

It obviously unsettled Ysaÿe. He was not not used to having anyone look at him as if he were wrong. He was a dignified man in the grand manner, with a full head of dark, wavy hair. He held himself proud as a Roman senator.

But there were cracks in the veneer. Maestro Everade had snarled at him. His wife had told him to get out of their bedroom and would not speak to him, and his daughter hated him. Add to that the rabbi . . . he'd never faced such unanimous censure in his entire life.

He had to admit there was some justification. There was the boy

273

with his swollen hand, a nice-looking young man whom those cretins struck!

He met with a representative of the law firm at the airport when he arrived, and lectured the man for a half hour, in the end threatening to sue the firm himself. He hadn't been able to take responsibility himself for his instructions to the lawyers

The maestro paced back and forth in front of the fireplace. Every so often he would go to Ailey and ask him how his hand was, after which he would turn toward the Frenchman and snarl.

Mrs. Everade and Miss Iris sat close on one side of the room, drawn together for strength.

At one-thirty, purposely a half hour late, the rabbi arrived. By that time the tension in the room was electric. Everyone transferred their attention to him.

He stood near the Stradivarius, diminutive, a strong presence. He looked around the room at each person individually. He smiled his sweet, child's smile. His voice seemed unnaturally loud in the high-ceilinged room.

He looked directly at Eugene Ysaÿe.

"Do you understand the meaning and nature of a Talmudic decision."

The silence was complete. Then the maestro nodded vigorously. He understood and obviously agreed.

Lucienne looked at her father. She didn't understand.

Ysaÿe understood. He was a storm about to explode.

"I see that some of you do. For those who don't, I will explain in a moment." He turned back to Ysaÿe and the maestro.

"Mr. Ysaÿe, Mr. Everade, all of you, I want your agreement to a Talmudic decision in the matter of the Stradivarius violin Hercules."

"Yes, of course," Everade said.

Ysaÿe stood abruptly. He towered over Rabbi Ben Ezra. Luther started to get up to intercede on the rabbi's behalf. Rabbi Ben Ezra held out his hand toward Luther. Luther sat back down slowly.

Ysaÿe looked at Luther angrily. "What is wrong with you! You idiot, did you think I was going to strike the rabbi."

Luther stood up straight and the room was filled with menace. "I don't care to be called an idiot by you, mister. As far as I can see it, any man who will send thugs to beat up a child ain't to be trusted around a man of the cloth.''

"I did not sent those idiots to beat up the boy. Those fools did that on their own, and I fired them the instant I heard about it.''

"Stop! Both of you sit down.'' The two men sat, still bristling. "Luther, be patient. Ysayë, you will apologize. I will not have such rudeness in this place.''

He grumbled. "Oh, all right, I apologize, Monsieur Cole.'' He stood up again. "I will not have it! The Hercules is Ysayë, and it shall remain Ysayë.''

"Sit down,'' the rabbi ordered.

Ysayë did so reluctantly.

"And what will you do, so full of pride, so right, Mr. Ysayë? Will you have your thugs hurt this fine young violinist again?''

Ysayë opened his mouth to protest again, and the rabbi rode right over him.

"Will you make your daughter so unhappy she cannot play at all?''

He pointed at Luther. "Will you have this old soldier put in jail to prevent him from seeking that which he most certainly saved from destruction?''

A somewhat deflated Ysayë answered. "I know the law; you cannot tell me what to do.''

"Do not tell me the law, young man! I speak for a higher law.'' Rabbi Ben Ezra walked closer to Ysayë. "I have studied the laws of man and God for more than eighty years. *Now''*—his voice filled every corner of the room—"now, will you have heartless legal trickery or a just decision that considers the unmeasurable knowledge of your faith?''

Rabbi Ben Ezra went on in a gentler, more persuasive voice.

"Or, will you have *goyische* judges, perhaps, who think your very legal laws of ownership favor the finder of an abandoned object? Or will you have consideration for the needs of all those here today.''

It was a telling argument. Ysayë's lawyers had warned him that a good lawyer could make a strong case against prior ownership, and when it came out in court what happened with the boy, the lawyer had cautioned him.

For the first time since he arrived he really looked at his daughter. The plea in her eyes was clear. His voice was quiet, reasonable.

"I have dreamed about finding the Hercules since the first time I heard about it when I was four years old. It is the talisman, the musical cornerstone of the Ysaÿe family.

"Lucienne, do you understand that if I submit to a Talmudic decision, it is binding on all who participate?"

"I don't care, Papa. No more lawyers. They care for nothing! Not violins, not music, especially not people. They don't know you, or Mr. Cole. They don't love or hate or feel anything except greed."

He looked at her as if she were someone newly met. Her passion and conviction were total. Ysaÿe sat silently and thought. The rest of those in the room held their breath. Finally, he heaved a long, weary sigh.

"I agree."

Rabbi Ben Ezra walked over to him and touched his face with the palm of his hand. Ysaÿe understood. It was recognition, an acknowledgment.

"Good, good. For the tough decision, the bigger man and always the greater reward."

He turned to Ailey and Luther.

"Now then, Ailey, Mr. Cole. I will explain to you what is this thing called the Talmud, and the decision that shall come from it. The Talmud is a living, growing document of Jewish law. It contains every decision on every subject talmudic scholars and rabbis have thought about and decided on for many centuries."

The rabbi told them about the Mishnah and Gemara, text and commentary. Luther and Ailey listened patiently.

"Now, Luther, you might wonder how spiritual law, Hebrew law, can render a fair decision for a Baptist."

There was no such question on Luther's face. "I ain't worried none. I look at the man, then I listens to the words."

"Good, your understanding does you credit, but I will speak on the subject anyway."

Ailey, who loved a good sermon, listened with great interest.

"Wisdom, real wisdom, is recognizable above and apart from questions of doctrine. When God gave the Hebrew prophet Moses the Law, he gave wisdom many religions have accepted without question or change, even as they went their own way regards doctrine.

"In making this decision, I will consider all the appropriate parts of the Talmud, and those higher laws which govern all men."

Rabbi Sholem Ben Ezra closed the violin case. His hand caressed the case lightly. "I will go now to study the Scriptures, in the meantime . . ." He looked around at all of them. "Jew and Christian, get to know one another. Like it or not, your lives are caught up in the net of this beautiful thing."

Rabbi Ben Ezra left the room carrying the case. No one moved for several moments, then Lucienne, embarrassed, got up and ran from the room. Both Ailey and her father looked after her. Ailey couldn't do what he knew was right.

Ailey got up and walked toward the rear of the house. He walked out across the patio toward the pines. In the distance he heard a violin. He recognized Lucienne's touch. He moved in that direction instinctively. He was having a difficult time being right and wrong at the same time.

He kicked at a pine cone. "Damn, I better pick one or the other, this being right isn't much fun."

At the cabin Ailey opened the door as quietly as he could. Lucienne stood with her back to him, attentive to the music. She sensed his presence and turned quickly, then as quickly turned back toward the music. She put the violin down and stood stiffly, as though waiting for a punishment she knew was coming.

Ailey took a breath, walked to her, and put his hand on her shoulder. She turned and threw her arms around his neck. They each tried to apologize faster than the other.

They kissed and embraced beneath the pines and swore never to hurt each other again. They were sitting on the couch, talking in low voices, when there was a knock on the door.

"Lucienne, it's your father. May I talk to you?"

She looked at Ailey, then toward the door. "You better do it, he is your father."

She got up, went to the door, and opened it. "Come in, Papa."

He saw Ailey on the couch and nodded as if he expected to find him there. Lucienne went back to the couch and sat close to Ailey. She took his hand and held it with both of hers in her lap.

"Good, I'm glad you are both here. This has been a very difficult time for me." He walked around the cabin and stopped in front of her music stand.

"The Paganini, Concerto Number Three. You will play this in Brussels?"

"Oui, Papa."

"Hmmm . . . well, perhaps."

Their eyes followed him as he moved around the room. "Does this hot plate work?"

"Yes, Papa. Would you like a cup of tea or coffee? I'm sorry, the coffee is instant."

"That's all right. I have a confession to make. I have been drinking instant for years. A terrible confession for a Frenchman, no?" He gave her a small smile.

She got up and went to the corner of the room to make the coffee.

"Ailey, may I make you some tea?"

"Yes, thank you."

It was as though there were something awful lying in the middle of the room that none of the occupants could bear to look at, so they moved about, pretending it wasn't there. But each knew they would have to look at it eventually.

Ysaÿe picked up a cane chair and set it down in front of Ailey. He sat down heavily. The chair looked very small beneath his bulk.

"You think I am a very terrible person, no? You don't have to answer that. If I were you, it is what I would think."

"I don't know what to think."

"Yes, it is very confusing. One has a certain viewpoint one's entire life. One has a dream. For me"—he waved his hand toward the music on the stand—"the music was always there. I was a part of the right family, there was never any doubt.

"My dream was the Hercules. My arrière-grand-père, from whom the Hercules was stolen in St. Petersburg, Russia, in 1908, wrote a history of the Hercules. Most of the information had been handed down to him as legend. It was supposed to have been Paganini's."

Lucienne brought her father his coffee, and Ailey, his tea. "Sit, Lucienne. I have to talk or I will go crazy."

She went back to the corner and made a cup of tea for herself, then came back to the couch.

"Monsieur Barkwood, you must believe me when I tell you I did not send those fools to hurt you. Even if I did not like you, because you might take my daughter away from me, I would never do anything that would harm you as a musician." He pointed to Ailey's hand.

"To do that was unforgivable. Are you able to flex the fingers?"

Ailey held his hand out and rolled his fingers. "It's just a little stiff. I've been soaking my hand in Epsom salts."

"The salts are very good. You must continue to use them, exercise, move the hand and fingers constantly." He paused for a moment. "So, do you accept my apology?"

It was so close to a demand, Ailey almost told him no, then he thought about the future, his future with Lucienne.

"Yes, I do, I reckon."

"*Bon,* I am glad for that." Ysayë was visibly relieved.

"And you, Lucienne, do you forgive your papa?"

"Oh, Papa, of course." He sighed and rubbed his face and head. "That is good, *chérie.* Now, I want you to call your mother and tell her, before she runs off with some juvenile cellist. She hasn't spoken to me since this mess began. I am sleeping on the couch, which is much too small. Celeste called and told me I was a Hun, and some things I will not repeat, and the cook has ruined all my meals."

Lucienne tried not to smile. "All right, Papa, I will call her."

"Are you able to play, Mr. Barkwood?"

"I don't know, I haven't tried since I hit that lawyer."

"Would to God you had killed that swine!"

"No, sir, I don't want to kill anyone."

"Will you try to play something? The papers say you are very good."

Ailey looked at Lucienne. She shrugged, leaving it up to him.

Ysayë watched the byplay. They looked at each other before they decided. Well, there you are, old man, she isn't yours anymore.

"Use mine, Ailey."

Ailey took Lucienne's violin and bow. "I need to loosen up a little, excuse me."

"But of course."

Ailey began a series of scales, legato, slowly, moving from one key to the other. Then, as he became more comfortable, doubled the velocity, and then doubled it again until he was rippling through the notes at double presto.

When he stopped, Ysayë asked him if it hurt.

"A little, but not much."

"May I suggest something? No, yes, it won't conflict with anything the maestro has said, I promise."

"Okay, sure."

"Good. Play the double presto again, Yes, right there when you change registers, there's a tiny pause. Here, may I?" He reached for the violin. Ysayë showed him a simpler fingering that made the whole passage flow as one piece."

"Ahh, that's very nice," Ailey said. "There's always different ways to get there."

Ailey tried it the way Ysayë demonstrated.

"Yes, yes, much smoother. My father taught me that and he told me his father taught him."

"Thank you very much."

"What about when you bear down for the double stops?"

Ailey tried a series of double-stop exercises. "Yes, that hurts a little. I think I would get tired quicker."

"That is to be expected. Lucienne says you will play the Bach. It is not the favorite of the judges, they will expect something more flashy. No matter, if you can play Bach well, you are a violinist, they will know the difference. You have the great touch. I wish you well."

Ailey bowed an acknowledgment.

"I am going back to my hotel now. For some reason I am very weary."

"I'll take you, Papa."

"You are going to drive?"

"Ah, *oui,* Papa. I have learned many things here."

He looked sour for a moment. "Yes, I can see that."

Korea, Early Spring, 1910

Golodkin slipped in and out of reality with only the barest percep-
tion of the difference. The fever was unending. He couldn't remember
when it started. In those few moments when he saw the world as it
was, he found himself looking at the back of a two-wheeled cart
pulled by oxen. A baby was strapped in the back between sacks
of millet.

The baby's black eyes seldom left Golodkin.

In a brief, lucid moment, Golodkin thought the baby was waiting
for him to die. The man driving the oxen had tied Golodkin's hand
with a bit of rope, then attached it to the back of the cart so that
he wouldn't wander off.

They stopped often, as much for the oxen's sake as for the crazy
northerner tied to the cart. The fog of delirium seldom lifted.

Every minute or so, like the pendulum of a clock Golodkin's hand
reached his shoulder and touched the pack. As long as it was there,
he could go on. His thoughts were never far from the violin, Her-
cules, and that terrible, mad moment when he took it. He could still
see Ysaÿe's face with total clarity.

The man on the cart looked back frequently, indecisive. Survival
did not include extra mouths to feed. But Golodkin didn't eat much.
The farmer's wife made him a soft gruel of millet and bits of pickled
vegetable. She had to feed it to him like a baby.

They stopped in a bowl between low hills. To one side were twenty

281

acres of rice paddies. Beyond the rice fields a narrow building with a peaked roof and a simple cross perched atop a hill overlooking the valley.

Years before, Methodist missionaries had come to the area. The missionaries had been gone for ten years, but their converts still used the church. Several women and men stood in the muddy water, repairing the dikes. A sturdy man with a mattock cut a new channel into the packed earth.

The man got down from the cart and talked with his wife. As they talked they looked back toward Golodkin, who stumbled into the back of the cart and hung on with grim determination. His world heaved and rolled drunkenly.

The owner of the cart walked into the rice paddies toward the man with the mattock. They bowed to each other and talked for a long time.

Golodkin stared at the baby, asleep, its fist in its mouth. The woman came around the back of the cart and untied the rope from his hand. She spoke in a strange tongue, not one word of which he understood. She eased him to the ground, patted his back gently.

They were not unkind, they simply didn't know what else to do. The stranger was dying and it was better that his last days be spent with those who might understand him.

The cart driver came across the fields with the farmer, who stood over Golodkin and shook his head sadly. The man, his wife, and the baby moved off down the road.

The farmer, who was also the minister to this forgotten congregation, got Golodkin to his feet and helped him across the dikes toward a small two-room farmhouse.

Golodkin reached up and touched the pack automatically. A brief, peculiar smile crossed his face.

Chapter 38

Luther sat on the veranda drinking coffee and reading a newspaper. Every few moments Mrs. Berenson came to the patio to ask if there was anything he wanted.

Before Mrs. Everade and Miss Iris left for the city, she had been literally gushing about Luther.

"Rose, have you seen him this morning? He looks just like Gary Cooper, and so polite. He gives me these little bows and calls me ma'am. Such a handsome man. You say he's"—she made a funny motion with her hands—"with that woman from West Virginia.'

"Louise, that woman from West Virginia? What are you talking about? She is like a mother to Ailey. She isn't that woman from West Virginia."

"Oh, she's so prim and proper. A beautiful man like that would be wasted on her."

"Louise! Take a cold shower and remember your age." She shook her head with disgust, and left.

"Remember my age, you're no teenager, Mrs. Overweight Rose Everade."

Mrs. Berenson went back to the patio. "Are you sure you wouldn't like a nice omelet, some more sweet rolls. You could use a few pounds, though I must say you're quite trim."

"Thank you kindly, ma'am. I ate breakfast at the hotel. But I'll look forward to lunch, that's a fact."

"Good, I'll make you something special to remember us by."

"I always remember a kindness, ma'am."

His smile sent a warmth through parts of her body that had mostly forgotten such feelings.

Eugene Ysaÿe came through the door with his newspaper. He saw Luther and headed for the other end of the patio.

Luther looked at him coldly. Mrs. Berenson glanced at the two of them and rushed through the house, searching for the maestro. When she found him in the library, working with Ailey, she began talking a mile a minute.

"Maestro, you'd better come with me right now. Mr. Cole and Mr. Ysaÿe are squaring away on the patio. Personally, I hope Mr. Cole gives him a good whipping."

"What? What's gotten into you, Mrs. Berenson? Ailey, you stay here, likely it won't come to anything. Good God! Will this lunacy never end?"

He left the room walking fast. Ailey looked at Mrs. Berenson curiously.

"Well," she said defensively, "he deserves it, he acted like a pig."

Ailey was startled by her vehemence.

On the patio Luther got up and walked toward the table where Ysaÿe was seated. Ysaÿe got to his feet as Luther approached. Luther stared at him coldly. They were both tall, able to look each other in the eye.

"What I want to know is why you set them lawyers to beat on my boy. Most everything else I can understand. I'd forgive most anything else, but that deserves a whippin', and unless I get a damn good answer, I intend to administer it."

Ysaÿe started to swell up, and his face got red. Almost as quickly it faded, and he slumped back down in his chair.

"Monsieur Cole, believe me or not, that was not my doing. Yes, I contacted my lawyers in Paris and told them to set about getting the violin, but violence, never. I would destroy the Stradivarius before I would cause harm to the hands of a great violinist." He sighed and looked pained.

"Maestro Everade says the boy plays as well as Heifitz when

Heifitz was twice his age. I heard him play. He is certainly much better than I was at that age, and I won the Tchaikovsky.

"If I thought it would do any good, I would personally beat that cretinous dolt to a pulp. You ... you must do what you think is right. Either way, I understand your feelings."

Luther looked at Ysaÿe for a long, quiet moment, then nodded. He walked to the coffee server nearby.

"You want a cup of coffee?"

Ysaÿe was startled. "*Oui,* yes, I would."

Luther fixed two cups and brought them back to Ysaÿe's table. "You and I better do like Rabbi Ben Ezra says. I'm here to tell you, God, yours, mine, whoever's talks to that man. This mess has to be cleaned up by us."

It was three days before Rabbi Ben Ezra called to say that he had reached a decision.

"So, Joachim, have them all in the library at one o'clock this afternoon."

"Yes, Rabbi ... you—"

"Just have them there, Maestro Everade." He hung up.

Everade looked at the phone. "You're getting as arrogant as that Frenchman, Rabbi Sholem Ben Ezra."

The participants began arriving in the library by twelve-thirty. It was one-thirty when Rabbi Ben Ezra arrived. He was carrying the violin case. He moved the end table to the middle of the room and placed the case on it. Everade thought he was really taking his time about it.

The rabbi opened the case dramatically. Golden-orange, the Maestro of Cremona's trademark. Its beauty held everyone's attention.

Ysaÿe leaned forward and devoured it with his eyes.

Rabbi Ben Ezra looked around and smiled.

"So ... so ... such a problem. Soloman shouldn't have to decide, but similar in a way." He paused. "Even I was caught up in its beauty. Both claims have merit. It came into these two families, and in each it became something greater than wood and metal." He paused again. "But in the end, the law, the Talmud, God's holy law is just."

There was growing impatience around the room, but Rabbi Ben Ezra wouldn't be hurried.

He looked around at each person in turn.

"It shall be thus: Ailey Barkwood shall have possession of the Stradivarius violin called Hercules for the rest of his life as a musician."

He paused. "At the time of his death, or if he stops playing for the world, it shall be returned to Mr. Eugene Ysaÿe or his heirs, and it shall be their property from that time forward. That is my judgment."

Eugene Ysayé sighed. "I thought it would be something like this. Well, Lucienne," he said, smiling, "now you will have to marry him, for my insurance."

She blushed and looked at Ailey. That was perfectly fine with her.

Luther nodded his head satisfied. "That's fair."

"Very well, do all parties agree completely to this settlement, without reservation?"

Luther spoke first. "I agree. It were the Christian thing to do."

The rabbi nodded.

"I agree, Rabbi Ben Ezra. It is fair," Ysaÿe answered.

The rest of them, each person in turn, agreed.

"Good, then it is done."

"Oh, Rabbi Ben Ezra, you are wonderful," Lucienne said. She ran to him and threw her arms around his neck and kissed his cheek.

"Yes, yes, it is true. Now can I have a nice glass of tea and something sweet? This being Solomon is hard work."

The maestro murmured, raising his head to the ceiling. "Thank God. You two won't manage tenth place if you don't practice."

Chapter 39

Brussels, Belgium, September 1989

They were gathered in an elegant suite in the finest hotel in Brussels, compliments of Monsieur Eugene Ysaÿe. Like coaches to a world-class team, much advice was passed, and like thousands of players, Lucienne and Ailey heard little of it. But it gave comfort to the coaches at their most helpless moment.

They were all there. Ailey Parkman Barkwood, tall, awkward, pulling at his bow tie, pacing nervously, showing signs of the small boy who liked to play in the dirt and sing "Rock of Ages" very loud. Lucienne Rosamond Ysaÿe, slender, reserved. The Maestro Joachim Everade and Mrs. Rose Everade. Martin Luther Cole and Miss Iris Bentley. Eugene Ysaÿe, looking very grand in tie and tails, with his wife.

Ailey was tremendously excited, pacing, snapping his fingers nervously. His black hair which usually hung to his shoulders was tied at the back of his neck with a hank of string, much to Mr. Ysaÿe's and Maestro Everade's disapproval.

Luther looked relaxed, quite at ease sitting in a damask-covered Louis XIV chair. The women were in one of the bedrooms with Lucienne. They had been in there for a long time.

"What's she doing in there, sewing the darn dress? It took me two minutes to get dressed. Would've taken less if it weren't for this hangman's noose around my neck."

The older men looked at him pityingly. They obviously knew something about women he did not.

287

"At ease, boy, you'll be fine," Luther said.

Ysayë laughed. "*Oui*, listen to your uncle, Ailee. Save your energy for the music. Look at your teacher, he is the picture of tranquillity."

This set them all laughing except Everade. He was a wreck. His bow tie askew, his hair disheveled, and he kept waving music at Ailey.

"Laugh, go ahead, have your fun. Why do I do this? Twenty-three of my students have been in the great competitions. Each time my life is shortened. They forget everything I have taught them. They do not listen to me. They add notes, take notes away, like . . . like . . ."

"Jazz musicians," Ailey finished for him.

"Yes, by God, exactly!"

"How many of your students have won, Maestro, fourteen of them, I think," Ysayë said.

"Well, of course!" Everade was not comforted.

Luther wandered over to a corner of the room, where a violin case rested on top of a small table. He opened the case of the violin Hercules. He touched the strings, the body of the violin, and listened for the voices of war. There were echoes, images without force, fading sounds. The voices were finally silent.

Lucienne glided out of the bedroom followed by Mrs. Everade, Mrs. Ysayë, and Miss Bentley. She caught the attention of everyone, which had been her intention. In a wine-red-velvet gown, her auburn hair piled artfully, strands falling to creamy shoulders, she was beautiful.

Ailey looked toward the bodice of her gown nervously. He'd never seen anything like it up close.

Judas priest, you can darn near see her . . .

She went to him and took his hands.

"You are so beautiful, I don't know what to say. How can I compete? No man in the world will listen to me after he has seen you."

She purred. "Music to my ears. I do not care what they think, only what you think."

He leaned forward and whispered in her ear, "I'll tell you what I think, you're showing more chest than when we went swimming in Blair's Pond."

"Impossible! I did not have a chest when we went swimming in Blair's Pond. Do you like my chests, Ailee?"

"That isn't fair. I'm trying to think of Bach and you're showing me your bosom."

He laughter rang merrily around the high-ceilinged room.

"Maybe you should put a shawl around your shoulders. You don't want to catch cold."

In the corner of the room Luther, who had been running his fingers over the velvet case, stopped and looked at the cover of the case curiously.

"Eugene, come over here for a minute."

Ysaÿe walked over to Luther.

"Look at this, the lining, it's come apart a little." Luther lifted up the lining where it was broken.

"*Ma foi!* It looks like paper. No, it cannot be."

The rest of the family crowded around.

"Ailey, may I open this a little more?"

"Sure. Let's see what it is."

Ysaÿe took a penknife from his pocket and slipped it under the lining. As he lifted the edge of the lining, a folded sheet of rice paper appeared.

Ysaÿe stopped and looked at the others.

"Go ahead, take it on out," Luther said.

Ysaÿe slipped the paper from its hiding place. The sheet of paper was small, the handwriting precise. It was in French. Ysaÿe was pale. He sat down in the nearest chair.

"Read it to us," Luther said.

Ysaÿe had to clear his throat several times. He translated the French into English.

"It says:

"To whom it may concern:
    "I, Nikolai Golodkin, am dying. There is no one to whom I may confess. In the summer of 1908 I took the violin Hercules from the apartment of Eugene Saint-Saens Ysaÿe in St. Petersburg, Russia. I was mad to do it, I know that now, but I desperately wanted to be a great artist like Ysaÿe. I thought, if I had a great instrument like the Hercules, I, too, could become fa-

mous! In fear and illness I left St. Petersburg and carried the Hercules across the breadth of Russia, Mongolia, and now this strange place called Korea. A hundred times I would have traded the Hercules for food, but I could not. It is worth far more than my wretched life. If you have found this note, I make my pleas to you, save this violin. It is truly worth more than a life. It can in the hands of a master bring joy and excitement to thousands. I ask this one last thing. Let it fall into the hands of one who can make it sing its wondrous song. I was not that man. If you are not that person, be a true man, find one who is. Let me go to my grave in peace, knowing that it will soar with the power of its namesake.

"*Merci,* many times, *merci.* Forgive me.

"I am Your Humble Obedient Servant

"Nikolai Golodkin

"January 1910, Korea."

Ysayë's hands fell to his lap. The tears ran down his cheeks. He took out a handkerchief and wiped his eyes.

Ysayë looked at Ailey sadly.

"I think Rabbi Ben Ezra and the rest of you, especially you, Luther, have done better than you knew."

Chapter 40

The Royal Opera House was packed to overflowing. Critics and teachers alike agreed that this year would be remembered for the quality of the music and the talented young men and women who made it.

The lights went down and Ailey Barkwood walked to the center of the stage and stood to one side of the conductor.

The conductor reached forward and took the microphone in his hand.

"*Mesdames et monsieurs.* Monsieur Ailee Barkwood has asked me to say these few words to you, as he does not yet speak French.

"He wishes to dedicate this work to Nikolai Golodkin, who in 1908 walked across Russia, Mongolia, and most of Korea to preserve the Stradivarius violin, Hercules, which he will play for you this evening. *Merci beaucoup!*"

The crowd cheered enthusiastically for the slender boy with black hair from the hills of West Virginia.